THE BOOK OF SURFING

Michael Fordham

THE KILLER GUIDE

itbooks

AN IMPRINT OF HARPERCOLLINS PUBLISHERS

THE SURFING PLANET

The Ride

THE VISION

Surf Legends

THE SEARCH

Surf Culture

CONTENTS

INTRODUCTION

I first glimpsed the surf dream on a Sunday afternoon in East London. It was the fag end of the seventies and I was nursing a broken wrist and a badly sprained ankle sustained while skateboarding the hill outside the family house. I was feeling bored and sorry for myself. Rummaging though an old pile of magazines in my uncle's bedside cabinet, I found a stack of old Aussie surf mags amid the dog-eared copies of *Playboy* and *Motorsport Magazine*. Despite the raging hormones of this moody thirteen-year-old, it was images of surfers riding the curvatures of tropical waves that burned into my cortex, far deeper than those of the honey-hued bunnies and classic Ferraris. The surf magazines evoked a world so exotic, so perfect, so beautiful – and so essentially 'other' to my suburban existence – that I was instantly intoxicated. From that moment I was determined one day to become a surfer.

Fast forward five years. I'm paddling out at dawn for the first time on a battered old board at Noosa Heads in Queensland, my stomach a nest of butterflies. Having failed to realise that it was possible to surf around the shores of England, I had spent two years of my teenage life toiling on building sites in London, working to save the money for a plane ticket to Australia. I eventually scored the airfare, flew in to Brisbane, bought a crappy old Mazda Bongo campervan, stuck in my well-worn *Best of the Beach Boys* tape and headed north.

A lot of water has passed under the keel since I caught that first wave at Noosa. Back then, in the mid-eighties, surfing was still very much a marginal coastal creed outside of Australia, California and Hawaii. In places such as Britain, Japan, South America and most of Europe it was practised resolutely under the radar by a small cadre of passionately committed pioneers. In the two decades since, surfing has become a billion-dollar industry that has penetrated ever deeper into the mainstream. Engaging with skate culture's thrash-and-burn ethos at the end of the eighties, the industry absorbed the global dollar generated by the explosion of snowboarding in the nineties. Surfing now lies at the heart of a truly global 'action sports' industry whose wealth and influence would have been unimaginable to preceding generations. In the process wave-riding has become one of the central elements in the lives of millions around the world, giving access to the kind of sustained euphoria that no other activity can bring. Not everybody has an ocean on their doorstep, but everybody's gone surfing.

Ever since its rebirth in late-nineteenth-century Hawaii, surfing has transformed the lives of the people it has touched. It has galvanised countless relationships in shared experience and lent purpose and piquancy to innumerable wandering adventures and inner explorations. Reflecting both technological and aesthetic trends, it has inspired musicians, photographers and artists to produce some of the most dynamic work of the last forty years. Many of the masters of the sport have proved themselves athletic giants, creative visionaries and cultural heroes – although their stories are largely lost to the narrative of popular culture. Surfing is rich in anthropological, historical and cultural resonance and is full of metaphoric potency. As well as being sun-kissed exponents of the rock-and-roll dream that gobbled up a planet, surfers are initiates of an intensely physical set of rituals and practices that can produce a state of pure, natural joy. And surfers have invented a word for that very specific type of joy: stoke.

It's this incredibly rich, diverse nature that *The Book of Surfing* attempts to express. Structured so that you can dip in and out, as well as reading it through from first page to last, the book builds up a multi-layered picture of wave-riding and the culture that it has created. It aims to entertain the old salts as well as to inform and inspire the newly surf stoked. It's naïve to think that any medium could adequately express the light and shade of a life that revolves around a wave. If a few readers of this book are motivated to make it their goal to find out for themselves what's so special about this surfing life, then my mission will have been accomplished.

Michael Fordham

" **WHERE BEFORE THERE WAS ONLY THE WIDE DESOLATION AND INVINCIBLE ROAR,** IS NOW A MAN, ERECT, FULL-STATURED, NOT STRUGGLING FRANTICALLY IN THAT WILD MOVEMENT, NOT CRUSHED AND BURIED AND BUFFETED BY THOSE MIGHTY MONSTERS, BUT STANDING ABOVE THEM ALL, CALM AND SUPERB, POISED ON THE GIDDY SUMMIT, HIS FEET BURIED IN THE CHURNING FOAM,

THE SALT SMOKE
RISING
TO
HIS
KNEES,
AND ALL THE REST OF HIM
IN FREE AIR AND FLASHING
SUNLIGHT, AND HE IS FLYING
THOUGH THE AIR, FLYING
FORWARD,
FLYING
FAST
AS THE SURGE ON WHICH HE
STANDS. **"**

Jack London

THE PERFECT WAVE

Over the last century, the search for the perfect wave has shaped surf culture. Always an elusive notion, it has been constantly re-defined.

Picture the scene at Waikiki, Oahu, around 1912. The tourists started arriving a few years ago, drawn by the hibiscus-heavy Hawaiiana propagated by writers such as Jack London. The small coterie of local 'beach boys', heirs to the grand old indigenous Hawaiian tradition of wave-riding, are making a living teaching the rich *haoles* to swim and to surf. The long finless boards, hewn from heavy timber, are well suited to the angles and trajectories of Waikiki's waves. The boys who ride them are the first proponents of the surfing lifestyle, and Waikiki becomes the earliest epitome of a wave's manifest perfection.

Cut to Palos Verdes Cove, California, some time in the mid-1930s. On the beach, the members of the Palos Verdes Surf Club are doing their best to replicate the Hawaiian lifestyle that had been introduced to the mainland by the likes of visiting Hawaiians Duke Kahanamoku and George Freeth. They're catching lobster and abalone. They're strumming ukuleles and drinking wine out of jugs around an open fire. Meanwhile, Tom Blake, visionary waterman, is paddling way outside of the peak on a big day. His hollow 'cigar-box' board, fitted now with a single fin, is more manoeuvrable than anything seen before. The relatively light board, with its stabilising skeg, enables Blake to draw tight turns and acute angles down the faces of the Cove's big, fast-moving walls. This is California's pre-war halcyon of unspoilt shorelines and rich inland forests, hills and pastures. Out beyond the beach, surf perfection is realised.

Come to Malibu in 1958. Surfers are riding First Point's long, peeling waves in the dynamic style known as hotdogging. Dewey Weber and Mickey Muñoz are at the cutting edge of the hotdog revolution. There's a crowd on the beach willing to be impressed by the new and the strange. The foam and fibreglass boards the heroes ride are increasingly light and dynamic. There's a rock-and-roll soundtrack to the parties on the beach, and the rides along the 'Bu's seemingly endless, gently tapered walls are just waiting to be filled with the new stylistic vernacular. Malibu is the canvas upon which modern surf style was painted.

Smell that patchouli oil? Yes, it's 1973 and we find ourselves at Uluwatu in a little-known island outpost called Bali. The left-breaking, fiercely pitching maw that's firing with razor-like sharpness down the southwestern tip of the Bukit Peninsular is at the edge of surf culture's consciousness. With short, spear-like boards a tuned-out core of a globally wandering surf tribe is exploring the limits of speed and hollowness. Waves of undreamt steepness and ferocity that would have sent Blake scampering back to the beach are being harnessed by the likes of Terry Fitzgerald, Gerry Lopez and Michael Peterson. The surf magazines back in California and on Australia's east coast have spread the dream of tapping into the power source no matter how impossible it might have seemed only a few years previously, and Uluwatu is the ideal aspiration for the children of the shortboard revolution.

1983. Greed is good and the thruster surfboard is unashamedly greedy on the wave. Three fins are by now ubiquitous and the thruster's bite has drawn tube riding deeper and deeper back into the heart of the wave.

Surfers are intent these days on satisfying their thirst for increasingly obscure, increasingly hollow, mind-bendingly fast waves. Professional superstars like Martin Potter and Tom Carroll are paring down their moves with the dynamics of an on-the-limit Lamborghini Countach. Indonesia's gravitational pull hasn't diminished – G-Land, Nias and Tavarua are now the spiritual homes of this new power generation. Glossy dispatches from the frontiers are populating a raft of full colour, globally distributed surf magazines whose cluttered ad pages are an explosion of DayGlo and aggression.

It's 1988 and the trajectory of the ideal line on the ideal wave is beginning to go ballistic. Inspired by skateboarding's third boom, and the early flights of Larry Bertlemann and Martin Potter, surf performance superstars and American gothic punks Christian Fletcher and Matt Archibold are beginning to reach out of the liquid parameters, busting out into aerials that flow back seamlessly into the ride. Surfing's aesthetic is beginning to merge with that of skateboarding, while up in the mountains surfers and skaters are riding steep and deep in powder snow and halfpipes.

2001. A virgin charter operation just the other side of the millennium. A pod of supergroms, sponsored by a major surf conglomerate, have been on wave-watch for months in the upper reaches of the Indonesian archipelago known as the Mentawais. Here, waves of intense power, consistency and geometric perfection wrap and bend off the reefs that surround these remote island communities. The perfect wave can't get better than this. Or can it?

2008. A crowded Saturday afternoon at the Côte de Basques, in Biarritz in July. An unusually powerful summer swell is pulsing in from the Bay of Biscay. Way outside, sculpted watermen are paddling into unbroken set waves riding statuesque on standup paddleboards. On their inside a flotilla of neo-classical longboarders cross-step towards the nose of their boards. Snagging the scraps, a pod of thruster-riding groms hustle to cut a bottom turn and bust an air. Further in, at the shorebreak, a hundred or so families on bodyboards launch themselves into the foam. This is wave-riding's perfect day, twenty-first-century style. It's a post-modern mishmash of wave craft and sensibilities, each individual enjoying a distinctly contemporary flavour of stoke, and each enjoying their very own perfect wave.

Overleaf: Jordan Heuer slots into a slice of tubular perfection at Lance's Right, Mentawai Islands.

ANATOMY OF A WAVE

No two ocean waves are, or have ever been, identical – it's this simple fact that provides the source of surfing's endless possibilities.

Although surfers' descriptions of waves are often shot through with adjectives such as 'perfect' or 'geometric', these can never amount to more than a platonic ideal. No matter how structurally sound a particular reef, sandbar or point, and no matter how stable the wind, swell and tide, two waves can never be cloned. There are certain basic elements, however, that apply to breaking waves regardless of where they stand on the philosophical scale of perfection. Waves contain these elements in unequal measure. Some waves, for example, may have a gently sloping shoulder and a wide, smooth face. Others may have a viciously throwing lip and absolutely no shoulder. The truth is that you can never accurately describe what is after all a shape-shifting, constantly transforming body of raw energy. But surfers spend a lot of their time trying.

A The lip
Often referred to by non-surfers as the 'crest', the lip is the upper edge of a breaking wave. As waves shoal on the ocean floor in shallow water, the lip begins to move faster than the bottom of the wave.

B The trough
The trough is the bottom, or 'foot', of a wave. It is the slowest-moving area of water closest to the ocean floor. In hollow waves, water in the trough is sucked quickly upwards and backwards into the lip.

C The curl

Although the curl is often used as a synonym for the lip, it is more accurately described as the moving edge of a breaking wave, formed as water is sucked up from the trough towards the throwing lip.

D The shoulder

The shoulder is a relatively gentle sloping area to the side of the curl.

E The barrel

The barrel is the area deep inside the heart of a hollow breaking wave. It is formed when a lip is thrown out above the trough. Riding back in the heart of a barrel requires great skill and experience but is also one of the most intense experiences in surfing.

F The face

The face of a breaking wave, where most surfing takes place, is the open expanse of water between the very bottom of the trough to the highest point reached by the lip. A wave's height is defined by the distance between these two points.

Surf contests were a favourite Church subject. This scene was shot from a crane at Huntington Beach in 1964.

RON CHURCH

Ron Church was a champion of ocean exploration and helped lay the foundations for modern water-based surf photography.

The scene is 1968, near Cabo San Lucas, Baja California, Mexico. Photographer Ron Church is helping to prepare the cameras aboard *Diving Saucer*, the submersible with which French sub-aquatic legend, Jacques Cousteau, is pioneering deep-water exploration. The winds are light and the water is clear but the usually focused lensman is curiously distracted. The skipper himself notices Ron's preoccupation. Peering out over the stern of the *Calypso*, Cousteau quickly realises what is causing the American's uncharacteristic lack of focus. A smooth, head-high set of waves is peeling into the bay a couple of hundred metres away. 'Ronnie,' says the Frenchman in the woolly hat, 'if you must surf, you surf. But we must dive.'

Although surfing and surf photography came relatively late in his short, dynamic life, Ron Church was a true aquanaut. In 1945, at the age of nine, he moved with his family from his birthplace in Colorado to San Diego. The kid was always fooling around with cameras, and attended classes at the prestigious Art Center school in Pasadena after high school. Marrying his teen sweetheart and becoming a father at the age of nineteen, he left full-time education early to find work as a photographer for aviation firm Convair. The ambitious Church, initially hired to take PR shots of aircraft interiors, accompanied test pilots in early supersonic flight with his own customised equipment. During the latter part of the fifties, he began to experiment with underwater photography, adapting the technical wizardry he had learnt up in the

stratosphere to explore 'inner space'. By 1958, his work was being published in popular titles such as *National Geographic*, *Popular Mechanics* and *Time*. By the end of decade he had gained a reputation as one of the best and most innovative underwater photographers in the world.

Church began to surf at Windansea, Calfornia, in 1960. Inevitably he was soon training his lens on surfers. Published by John Severson in very early editions of *Surfer*, Church's pictures were characterised by a compositional elegance as well as a precision that hadn't been seen before in the fledgling surf media. Church went on to document the human life lived in and around the ocean with the same energy with which he had explored the deep. Although he was a master of water work, some of Church's most interesting pictures are the portraits he took of surfers on the North Shore of Oahu in the winter of 1961 and in his native California.

Ron Church died of a brain tumour in 1973 at the age of thirty-nine. During his short life he was widely recognised as a tireless champion of the ocean environment. Surfing might have been a passion that arrived late, but the meticulously crafted body of work that he left schooled a generation of lensmen in the possibilities of surf photography.

Above: Church used the technical expertise
acquired in his underwater work
to capture the peaks of Sunset Beach.

Right: Out of the water, Church was equally
adept at conjuring up the perfect shot.

ANATOMY OF A BOARD

Surfboard design – including materials, shapes, and dimensions – has been subject to continual refinement and revision. Some of the basic elements, however, have remained constant since the first boards as we know them were shaped – probably by the ancient kings of Polynesia.

Stringer

The thin piece of wood that runs from nose to tail and helps strengthen the board is called the stringer.

Deck/Bottom

The outline of a surfboard when viewed from the deck (the top) or the bottom is known as 'plan shape' or 'template'. The plan shape, along with the fins (this is a subject in itself, so check out p.180), gives a board its most telling characteristics.

Rocker

Rocker is the degree of curve in a board from nose to tail. 'Entry rocker' refers to the curvature in the front-to-middle area; 'tail kick' to the curvature from the middle to the rear. A low, flat rocker enhances a board's wave-catching abilities but decreases its speed in the turn. An increased tail kick improves lift and turning ability, but at the same time reduces drive.

nose width

rail

stringer

rail

board width

tail width

fin

fin

Deck

Bottom

Rocker

The Ride

Tapered   Hybrid   Rounded

50/50 rail

Nose

A surfboard's forward area is known as 'the nose'. This can be rounded (mostly longboards) or 'tapered' (most shortboards) or any gradation between. A rounded nose is more stable and will promote greater forward projection than a drawn-in or tapered nose. The latter decreases 'swing weight', making it easier to turn the board quickly, but providing less stability.

Down-rail

Rails

The profiles of a board's outside edges are called 'rails'. Modern designs often feature a variety of different rail profiles from nose to tail. Rounded profiles, such as egg rails (also known as 50/50) are more commonly found on traditional longboards. Down-rails bite into powerful, steep faces but are more difficult to turn with grace and flow. Most boards feature softer rails in the middle area, with harder rails toward the tail area.

cross-sections through one rail of the board

Foil

Foil is the thickness of a surfboard from deck to bottom. In most designs, this varies from tail to nose and from rail to rail.

Tail

Tail designs are the most important element in determining turning characteristics. Square tails provide more drive and lift but will be harder to tip on the rail to turn, whereas sleeker, tapered pintails lend themselves to smooth turn transitions with some loss in drive. Hybrid designs between square and pintails are a trade-off between loss of drive and lift and flow of turn transition. In big, powerful waves, pintails make sense: the power of the surf compensates for loss of drive. Conversely, in smaller waves, square tails give more drive and will therefore catch more waves.

NB: MEASUREMENTS

The width of a board is measured at its widest point whereas the width of the nose and tail are measured 12 inches from the front and rear of the board respectively. Surfboard measurements are generally given in imperial measurements. This is because, prior to its closure in 2005, up to 90 per cent of the world's surfboard 'blanks' (the raw lumps of extruded polyester cores from which surfboard builders sculpt boards) were made by Clark Foam in California.

Swallow   Square   Squash   Diamond   Rounded pin   Wingpin   Pin

DUDISH DECONSTRUCTED

No cult vernacular has been adopted so enthusiastically by the mainstream as the alternative language used by surfers. Pre-dating the ubiquitous jive of greaser culture and the hipster argot of jazz, the California-born dialect that is dudish is a constantly evolving language.

The scene

A super-crowded beachbreak somewhere on the surfing planet. The waves are six to eight feet, and a light offshore wind is blowing. Two young surfers, just towelled down and quaffing a bottle of water between them, stare out into the jammed line-up, talking about their morning's surf.

SURFER ONE

DEEP CEREBRUM STOKE [1], DUDE.[2]
I GOT SO SHACKED [3] OUT THERE.
IT'S [4] CRISP [5] AND GLASSY, [6] AND WAY [7] SUCKY.[8]

SURFER TWO

DID YOU CHECK THAT GOAT-BOATER [9] DROP IN [10] ON ME THOUGH? THAT WAS SO GAY.[11] TREACHEROUS.[12]
SHOULDN'T BE OUT THERE WHEN IT'S WAY HOLLOW[13] LIKE THIS. I WAS LIKE, 'I'M GOING[14] AND HE JUST, LIKE TOTALLY [15] BACKDOORED [16] ME, EVEN DINGED [17] MY RAIL [18] WITH HIS PADDLE. DO THAT TO THE LOCALS [19] ROUND HERE AND YOU'RE RAGGED,[20] MAN.

SURFER ONE

LOOKS LIKE IT'S BUILDING [21] TOO.
GETTING MORE GNARLY [22] BY THE MOMENT.
THERE'S A LOT OF WEST [23] IN IT, AND WHEN IT'S LINED UP [24] LIKE THIS IT JUST HITS THE BANK [25] AND THROWS, [26] DUDE.

SURFER TWO

I GOT THIS ONE MACKER. [27] NICE BOWLY DROP, [28] THEN INTO A TOTALLY SCHWACKABLE WALL,[29] THEN IT JUST DREDGED OUT [30] AND I GOT WAY BACK,[31] MAN. THIS GROM [32] WAS HOOTIN'! [33]

SURFER ONE

CRUCIAL,[34] BRAH. [35] TOTAL GREEN ROOM. [36]

Surf
Culture

1 **stoke**: ephemeral but tangible sense of boundless euphoria (probably produced by a cocktail of endorphins and adrenalin) that can only arise after surfing. Remember, however, that the only true path to stoke is through surfing. Snowboarding, skateboarding, football or fishing may lead to good feelings, but only surfing produces stoke.

2 **dude**: universal surfer nomenclature for a fellow surfer. Hijacked by jive-talking subcults and the metropolitan media savvy the world over. Rendered more or less meaningless because of the latter's ubiquitous use of the term.

3 **shacked**: to ride inside the barrel or tube – the tunnel-like formation of a wave that forms when its lip reaches out and over the surfer.

4 **it**: universally replaces 'the waves' or 'the surf' or 'conditions'.

5 **crisp**: describes well-formed, evenly breaking waves perfect for surfing.

6 **glassy**: describes low or no-wind conditions augmented by favourable light, so that the waves take on the transluscent appearance of sheet glass.

7 **way**: universally replaces 'very'. Synonyms: 'total', 'totally', 'super'.

8 **sucky**: describes a wave that is hollow and that dredges or sucks up water from the trough of the wave quickly to its lip or 'crest'.

9 **goat-boater**: generally derogatory term for a rider of a surf ski or sea kayak.

10 **drop in**: one of surfing's deadliest sins. To take off on a wave that someone is already riding.

11 **gay**: quasi-homophobic term for anything regarded as uncool.

12 **treacherous**: example of the hyperbolic and often misappropriated use of adjectives when describing waves or surf conditions.

13 **hollow**: *see* 8 **sucky**

14 **going**: paddling for and taking off on a wave.

15 **totally**: *see* 7 **way**

16 **backdoor**: to take off on a wave from the opposite side of the peak to the direction the wave is travelling.

17 **dinged**: universal term for damage to a surfboard.

18 **rail**: the outside edge of a surfboard.

19 **local**: usually grumpy, often small-minded surfer who never had the imagination to get out of the seaside town he grew up in and, as a result, labours under the misapprehension that he owns the rights to all the waves that break there.

20 **ragged**: to be beaten, worked over. From 'rag-dolled', which refers to the pounding you get when held under by a powerful wave.

21 **building**: when waves increase in size gradually, usually due to the arrival of a new groundswell created by a storm at sea.

22 **gnarly**: refers to heavy, stormy or dangerous surf conditions, but can also relate to heavy or dangerous situations out of the water.

23 **lot of west**: when a swell brings waves directly from a given direction, it is referred to as having a 'lot of west' or a 'lot of south' in it.

24 **lined up**: describes long, evenly spaced swells from a favourable direction.

25 **bank**: sandbar upon which swells interact to produce beachbreak waves.

26 **throw**: when a swell meets a shallow spot on sandbar, it breaks quickly and suddenly, throwing out the lip, or crest of the wave to form a tube.

27 **macker**: a big, powerful wave.

28 **bowly drop**: refers to a not particularly steep start of a ride, where the first turn is made in a part of a wave's face that appears rounded, smooth and 'bowl-like'.

29 **schwackable wall**: a long, evenly breaking section of a wave perfect for performing dynamic manoeuvres.

30 **dredged out**: *see* 8 **sucky**

31 **way back**: riding deep in the tube.

32 **grom**: a young surfer.

33 **hootin'**: appreciative hoot made by a surfer when another surfer gets a good wave or performs an impressive manoeuvre.

34 **crucial**: *see* 12 **treacherous**

35 **brah**: brother.

36 **green room**: the tube, barrel, etc.

SURF SPOT

MALIBU

Malibu is one of California's most beguiling spots. A star-spangled confluence of geography, meteorology and history, it is where modern surf culture was born and raised.

The Native American Chumash people named their village, where Malibu stands today, 'Hanaliwu' – 'the place where the surf sounds loudly'. With the endless bounty of the ocean, backed by majestic canyons cutting into mountains teeming with game, it's hard not to think they must have had it pretty good. And how about that surf? Surely a stoked brave or two must have eyed up the perfect waves peeling into the beach from way outside and ridden them with supreme joy in the canoes the tribe made so diligently. Until 1542, when Spanish colonists sailed north from Mexico to claim the Malibu headland for the Spanish Crown, the Chumash had it all to themselves, too. They didn't leave any written records and the Conquistadors failed to mention wave-riding in any of their dispatches of the time, so the prevailing line that pioneer watermen Tom Blake and Sam Reid rode the very first waves there in 1927 just might be an unassailable truth. Although Malibu was surfed sporadically throughout the thirties, it was San Onofre in Orange County to the south that was the epicentre of straight-to-the-beach surf-riding on redwood planks. It wasn't until after the Second World War that this northern outpost became the seedbed from which the edgy beach culture that gobbled up the planet grew.

Situated just over the hill from the sprawling San Fernando tracts, Malibu is where the disparate tribes of America's post-war boom chose to congregate and lay the bedrock of youth culture's new creed. The availability

Malibu, with a beautiful setting, a vibrant beach scene and mechanically perfect waves, was the birthplace of surfing as a post-war youth cult.

The waves at Malibu range from mellow to radical,
depending on the power and direction of swell.
Typically the surf here rarely reaches above head high.

of materials pioneered during the Second World War had inspired local shapers such as Bob Simmons, Joe Quigg and Matt Kivlin to produce balsa-wood-cored, fibreglass and resin-coated surfboards with stabilising fins perfect for angling down the faces of waves. These boards became known as 'Malibu chips', and the evenly peeling rights of the 'Bu were perfect for the stylish, dynamic form of surfing that the boards facilitated. Soon surfers such as Miki Dora, Dewey Weber and Phil Edwards were creating the hotdog culture and an edgy new archetype of youth. It just so happened, too, that Malibu drew the best south swells in the summer months. With the influx of thousands of teenagers, by the late fifties Malibu was the perfect environment for surfing to become the embodiment of cool. ▶▶

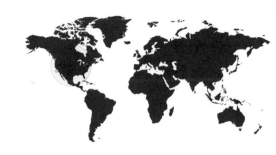

SURF SPOT
MALIBU

◀◀ Today, the place is a cacophony of clashing surf culture. On any given day you can see an armada of trad loggers flowing in a syncopated rhythm – a counterpoint to the post-modern bebop of floppy-haired shortboarders bobbing and weaving for wall time. Punk-ass DayGlo groms, for whom the eighties were the cradle of all things aesthetic, boost airs outside on the short lefts that bowl toward the lagoon off Third Point – while colonists from Hollywood clog up the arteries at First Point as they learn to surf with a battalion of paparazzi and starstuck punters gazing from the beach. In the strip behind the pier, meanwhile, you can breakfast with a moneyed, motley crew of C-listers, surf legends, plastic surgeons and screen scribes. Pull up at the 'Bu to greet one of California's easy-to-call south swells and you'll meet the whole of the Californian surf diaspora hustling for a slice of Malibu's mythic potency.

The break is a series of cobble-bottomed rights that form as a series of perfectly foiled banks. These radiate away from a huge sandbar that forms a lagoon inside the headland. There are three distinct take-off zones. First Point, the longest ride of the three, is where the Malibu myths have been made, where modern surf style as we know it evolved in the feline grace of Miki Dora and the radical elegance of Lance Carson's cutbacks. The names have changed, but First Point's core influence has remained the same. Contemporary young guns such as Josh Farberow and Jimmy Gamboa and a veteran Allen Sarlo rule First Point peelers. Second Point's takeoff is roughly in front of the Adamson Residence,

which was one of the earliest houses in Malibu and is now a tourist attraction owned by the State Parks organisation. Close by Second Point's takeoff area, the wave winds into a fast, bowling high-performance section known as Kiddie Bowl, where local young hotsters flex the full armoury of progressive manoeuvres. Third Point is situated at the furthest extremity of the spot, out in front of the lagoon. This is a zippy wave with steep take-offs and a quickly forming wall ruled by a highly accomplished local crew of shortboarders. It can be prone to closing out, reforming on the biggest swells inside and hooking up with the other two points.

The whole of Malibu works best on huge swells directly from the south, during which the prevailing north-west winds will be cross-offshore. Oriented due south, it's only a rare direct onshore wind that closes down the spot. The dream ride at Malibu is to thread a single wave right through from Third Point back into the pier, a feat possible only on the most perfect of big, lined-up swells. It's something that is achieved only rarely, even by seasoned locals. To link that wave isn't quite the surfing equivalent of the Hajji turning seven revolutions of the Ka'aba. But it just might come close.

Jimmy Gamboa, with toes on the nose, surfs First Point. For over fifty years, Malibu has been one of the great arenas for classic style.

READING THE SPOT

Before attempting to paddle out into an area of breaking waves, it is important to get your head around what is happening out there.

Seasoned surfers are experts at 'reading' a surf spot, even though the vagaries of sandbar, wind, tide and swell vary wildly from place to place and from wave to wave. Recognising the key features that exist at almost every surf spot is an essential skill for surfers starting out on their wave-riding journeys. When surfing a new break, however, be careful. Whether you're a beginner or have years of experience, the sea has a habit of making you feel humble.

Two surfers ride the right and the left at the peak at Bundoran, Co. Donegal, northwest Ireland. This spot, which has been threatened by a proposed marina development, is one of the highest-quality reefbreaks in Europe.

Ⓐ The peak
This is the point where the wave reaches critical mass and begins to break. The peak is the ideal spot from which to catch the wave. The surfer who is taking off from the peak, or is closest to it, has priority on this wave.

Ⓑ The right
A 'right' is the wave that breaks from right to left as you look at it from the beach. If you're a 'regular foot' (someone who rides with your left foot forward), you surf a right-breaking wave frontside (facing the wave). If you're a 'goofy foot' (someone who rides with your right foot forward), you surf a right backside (with your back to the wave).

Ⓒ The left
A 'left' is a wave that breaks from left to right, when seen from the beach. A goofy foot rides a left-breaking wave frontside, while a regular foot rides it backside.

Ⓓ The line-up
The place where surfers wait for waves, outside the peak.

Ⓔ Outside
This is any part of the water behind the line of the breaking waves.

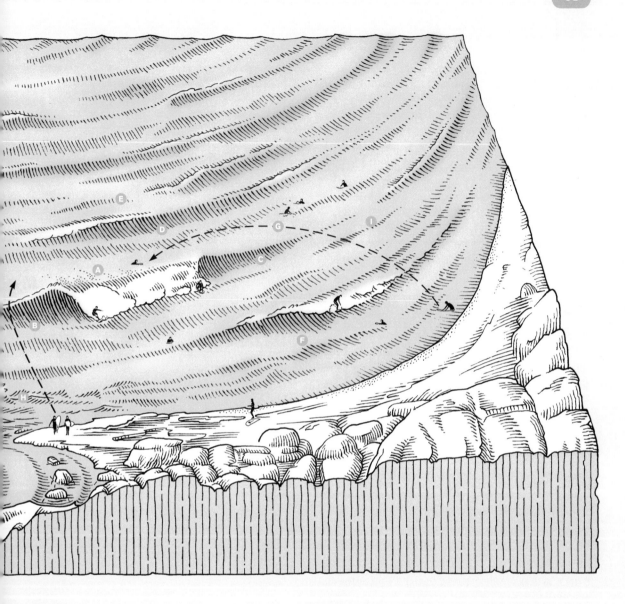

F Inside

This is any part of the water in front (shoreside) of the line of the breaking waves. If you are 'caught inside', you must paddle either side of the peak to find the channel, in order to take your place in the line-up.

G Outside paddle

The longest, but safest option, is to paddle 'outside', around the line of the breaking wave as it peels left and right. It is every surfer's responsibility to take note of the line of the ridden wave and to avoid it, where possible, when paddling out.

H Rips

The area of water directly in front of these rocks contains currents known as rips. These are caused by water rushing back out to sea from the shore. Rips can be a surfer's friend, as they ease the transition from the inside to the line-up.

I Channels

These are areas of deeper, calmer water to the side of the breaking wave, giving relatively easy access to the line-up.

DUKE KAHANAMOKU

Duke Kahanamoku, supreme athlete and globe-trotting 'ambassador of aloha', is universally recognised as the founding father of surfing.

Out of the water, I am nothing. Staring out of the window of a dusty, steel-seated bus somewhere deep in the American continent, he couldn't get the thought out of his head. He was a magnificent man. Six foot two, 190lbs. Not an ounce of fat on him. He had a stillness about him as well as something unfathomable. No one on the bus sat close to him. He was like an alien from another planet. *Out of the water, I am nothing.*

It was 1912 and Duke could swim faster than anyone on earth. Crossing America en route to Atlantic City to join up with the Olympic swimming team, this regal Polynesian was a man out of place, but thoroughly of his time. The twenty-two-year-old Hawaiian was already one of the most celebrated watermen in the Islands, supremely adept at not only surfing, but swimming, outrigger canoeing, game fishing and diving. He had a grace of movement about him and tremendous natural athleticism in the water. Because of this he had quickly become one of the most recognised members of the loose brotherhood of Waikiki 'beach boys'. The sport of the Hawaiian ancestors, decried as ungodly by the missionaries a hundred years previously, had almost disappeared by the time Duke was born. But, with the approaching twentieth century and a booming American economy, the Hawaiian Islands had become a symbol of Eden in the American imagination. The beach boys taught the ways of Hawaiian surf to the rich *haoles* who had begun to flock to Waikiki. Duke slipped perfectly into the role of an aquatic Adam.

Date of birth: 24 August 1890
(died 22 January 1968)
Place of birth: Honolulu
Defining wave: Waikiki

Duke Kahanamoku combined an unmatched athleticism with a flamboyant style in the surf. This photograph was taken in December 1914 at Freshwater, near Sydney, when thousands flocked to witness the 'bronzed Duke' in action.

Surfing had been reborn, and it fell to Duke with his imperious, straight-backed, straight-legged style and guileless ease with people, to communicate the magic of wave-riding across the world. It was the east coast of America first, then, after taking gold in the 100 metres freestyle swimming event in the Stockholm Olympiad, he travelled to Australia and New Zealand, spreading the surf creed along the way. Winning more gold medals at the 1920 games in Antwerp, he met Tom Blake in a movie theatre in Detroit on the way home, thereby inspiring a whole new chapter in surf history. Taking silver in the 1924 games in Paris, he was by this time a fully fledged friend to the stars. In the thirties he was elected ceremonial 'sheriff' of Hawaii, (and was re-elected twelve times) and scored one of the longest and most celebrated single rides in surf history, from 'zero break' outside Waikiki all the way to the beach – a distance of over a mile. During the thirties and forties, he frequently popped up in Hollywood movies, playing cameo roles opposite stars such as John Wayne and Johnny Weissmuller.

It was during the surf boom of the post-war years, however, that Duke became celebrated by surfers for his fundamental role in surf culture. As if his athletic achievements weren't enough to seal the deal, Duke seemed to embody the essential spirit of surfing – a living, breathing bridge between ancient Hawaii and modern surf culture. If, out of the water, Duke Kahanamoku was nothing, in the water, he would become a symbol of everything.

THE RIDE

Our current idea of a well-ridden wave is the result of a century of evolving surf technique.

The high-frequency lateral lines traced upon waves by twenty-first-century surfers are a far cry from the straight-to-the-beach surf-riding style of the early 1900s. This evolution reflects aesthetic shifts within surf culture as well as improved performance of the boards themselves. One of the most appealing things about contemporary surfing is that – apart from in competition – there are no rules set in stone. The surfer can either pick and choose from a hundred years of tradition – or throw out tradition itself and improvise freely upon a handful of classic moves, some of which are illustrated here.

No two waves, of course, are ever the same. What follows is a sequence of manoeuvres on a high-quality, right-breaking wave (breaking from left to right from the surfer's perspective) that includes a tube section. Master these building blocks of technique and you'll be able to make the most of every wave you encounter over a lifetime of surfing.

❶ Sprint paddling
accelerates the rider to the speed of the breaking wave

❻ The tube ride
takes the surfer to the heart of a hollow wave

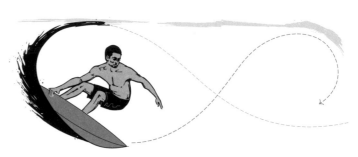

❼ The cutback
takes the surfer back to the powerful and breaking part of the wave

2 The take-off

sets up the beginning of the ride

3 Bottom turn A

turns the energy of the take-off into forward projection

5 Bottom turn B

harnesses speed and power for the tube ride

4 The top turn

returns the surfer to the bottom of the wave

8 Bottom turn C

harnesses speed in order to perform an aerial manoeuvre

9 The aerial

takes the surfer up and over the lip and can stylishly end a ride

CLASSIC SURF WAGON

THE WOODY

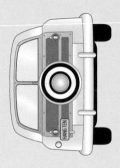

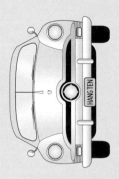

Surf
Culture

The surf wagon – almost as much as surfboards – has come to define modern American surf culture. And during the first surf explosion of the fifties, the 'woody' became an automotive icon.

Generically denoting any wood-panelled sedan, station wagon or van, the woody of popular surfing lore had two outstanding qualities. It was cheap and it was practical. This talisman of California cool, was, in reality, a heavy, lumbering 'sideboard on wheels'; the automotive equivalent of powdered egg: a memory of pre-war austerity crossed with a distinctly American idea of rustic nostalgia.

The ascendancy of the all-steel station wagon during the fifties meant that what were once the wheels of the leisure-focused wealthy became hand-me-down wagons that could be loaded with surfboards and surfing buddies without fear of incurring the wrath of Mom and Dad. The good citizens of boom-time America had gone out and purchased their chrome-clad behemoths from Detroit. Their surfer kid got the woody.

Ford's woody was the biggest seller throughout the forties and fifties, although Chrysler provided a strong contender for the woody crown with the introduction of the 'Town and Country' series in 1941. By the fifties, when the industrial innovations wrought in wartime began to filter into the mainstream of American industry, Detroit had fallen out of love with wood. Steel didn't rot, fade or buckle and steel wagons began outstripping the sales of traditional woodys. An era had ended, but woodys remained a fixture in California beach car parks until the end of the sixties.

A **Ron is stoked with his 1950 Woody**

It's an eight-year-old Ford wagon framed in blond maple with mahogany panelling. Under the bonnet it's running a '51 Mercury Flathead V8.

B **Barbara isn't really into surfing …**

But she's fascinated by the guys and girls down at Malibu. That Miki Dora is just the most. She discovered the beach scene a couple of years back through this little novel called Gidget: The Little Girl with Big Ideas. *They're making a movie out of it next year, apparently.*

C **Ron's Velzy**

Ron saved up and convinced Dale Velzy to build him this board for that one point he found down in Baja last summer. He and Barbara are heading down this weekend with nothing but a crate of beer and his baggies.

D **On the road**

There's this writer cat called Kerouac who Ron's starting to dig. Something about reading him just makes him want to load up the woody, stick the Art Pepper and Shorty Rogers concert on the radio and pop out some bennie.

HOW TO

READ A PRESSURE CHART

An educated glance at the weather chart can take much of the guesswork out of predicting rideable waves in a particular area.

The rise of forecasting technology and the availability of detailed, accurate information on the Internet has produced a fervent cult of amateur meteorology within the global surf community. Knowledge of local conditions remains key to predicting the arrival of quality waves at a particular spot. A quick, informed look at the local pressure chart, however, can give a surprisingly accurate indication as to whether there will be rideable waves on any given day.

A low-pressure system is an area of cool air that draws in warmer air from around itself, creating winds. In the northern hemisphere wind blows in a counter-clockwise direction around these areas of cool air. Lows are represented on a weather chart by lines with numbers along them. These lines are called isobars and represent areas of equal pressure measured in millibars. The lower the pressure, the closer together the isobars appear on the chart. The lower the number, the more severe the storm and the more powerful the swell it is likely to produce.

Swell radiates away from the centre of a low-pressure system, roughly along the lines of the isobars, like waves made by a pebble thrown into a pond. Low-pressure systems in the North Atlantic can produce swells that generate waves from the far northwest of Ireland to the desert coastlines of Morocco. The further away from the coastline a low appears, the greater the 'period' between waves that break on shore and the higher the quality of those waves. If the low is too close to land, the waves it produces will be chaotic and unrideable on that coastline. But one European surfer's nemesis will be another's dream. A low-pressure system located just off the coast of Ireland, for example, will produce big, stormy seas that are more or less unrideable up and down Ireland and southwest England. This same low, however, will produce beautifully spaced, long period waves in northern Spain.

The ideal chart for southwest England will see the United Kingdom under an extensive area of high pressure, (which usually produces sunny skies and light winds). Out in the Atlantic, however, to the south of Greenland, a large area of low pressure will form, held at bay by the high-pressure system that sits over the land. This will mean that big, powerful, long-distance waves will radiate to the north coast of Devon and Cornwall, and that local conditions on the beaches will be blessed with light winds – perfect surfing conditions.

A Low-pressure system

Isobars close together indicate a large, powerful low-pressure system situated south of Greenland. Near to the centre of the storm, pressure is lower and winds are higher.

B Severity of storm

The tightly spaced isobars radiating outwards indicate a big and powerful swell is on its way. In the northern hemisphere winds travel around the storm in an anti-clockwise direction.

C High-pressure system

Winds in a high-pressure system travel in a clockwise direction along the lines of equal pressure. Here, relatively light winds will be blowing toward the the coastline of southwest England.

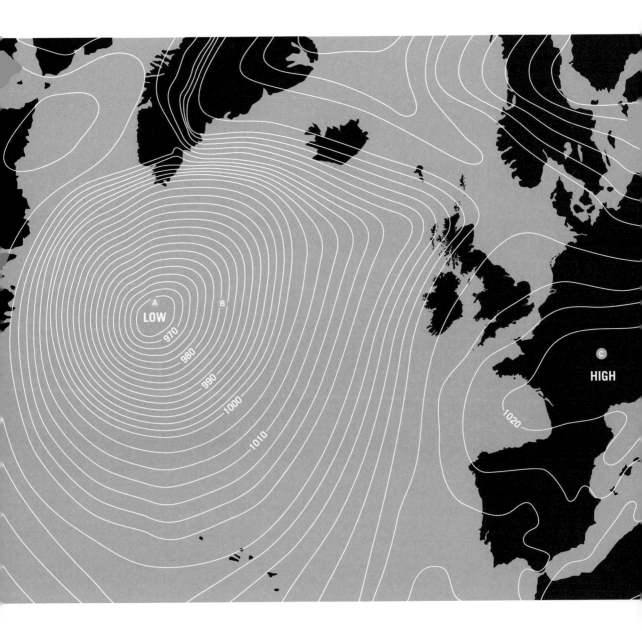

TECHNIQUE ONE

PADDLING

Paddling is the most fundamental of surfing skills. Only once this is mastered can the business of wave-riding truly begin.

There are two phases to paddling. The first is used when paddling out from the beach to the line-up – the area where surfers wait for a wave – and postioning yourself there. The second is sprint paddling, which you need to catch your wave (or in order to get out of the way of a set of breaking waves). To reach the line-up it is important to paddle in a relaxed but purposeful manner. You should keep your head up and remain aware at all times of the position of the waves and the other surfers around you. When you're in the correct position to catch a wave (as close to the 'peak' as possible), paddle strongly towards the shore and take one last glance over your shoulder to the wave. This will enable you to make any last-minute adjustments prior to committing to the wave and the take-off.

During the longboard era, when boards were heavy and had plenty of flotation, most paddling was done on the knees. Whilst many contemporary longboarders still use the knee-paddling technique, by far the most common and practical form of paddling on a modern surfboard is the prone paddle.

A surfer about to sprint paddle for a wave

A *Head*

When paddling out, arch your back, keep your head raised and look straight ahead. This will keep the nose of your board up and help you glide more cleanly through the water.

fig. I: Paddling

B *Hands*

Your focus should be on displacing as much water as possible with long, steady and rhythmical strokes.

C *Arms and hands*

When in position close to the wave's peak, paddle hard directly towards the shore, until you feel the board planing beneath you. (At this point you'll be ready to pop to your feet for the take-off.)

D *Legs and feet*

When sprint paddling it is possible to gain extra momentum by kicking with the legs and feet. Be careful, however, not to undermine your core stability when doing this – your arms and shoulders are all-important in paddling, and they need a stable base from which to work.

fig. I.I:
Sprint Paddling

E *Head*

When sprint paddling your head should remain low, close to the deck of the board. This will help tip the board forward, enabling you to achieve the necessary speed for a successful take-off.

The Search for the Perfect Wave

On any day of the year it's summer somewhere in the world. Bruce Brown's latest color film highlights the adventures of two young American surfers, Robert August and Mike Hynson who follow this everlasting summer around the world. Their unique expedition takes them to Senegal, Ghana, Nigeria, South Africa, Australia, New Zealand, Tahiti, Hawaii and California. Share their experience as they search the world for the perfect wave which may be forming just over the next horizon. BRUCE BROWN FILMS

One-time art director of *Surfer* magazine, John Van Hamersveld created one of the most enduring images of surf culture with his poster design for *The Endless Summer*.

CLASSIC SURF MOVIES

THE ENDLESS SUMMER
AND *FIVE SUMMER STORIES*

The makers of surf movies are the chief architects of the surf dream. Here are two era-defining moments in surf-movie history that changed for ever the way we looked at waves.

The Endless Summer (1964)

Bruce Brown's cinematic odyssey, based on 'the search for the perfect wave', took young Californian surfers Robert August and Mike Hynson around the globe in an exploration of the world's waves. It's an arrestingly simple movie that pulled off the complex task of drawing in a huge mainstream audience whilst retaining credibility with its central audience of surfers. We follow the slick-suited, Brylcreemed Californians to West Africa, then on to South Africa, and across the Southern Ocean to Australia and New Zealand before circumnavigating back to California via Tahiti and Hawaii – with Brown's enthusiastic, understated Californian lilt guiding us all the way.

Rather than ground-breaking surf action or breathless derring-do, it's the timeless sentiments the film manages to evoke – the beauty of the surfing lifestyle, the friendship hewn out of the spirit of common adventure – that make the film such an enduring classic. Its definitive sequence is that of the flawless, endlessly peeling waves the boys surf at Cape St Francis, on the southeast coast of South Africa. As a result of the film's widespread distribution, the spot became the archetypal 'perfect wave' of the longboard era.

Those waist-high walls may have long ago ceased to be the surfer's supreme slice of heaven, but *The Endless Summer* remains a jewel that has found a place in the heart of the most cynical of contemporary surfers. It became the template for a new genre of globally successful surf films and introduced a generation to the seemingly infinite possibilities of surf travel. 'You think the surf's good here,' told its audience, 'look at what wonders await the intrepid.'

Five Summer Stories (1972)

Five Summer Stories was the high point of prolific film-makers Greg MacGillivray and Jim Freeman's surf movie success. It encapsulated the groovy, colourful world of the early seventies – a time when the changes introduced by the shortboard revolution had taken deep root. Over the four or five years before the film's release, the length and volume of the average surfboard had reduced drastically. The tube became the beating pulse of the wave and a generation of turned-on, dropped-out surfers sought to commune with its power. In the search for this holy grail, all surfers aspired to draw long, arcing lines in the ocean. *Five Summer Stories* defined that aspiration. Gloriously colour-saturated with in-the-water photography from surf-movie pioneer Bud Browne and cut together with a suitably far-out soundtrack, the movie's arresting visual presence was defined by the flow of Hawaiian tube-riding guru Gerry Lopez.

Bruce Brown's mellow utopia was replaced by the dangerous waves of the North Shore of Oahu. Here, along

THE VISION

Overleaf: action sequences from *Five Summer Stories.*

Artist Rick Griffin evoked the period perfectly in his design for the poster of *Five Summer Stories*.

The two main protagonists of *The Endless Summer*, Robert August (*left*) and Mike Hynson (*centre*), together with film-maker Bruce Brown, set off on their global odyssey.

with Lopez, surfers such as David Nuuhiwa, Billy Hamilton and Jeff Hakman led the attack on their sleek, Lightning Bolt-branded boards, pushing into what had been an unridden realm of power, speed and inside-out geometry. The film had everything the era required of it, including the superstars of a revolutionary period surfing at the edge of their formidable talents and a tripped-out soundtrack. It even had an achingly cool poster designed by esteemed psychedelic pioneer and surf artist Rick Griffin. With Vietnam raging, *Five Summer Stories* served as a powerful promotional tool for surfing as counter-culture.

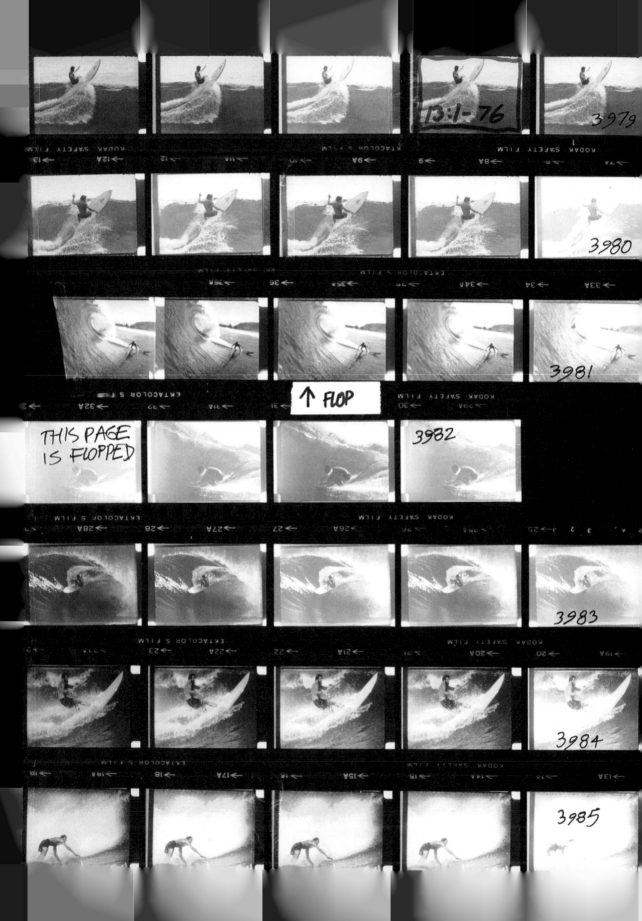

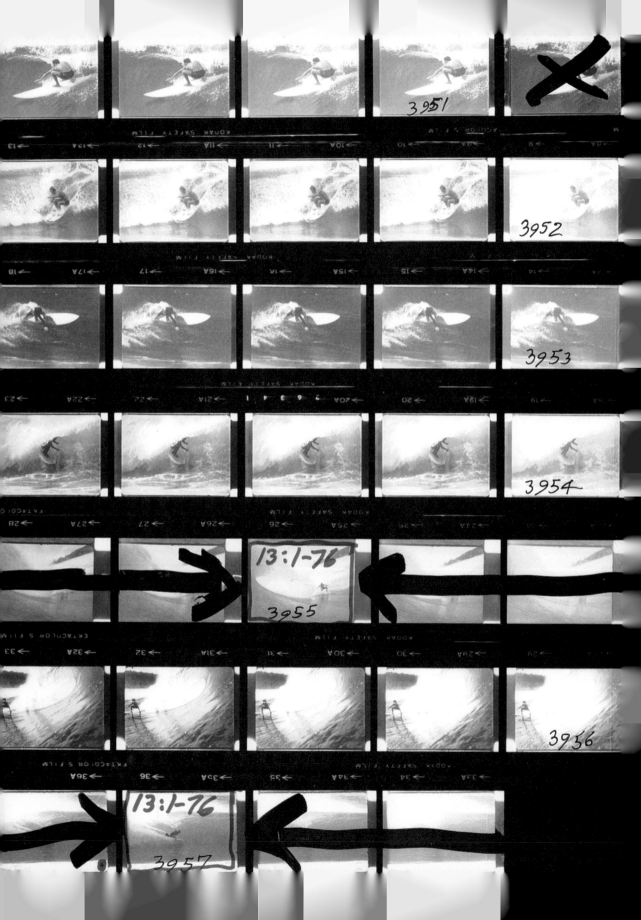

WHY HAWAII?

Pounded by Pacific swells and shaped by a complex history that is often overlooked, Hawaii occupies centre stage in the surfing universe.

At Ehukai Beach, on the North Shore of Oahu, Hawaii, in the middle of December, the swell is building. Just a few metres from where you stand, a surfer pulls deep into a screaming left-hand barrel and disappears behind a razor-sharp falling curtain. A little in the distance, to your right, at Sunset Beach, an A-frame peak collapses, crashing forward like a freight train through the line-up. Meanwhile, a couple of kilometres to your left, big-wave boards are being waxed up ready to take on Waimea Bay at twenty foot and rising. Take a deep breath and enjoy the moment. If wave-riding is your creed then you've arrived at its spiritual home.

Made up of 130 islands, Hawaii is an archipelago stretching over 2,400 kilometres and located 3,200 kilometres southwest of the California coast. There are four main islands: Oahu, Maui, Kuai and Hawaii (otherwise known as Big Island). Each has its own distinct character. Oahu is the jewel in the surfing crown and the most populated of the islands, while wind-blown Maui is home to the performance waves of Honolua Bay and Maalaea. Peahi (otherwise known as Jaws), on the north coast of the island, defined the emergence of tow-in surfing during the nineties. Kauai is a small, relatively quiet island whose surf is characterised by intense localism, while the Big Island has a down-home country atmosphere and, although eclipsed by the other islands' surf spots, its own surf hotspot – the Kona Coast. Although the islands have rideable surf throughout most of the year, it's during the months from November to February that their shores resound with the impacts of big, powerful swells pitching into the lava reefs that surround them. The islands, formed by volcanoes, rise abruptly from the sea floor, with no continental shelf to slow down or dilute the raw power of the swells that arrive from every direction. One of the consequences of this geography is that the North Shore of Oahu is a stretch of northwest-facing coastline blessed with the world's greatest concentration of A-list surf spots. To recite the full list of locations from Velzyland in the north down to Haleiwa in the west, is to utter a breathless litany of hallowed names that have mythical status in surf culture.

Wave-riding had played a central role in the lives of the islanders long before the first recorded European contact towards the end of the eighteenth century. It is possible that small boards may have been ridden, probably prone, by Polynesian settlers over 1,500 years ago. In any case, it is generally accepted that by the turn of the first millennium, surfing had grown into a complex and essential part of indigenous culture. It wasn't until the first successful colonists began sending dispatches back to the Old World that the earliest written accounts of surfing began to filter into European record. In 1778, members of Captain Cook's crew described in various accounts that the native islanders took great pleasure in riding waves. During the early colonial period, these reports, and others that came after, documented that surfing was an inclusive, integral part of Hawaiian culture. Women, children and men from all strata of society would take to the surf when the waves were up, mostly on the shorter, narrower Alaia boards, with the longer, heavier Olo reserved for nobles. Bets would be placed on who could ride the biggest wave and for the longest time, and courting couples would take to the ocean naked as a prelude to love. ▶▶

The Pacific Ocean

1 Hawaiian Island chain

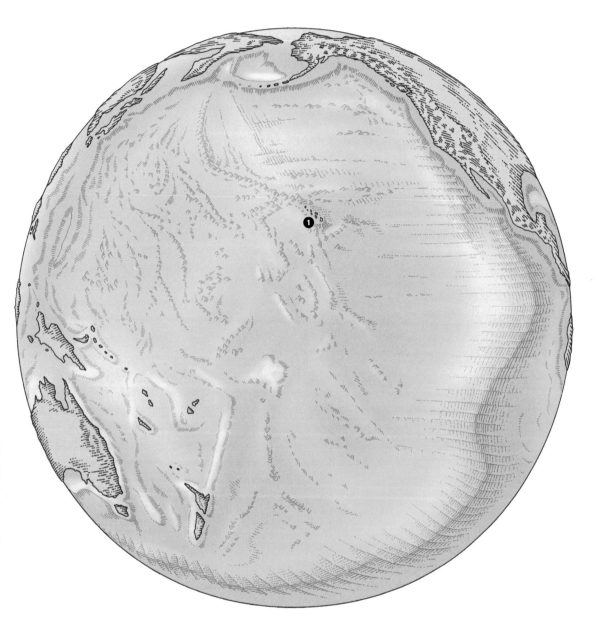

A volcanic archipelago set amid the huge expanse of the Pacific Ocean, Hawaii is exposed to huge swells generated by storms in the North Pacific. The reefs around its northern shores form some of the most powerful surfing waves in the world.

WHY HAWAII?

◀◀ Although the details have been buried under a fragrant heap of hibiscus and tourist-friendly 'aloha', the fact remains that contact with European culture at the end of the eighteenth century was a disease-ridden, blood-stained disaster. Within decades of Captain Cook's arrival, diseases borne by the European settlers, particularly smallpox, measles, influenza and gonorrhoea – infections for which the Hawaiians had no natural immunity – decimated the indigenous population. In addition, the traditional Hawaiian systems of law and economy were gradually undermined by an emerging market economy that meant that for the first time, Hawaiian land, products and labour came under private ownership to be bought and sold. Unable to survive economically under this new regime, many young Hawaiian men left their homes to crew on the ships that would trade across the Pacific, putting additional pressure on the shrinking indigenous population. Exacerbated by the preaching of the missionaries, by the early nineteenth century, many Hawaiians were convinced that their fate was a result of ungodly depravity. Surfing, perhaps the most visible and vibrant token of Hawaiian identity, more or less disappeared, decried as the work of the devil. Up to 250,000 migrant workers came from China, Japan and Portugal, and later Korea and the Philippines, to work the newly introduced sugar and pineapple plantations. Inevitably, this further undermined what, precariously, remained of traditional Hawaiian culture. It has been estimated that in the period immediately before the arrival of Cook's flotilla in 1777, the Hawaiian 'full blood'

population may have been anything up to a million. By the end of the nineteenth century, the number had shrunk to under 40,000. This impoverished group of people had an average life expectancy of just thirty-five years.

It's a bitter irony that by the turn of the twentieth century Hawaii and surfing itself would come to represent exactly the kinds of garlanded Eden that it actually had been prior to the arrival of the *haoles*, or foreigners. The surfing renaissance that came with this development was centred around Waikiki, on Oahu's south shore, and led by a small group of surfers, swimmers, divers and canoe-paddlers who congregated around the Hui Nalu and Outrigger Canoe Clubs. Full-blood waterman Duke Kahanamoku was among them, as well as Irish-Hawaiian surfer George Freeth and the energetic proselytiser of all things Hawaiian, Alexander Hume Ford. Earlier, during the 1860s, the American novelist Mark Twain had written a series of travel pieces on Hawaii which had been syndicated in the weekly magazines. These enjoyed huge circulation on mainland America, sowing the seeds of Hawaii's growth as a popular tourist destination. In 1907, adventurer and writer Jack London travelled to Waikiki and paddled out with Freeth and Hume Ford and wrote an account of the experience, which was widely published in the popular journals and reprinted in his 1911 travelogue *The Cruise of the Snark*. London evoked Hawaii and surfing as a new frontier, paradise-like in its beauty and simplicity, and referred to the sport's practitioners as the 'natural gods of the earth'. Surfing was soon enjoying a rapid and widespread popularity thanks to writers such as London along with the wildly successful demonstrations of the sport by George Freeth and Duke Kahanamoku, its roving ambassadors.

As surfing was exported to the rest of the world, Hawaii remained surf culture's beating heart. For mainland surfers, a visit to the Hawaiian Islands became a rite of passage, and some of these visitors, of course, never left. Surfers such as Tom Blake and Lorrin 'Whitey' Harrison, who settled here, helped to create the archetypes of a surfing lifestyle to which every contemporary wave-rider is heir. ▶▶

The Hawaiian Islands

1. Kauai
2. Oahu
3. Molokai
4. Maui
5. Lanai
6. Kahoolawe
7. Hawaii

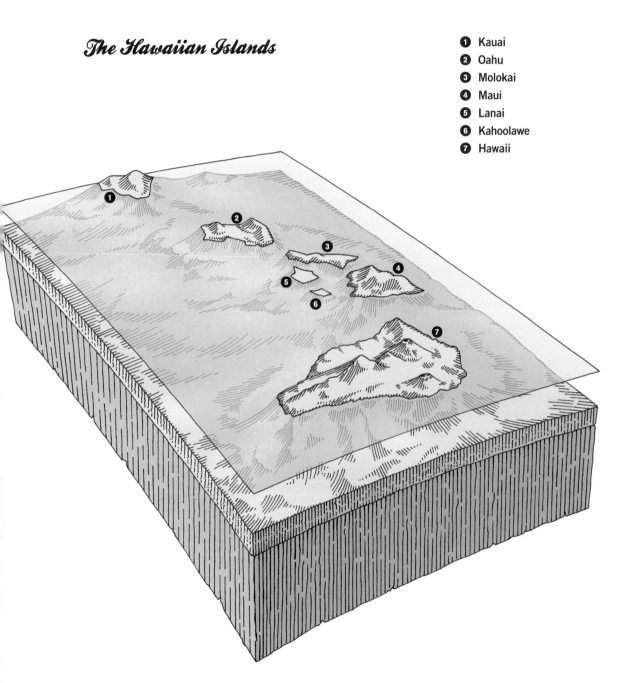

There are four major islands in the far-flung Hawaiian archipelago – Hawaii (otherwise known as 'Big Island', Oahu, Maui and Kauai. Hawaii itself is a relatively quiet surfing backwater; its Kona Coast, however, was once one of the centres of native surf culture, and where Captain Cook was killed by a group of islanders in 1779.

WHY HAWAII?

◀◀ Many of the important developments in surfboard design, such as George Downing's experiments with big-wave boards, took place here. The big waves of Makaha on Oahu's west coast, and the intense crucible of the North Shore were pioneered in the forties and fifties by a new generation of visiting surfers that included Pat Curren, Mickey Muñoz, Greg Noll, Ricky Grigg and others. During this time, surfing's place in the pantheon of popular culture was fully and irrevocably sealed, with Hawaii as its Mecca. Since then Hawaii has enjoyed an almost uninterrupted period in the spotlight of surf consciousness. Big-wave spots continue to be discovered elsewhere that eclipse in their intensity those found in the Islands – locations such as Indonesia and South Africa enjoy surf every bit as powerful as Hawaii. However, as a place so inextricably linked with the birth and development of surfing in modern times, its position remains unassailable.

One of the consequences of its pre-eminent status is that today it's difficult to see Hawaii other than through a veil of cliché. Take, for example, the way that the Hawaiian word 'aloha' has been reinterpreted in Hawaii. It is everywhere in the Islands. But, rather than a term that represents the spirit of love, kinship and welcoming, it is most often seen on the signs of dry cleaners, on the business cards of spam wholesalers. The guy behind the car rental desk will beam and smile while he says it. So will the bug man who comes to

Oahu

From the relatively mellow peelers of Waikiki in the south to the fierce surf of the North Shore, Oahu's fabled spots are among the most iconic in surf culture. Over 75 per cent of the Islands' total population live on Oahu and the state capital, Honolulu, is found here.

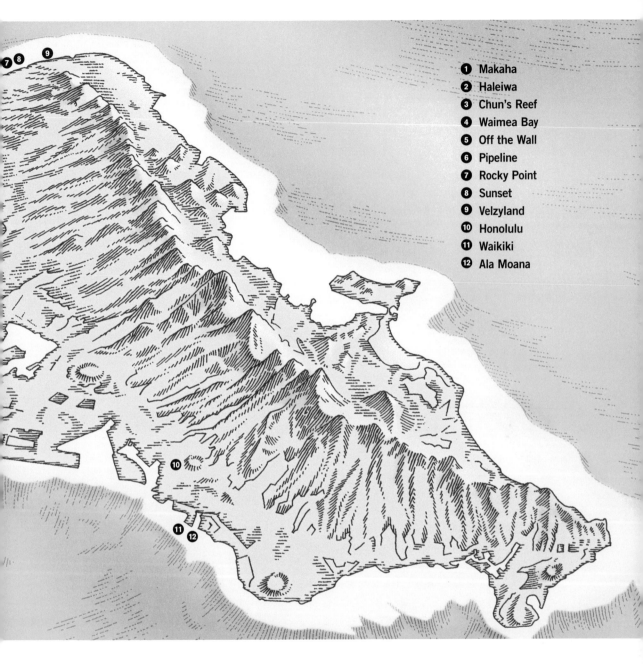

1. Makaha
2. Haleiwa
3. Chun's Reef
4. Waimea Bay
5. Off the Wall
6. Pipeline
7. Rocky Point
8. Sunset
9. Velzyland
10. Honolulu
11. Waikiki
12. Ala Moana

exterminate the termites in your apartment. And so will the pidgin-drawling white boy from Minnesota as he steals your wave at Ala Moana Bowls. In Hawaii 'aloha' is an idea that is one of many encoded in a culture of romantic primitivism. Like the ubiquitous Hawaiian shirt, it is everywhere and, at the same time, strangely absent, marketed to death like a greasy burger loaded with pineapple.

With a past shrouded in Eden-like myth, cut short by violent historical fact, it's hardly surprising that Hawaii has a confused and confusing identity. But its considerable assets will continue to draw wave after wave of surfers. It's a place to which every surfer must one day travel, and it's a place that will batter either your body or your romantic preconceptions – perhaps both.

"I DROP IN,

SET THE THING UP AND BEHIND ME, ALL THIS STUFF GOES OVER MY BACK; THE SCREAMING PARENTS, TEACHERS, POLICE, PRIESTS, POLITICIANS

– THEY'RE ALL GOING OVER THE FALLS HEADFIRST

AND WHEN IT STARTS TO CLOSE
———————— OUT,
I PULL OUT THE BACK, PICK UP
ANOTHER WAVE AND DO THE SAME
GODDAMN THING. "

Miki Dora

LEROY GRANNIS

Over the last fifty years, no other photographer has documented surf culture more eloquently than LeRoy Grannis.

Born in Hermosa Beach in 1917, Grannis was among the first generation of Californians to take up the surfing way of life. The Californian halcyon of the thirties he experienced as a teenager, with its unspoilt beaches, crystal-clear waters and uncrowded waves, proved to be the perfect seedbed for the photographic sensibilities that emerged much later. After the Second World War, a full-time job as a telephone engineer and a young family to support meant that he surfed only occasionally. In 1959, however, under doctor's orders to find a relaxing pastime to counteract the stresses of his working life, he began to photograph the surf culture that was developing around him.

During the late fifties and early sixties, surfing was in the throes of a rapid transformation from left-field coastal cult to a fully fledged youth phenomenon, spurred on by the release of *Gidget* and a slew of other surfsploitation movies. By the mid-sixties, the middle-aged LeRoy Grannis was one of the most prolific lensmen working for surf magazines and industry ad campaigns. Shooting predominantly on the Californian coast and Hawaiian Islands, he brought a candid, outsider's eye to the material, coupled with superlative technical precision. Despite his success, he continued to hold down his day job and, contrary to the current of surfing through the sixties and into the seventies, he remained a passionate advocate of competitive surfing.

There are thousands of perfectly framed moments of wave-riding in the Grannis archive, shot beautifully from the beach as well as from deep inside the action. Above all, his photographs offer an intimate insight into the lives of a group of blessed individuals. His lens captured the leading surfers of a generation growing to maturity while the surf culture, which they had helped to create, flowered around them.

Grannis captures the essence of surfing's soul in this 1968 shot of Midget Farrelly giving in to the glide at Makaha, Oahu.

TOM BLAKE

—

Date of birth: 8 March 1902
(died 5 May 1994)
Place of birth: Milwaukee, Wisconsin
Defining waves: Malibu, Waikiki

*As well as revolutionising the technology and practice
of wave-riding, Tom Blake pioneered the surfing lifestyle.*

Milwaukee, 1916. It was something about water. It seemed to set fourteen-year-old Tom Blake free. He had seen pictures of the Hawaiians in the little illustrated magazines his aunt kept in the dresser in the house out in the Wisconsin woods. Next to tales of the war in Europe, there were exotic images of brown boys in woollen one-pieces frolicking in the surf, the backdrop a scene of palms and mountains. He felt a little guilty looking at the pictures, flicking through the pages of the magazines in the rough fingerless gloves his aunt had knitted him at Christmas. He was meant to stoke the fire that freezing dawn but through these pictures he could feel the warmth of the sun on his skin. He recognised the feeling. It was the same feeling he got in the pool. In the water, lost deep in the physicality of the stretch and the roll and the breath of his stroke, he would picture those Hawaiians. He would get so deep inside himself swimming lap after lap after lap that the noise of the pool and the cries of the instructors and the laughter of the kids would fall away and his mind would fill with the ocean, the palm trees, the creatures of the sea, the sound of the surf and the strumming of a guitar. If he hadn't been bounded by the copings of the pool, he could carry on swimming for ever. At least until he got to Waikiki.

Detroit, 1920. Blake had been trying to make it to Nantucket. He thought he might work a passage on a whaler or some other vessel. Or maybe he'd join the navy. He'd heard that the Hawaiian swimmer called Duke Kahanamoku had won gold at the Olympics in Europe. He spent a dime to see the newsreel, and, to his amazement, Duke was there, at that very movie theatre, en route back to Hawaii. He strode up to Duke after the show and stretched out his hand. The champion smiled at him broadly. As they shook hands, Blake experienced the same feeling he got after a hundred and twenty laps of the pool. He felt as if he could swim for ever.

Rather than heading east to Nantucket, Tom Blake turned west, towards California. It wasn't until 1922 that he paddled out on a surfboard. It was a while before he ventured out again, but soon he had mastered the hydrodynamics of surfing. In 1926 he pioneered Malibu, the seedbed of modern surf culture. The following year he created a lightweight version of the ancient Olo surfboard, using large drill-holes which he then covered with a thin skein of timber. In 1929 he made a paddleboard constructed from a chambered hull which dramatically improved speed and agility (and therefore surf-rescue effectiveness). That year, Blake also fashioned a primitive water housing for a camera that he had been given by Duke, and began to take some of the first surf photographs shot from the water. Winning a number of high-profile and prestigious paddling races with his new, lighter board in 1931, and now living in Hawaii full time, Blake patented a hollow surfboard based on the same principles. The hollow board was so light it brought a whole new set of surfers to the beach. In 1935, he attached a powerboat skeg to the underside of one of his surfboards, inventing the surfboard fin. The same year, a folio of water shots were published by *National*

Blake published the details of his surfboard innovations in various magazines, including this 1937 issue of *Popular Mechanics*.

Tom Blake (*left*) and his mentor and hero Duke Kahanamoku pose with the hugely influential hollow 'cigar box' surfboard in the mid-thirties.

Geographic, making him probably the first extensively published surf photographer.

Although Blake's most tangible acheivements came during this decade of breathless creativity, he will be remembered equally for evangelising the surfing lifestyle. For Blake, surfing was an all-encompassing way of living, rooted spiritually in what he later called 'the church of the open sky'. He lived a life in which the wave is the primary imperative. In the process, his pioneering vision, which brought together the idea of the multi-talented waterman with the importance of a healthy mind, body and spirit, inspired an entire culture.

MILESTONES IN SURFBOARD DESIGN

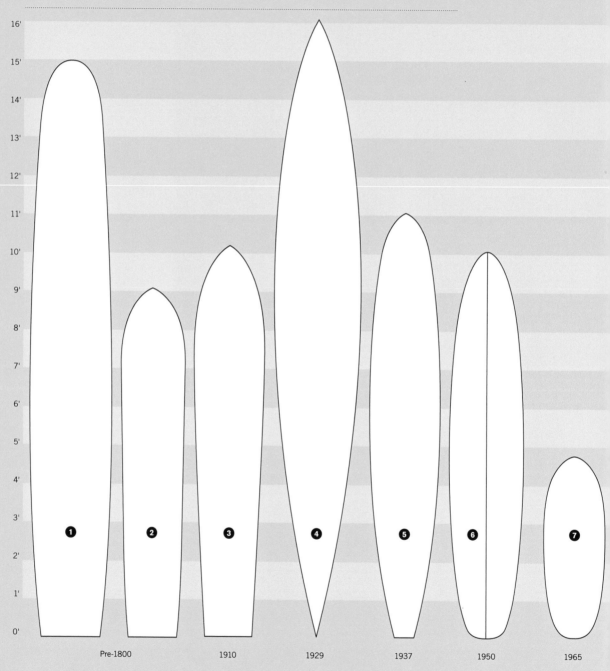

16'
15'
14'
13'
12'
11'
10'
9'
8'
7'
6'
5'
4'
3'
2'
1'
0'

❶   ❷   ❸   ❹   ❺   ❻   ❼

Pre-1800   1910   1929   1937   1950   1965

The perfect example of form reflecting function, the surfboard has evolved from hand-hewn lump of solid wood, to mass-produced, CAD-designed composite.

The general trajectory of surfboard design over the last seventy years has been from big, heavy crafts towards lighter, smaller and sleeker boards. The first major advance on the ancient designs of Hawaiian boards came with Tom Blake's innovative chamber-hulled 'cigar box' board of 1929. Lighter and more manoeuvrable than the cumbersome 'plank' of the early 1900s, it introduced a new generation to the joys of wave-riding. In the post-war years, breakthroughs in materials technology led to foam and fibreglass replacing balsa-wood cores and timber veneers, and by the mid- to late fifties, shapers such as Dale Velzy and Hobie Alter were among the first to mass produce what we now know as 'longboards'. During the following few years, the experiments of innovators such as George Greenough and Bob McTavish inspired an exploratory avant-garde to chop up their longboards into quicker-turning, shorter, lighter, thinner experimental designs. ▶▶

❶ Olo
❷ Alaia
❸ Redwood plank
❹ Tom Blake Cigar
❺ Hot Curl
❻ Velzy Pig
❼ George Greenough Spoon
❽ Bing Pipeliner
❾ McTavish Deep V
❿ Steve Lis Fish
⓫ Egg
⓬ Lightning Bolt Single Fin
⓭ MR Twin Fin
⓮ Thruster

The history of surfboard design has been one of endless experimentation, including huge variations in board length, shape and volume. Most of the developments during the last twenty years, however, have come in the form of improved materials and construction techniques.

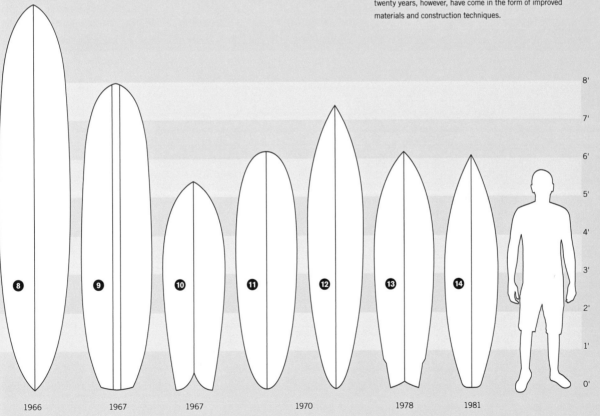

1966   1967   1967   1970   1978   1981

MILESTONES IN SURFBOARD DESIGN

◀◀ By the early seventies, the shortboard revolution was in full swing. The new boards reflected the spirit of the times, and allowed their riders to re-imagine the ridden wave as something to be attacked, where previously it had been all about teasing out easy-flowing glide. Ten years later, Simon Anderson's all-conquering three-finned Thruster, which was more forgiving than any previous design, proved a highpoint in the development of shortboards. Since then, composite materials, sophisticated sandwich construction and a wealth of hybrid and 'retro-progressive' models, based on earlier designs, have came to the forefront of a truly globalised surf culture.

Today's surfer is in an incredibly privileged position, able to pick and choose from a century and more of surfboard design. Even the ancient alaia design has been revived, and has sparked renewed interest in the possibility of fin-free surfing. With the turn of the twenty-first century, environmental imperatives have fuelled the search for the non-toxic, perfectly sustainable surfboard: the clean and green surfboard is the Holy Grail for surfboard design. If it can be found, then it may help the surfing tribe collectively become the natural custodians of the ocean environment.

See also

(Numbers refer back to the illustration on the previous pages)

Pre-20th century

Caballito Pre-Incan fishermen on Peru's west coast may have used reed craft to ride waves.

Olo Hawaiian solid-wood board, reserved for noble lineages, and surfed standing up. ❶

Alaia Hawaiian board made from koa or wili-wili. Ridden prone or on the knees by commoners and children. ❷

1900s to 1930s

The plank (early 1900s) Flat-bottomed, ten-foot-long varnished redwood boards weighing up to 100 pounds are used by Duke Kahanamoku and his contemporaries. ❸

Cigar board (1929) Hollow, flat-bottomed board, designed by Tom Blake. It is lighter and more streamlined than the plank. ❹

Hot Curl (1937) Finless, solid-redwood and balsa-laminate board developed by John Kelly for big waves. ❺

1940s

Malibu Chip (1945) Bob Simmons, Joe Quigg and Matt Kivlin develop a lighter, balsa-cored board, ten-foot long and weighing 25lbs, with a resin-saturated fibreglass layer.

1950s

Velzy Pig (1950) Early models have a balsa core with resin and glass finish; by 1958, polyurethane foam replaces balsa. The ubiquitous board of the early Californian surf boom. ❻

Big-wave boards (early 1950s) George Downing attaches a fin to the rear of Hot Curl board, creating the first big-wave board of the modern era.

Signature longboards (mid- to late 1950s) Companies such as Hobie begin to mass produce commercially successful pro-signature models.

Pat Curren Gun (late 1950s) Curren fashions boards from balsa specifically for the newly pioneered big waves of Waimea Bay. The term was coined by Buzzy Trent: 'You don't go hunting elephant with a BB gun,' said Trent. 'If you're going to hunt big waves, take a big gun.'

1960s

George Greenough Spoon (1965) Short knee-ridden design, for dynamic top-to-bottom turning. **7**

Bing Pipeliner (1966) Dick Brewer produces his Pipeliner model under the Bing Copeland label. Perfect for fast, hollow waves, this proves to be one of the most influential longboards of the sixties. **8**

Stubbies and displacement-hulled shortboards (1966) Malibu-based coterie of surfers, centred around Greg Liddle, attempt to produce a standup version of Greenough's spoons. These are at the cutting edge of the California branch of the shortboard revolution.

Bob McTavish V-Bottom (1967) Inspired by Greenough's kneeboards, Australian shaper Bob McTavish begins experimenting with eight-foot-long boards with a V bottom, wide, square tails and 'high aspect ratio' single fin. McTavish's design helps spark the 'shortboard revolution'. **9**

Steve Lis Fish (1967) San Diego-based kneeboarder Steve Lis designs split-tailed, twin-pintail shortboards. Used to ride standup by the mid-seventies. **10**

1970s

Egg (1970) Skip Frye produces wide, thin boards with rounded planshapes in the seven-to-eight foot range. These heavily influence hybrid designs of the nineties. **11**

Lightning Bolt Single Fin (1970) Gerry Lopez's pintailed, beak-nosed design becomes the dominant shortboard by the middle of the decade. **12**

Bonzer (1972) Ventura-based Campbell brothers experiment with a double concave tail set-up with two side-biter triangular fins in addition to the central single fin.

MR twin fin (1978) Australia's Mark Richards wins world championship on a twin-finned swallow tail. **13**

1980s

Thruster (1981) A three-finned board with a centrally placed single fin solves the twin-fin's skittish problems. Simon Anderson's design becomes ubiquitous. **14**

The Thruster refined (late 1980s) Santa Barbara-based Al Merrick and other shapers hone the Thruster design. The drop in weight and volume, however, creates a schism in surfing, and this contibutes to the longboard renaissance.

The performance longboard (late 1980s) Older surfers rediscover longboard designs, often adding hard rails and three fins.

Tow-in boards (late 1980s) A small tribe of surfers based in Maui and Oahu, led by Laird Hamilton, use zodiacs, and later jetskis, to tow into huge, fast waves. Boards evolve into short, heavy designs resembling snowboards.

1990s

Hybrids (mid-1990s) The decade following the re-emergence of the longboard is characterised by experimentation with hybrid designs that take classic designs – Eggs, Fish and Bonzers, for example – and re-interpret them with modern materials and construction techniques.

2000s

Standup paddleboards (2004) Inspired by Laird Hamilton's experiments, large, wide, thick surfboards emerge that are paddled while standing.

Post-Clark shortboards (2005) The closure of Clark Foam, which provided 90 per cent of the world's surfboard blanks, gives a boost to an already burgeoning scene of alternative surfboard technologies, including those championed by companies such as Aviso and Firewire.

Finless boards (2005) Australian-based Californian shaper Tom Wegener experiments with ancient designs made from sustainable, fast-growing Paulownia wood.

Stubbies and displacement hulls (2007) Designs are based around early transitional-era shortboards from the sixties.

CLASSIC SURF TRIP

EAST COAST AUSTRALIA

Clement waters, consistent swell and the sheer number and variety of jaw-droppingly beautiful spots make a journey from Sydney to the Superbank an unmissable surfari.

There are few places in the world where surfing and surf culture are so seamlessly interwoven with the daily life of the people as they are in Australia. Although there were reportedly a number of lifeguards who had started to standup surf on paddleboards in the very early twentieth century, the received wisdom is that in 1915 Hawaiian waterman Duke Kahanamoku pushed fifteen-year-old Aussie girl

AUSTRALIA

A beautiful environment combined with a comfortably stable European culture make Australia a paradise for surfers who journey there.

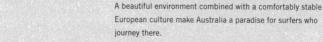

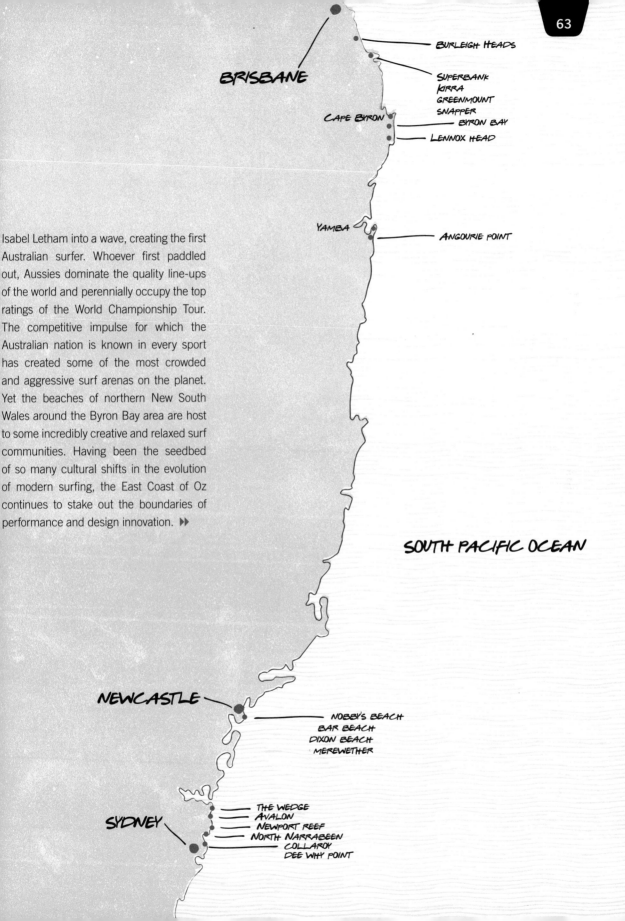

BURLEIGH HEADS

SUPERBANK
KIRRA
GREENMOUNT
SNAPPER

BRISBANE

CAPE BYRON ─── BYRON BAY

LENNOX HEAD

YAMBA ─── ANGOURIE POINT

Isabel Letham into a wave, creating the first Australian surfer. Whoever first paddled out, Aussies dominate the quality line-ups of the world and perennially occupy the top ratings of the World Championship Tour. The competitive impulse for which the Australian nation is known in every sport has created some of the most crowded and aggressive surf arenas on the planet. Yet the beaches of northern New South Wales around the Byron Bay area are host to some incredibly creative and relaxed surf communities. Having been the seedbed of so many cultural shifts in the evolution of modern surfing, the East Coast of Oz continues to stake out the boundaries of performance and design innovation. ▶▶

SOUTH PACIFIC OCEAN

NEWCASTLE ─── NOBBY'S BEACH
BAR BEACH
DIXON BEACH
MEREWETHER

THE WEDGE
AVALON
NEWPORT REEF
SYDNEY ─── NORTH NARRABEEN
COLLAROY
DEE WHY POINT

CLASSIC SURF TRIP

EAST COAST AUSTRALIA

The urban madness of Sydney's Bondi Beach is offset by consistent, beginner-friendly surf.

◀◀ SYDNEY: THE NORTHERN BEACHES

Sydney is one of the maddest, baddest and endlessly entertaining surf cities on the planet. There are probably more top-level surfers per square kilometre here than anywhere else, and as many ways to enjoy yourself as there are excellent places to surf. Narrabeen, one of the cradles of contemporary Australian surfing, is at the heart of Sydney's beautiful northern beaches. Names such as Avalon, Newport Reef and The Wedge, as well as North Narrabeen, provide serious challenges stalked by local legends. Despite the intense crowds peppered with highly talented surfers, there's usually enough space on the widely dispersed peaks up and down the beaches to cater for every level of skill and commitment. The closest stretch of surfable beach to the city is Bondi, a very urban, intense scene with fickle banks and crowds of tourists and ex-pats. Don't even think of tackling Moroubra and the other southern beaches, unless you enjoy scrapping for your waves.

IDEAL SWELLS: *Southeast–northeast*
IDEAL WINDS: *Northwest (offshore in the morning glass)*
HIGHLIGHTS: *Loads of spots, loads of culture*
LOWLIGHTS: *Surf machismo and pollution*

Avalon, well-exposed to northeast and southeast swells, is home to a range of spots and legions of talented surfers.

NEWCASTLE TO ANGOURIE

Heading north out of Sydney's white surfing heat, you might want to slug it out with the locals at the industrial city of Newcastle, home to a variety of challenging spots and most famously the home town of Mark Richards, two-time world champ and pioneer of the twin-finned surfboard. If an industrial backdrop and an urban population is not your bag, however, then it's a simple push north towards the staggeringly beautiful national parks of northern NSW and the classic right-hand pointbreak at Angourie just south of the village of Yamba. Situated at the foot of Yuraygir National Park, the wave at Angourie bends and tapers into the shelter of the point, creating a perfect canvas for performance surfing. The place is resonant, with its rural setting and endlessly peeling walls, of the 'country soul' period of Australian surfing. Angourie at the end of the sixties was one of the waves where Nat Young, Bob McTavish and others ripped up the rulebook of how waves could be ridden, sparking the shortboard revolution. It was also one of the prime locations featured so beautifully in Alby Falzon's 1972 film *Morning of the Earth*. Angourie has been rated by many as one of the top performance waves in the world and despite the burgeoning crowds retains a uniquely soulful beauty. ▶▶

It may look like heaven on earth, but the powerful waves and slippery, razor-sharp rocks at Angourie can challenge even the most experienced of surfers.

IDEAL SWELL: *East*
IDEAL WIND: *South*
HIGHLIGHTS: *Cyclone swells*
LOWLIGHTS: *Humbling crowds*

Carpark Rights is one of three high-performance breaks at Narrabeen, which was immortalised by the Beach Boys in their 1963 hit 'Surfin' USA'.

EAST COAST AUSTRALIA

◀◀ LENNOX HEAD TO THE GOLD COAST

An hour or so north of Angourie lies Byron Bay, an area once fragrant with patchouli oil and counter-culture. Although massive development and spiralling property prices have completely changed the tuned-out feel of the area, Lennox Head still retains much of the atmosphere that made surf culture fall in love with its verdant utopia. Even more than Angourie, Lennox was where the shortboard revolution was inspired and, according to many seasoned surfers, is as good a right-hand pointbreak as any on the planet. It was at Lennox that film-maker George Greenough introduced audiences to the inside of the ridden barrel in his paradigm-shifting film *The Innermost Limits of Pure Fun*. Despite the country vibe and the history of soulful creativity, Lennox is not a particularly forgiving wave. The sharp, slippy boulder pointbreak holds the biggest of swells and produces wicked hold-downs and broken boards – and to cap it all it's got one of the trickiest get-outs and get-ins in surfing. But shut your eyes to the crowds, paddle out early and infuse the atmosphere.

Right: Superbank's awe-inspiring series of long right-handers is the result of nature being manipulated by dredging and redistribution.

Snapper (*below*), a world-class wave in its own right, provides the opening section of Superbank.

IDEAL SWELL: *South-southeast*
IDEAL WIND: *South-southwest*
HIGHLIGHTS: *Eden-like in appearance*
LOWLIGHTS: *Heavy punishment, sharp rocks*

SUPERBANK

Further north you hit quintessential modern Australian surfing at the Gold Coast. The artificially created series of linked right-handers known as the 'Superbank' at the southern extremity of the 'Goldie' is contemporary surfing's apogee of performance. What was once a series of superlative sand-bottomed waves in their own right have become, though a programme of redistributive dredging, the longest barrelling wave in the world. On a solid swell, rides at the Superbank can run for as long as three to four minutes, and up to two kilometres. On the perfect day the wave seems to peel for ever as it negotiates the tapering banks with especially shallow, tubing sections that throw their hefty lips down the coast with the sort of geometric perfection surfers dream about. But be warned – the sucky, fast take-off, constant drop-ins and disregard for the niceties of etiquette make a proper ride at the Superbank a very rare experience for the vast majority of visitors. It's worth the effort, though, to witness a wave so perfectly plastic, and a testament – whether you approve or not – to our ability to shape the natural world.

At Kirra (*below*), the most northerly section of Superbank, Wayne 'Rabbit' Bartholemew and his contemporaries famously honed their tube-riding skills during the seventies.

IDEAL SWELL: Southeast–northeast
IDEAL WIND: Southwest–west
HIGHLIGHTS: Just seeing it working
LOWLIGHTS: Scrapping for a shoulder hop

Lennox (*left*) is at the pinnacle of performance surfing. Here, Joe Hudson makes a radical turn off the top of the wave.

WHERE DO WAVES COME FROM?

A breaking wave is the release of a mass of energy accumulated over vast distances. A basic understanding of a wave's journey enriches the surf experience.

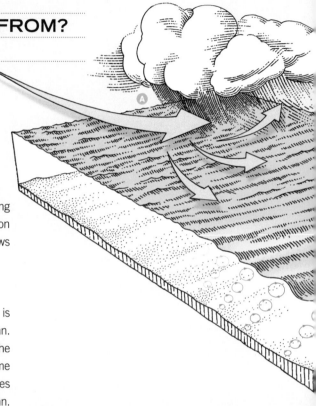

The beginning

Disturbance on a calm ocean is caused by winds blowing over its surface. Ripples, then chop, is formed by the friction of wind over the surface particles of water. If the wind blows hard enough, and for long enough, a 'sea' develops.

The middle

When the sea begins to form, most of the wind's energy is confined to the surface, or near the surface of the ocean. The area where seas develop is known as 'the fetch'. As the waves grow across the fetch, the waves' profiles become greater and the circular particle movement of water moves deeper and deeper, below the surface of the ocean. As the waves travel further from their origin they organise themselves into defined lines of swell, which increase in speed as they radiate downwind. Wavelength (distance between the peaks of the waves) increases as the swell travels away from the centre of the storm.

The end

When smooth, organised, open ocean swells move into water less than half their wavelength in depth, they begin to interact with the texture of the sea floor. Scientists call this process 'refraction'. As the water becomes shallower, the waves 'peak' upwards – their height increases rapidly, as does their steepness. The shallower water also decreases wavelength: as a preceding wave slows, the one behind it starts to catch up. When a wave reaches water that is around 1.3 times deeper than the wave's height, it becomes unstable, and begins to 'break', creating surf, returning to the apparent chaos of unordered energy that gave it birth.

A The storm

Low-pressure systems create storms out at sea. Water particles move in a circular motion away from the centre of the storm, forming 'chop', then a 'sea'.

B Swell

As the energy created by the storm moves further away from the storm, the chaotic sea organises itself into lines of swell.

C Breaking waves

When lines of swell begin to approach the shore, they slow and 'focus'. When the water becomes shallow enough, the upper part of the wave will 'overtake' the bottom of the wave and begin to break.

D Backwash

After a wave has broken, water escapes back out to sea from the shore, often creating currents.

The picture that launched a thousand Hawaiian surfaris. Once this image was published, the secret of the Hawaiian heavies was out.

BIG-WAVE PIONEERS

When a new generation of Californian surfers first glimpsed Makaha during the fifties, it sparked a big-wave revolution.

It was a photograph that did it. In early November 1953, Californian surfers saw a black and white image on the front page of the local papers that would change the course of their lives. They could hardly believe what they were seeing. In the photo three Californians – George Downing, Buzzy Trent and Wally Froseith – were taking off on a wave of impossible size and beauty. This decisive moment was captured at Makaha, on the west side of the Hawaiian island of Oahu. The image would send shock waves through California's seedling surf culture.

By the early fifties, Californian surfing was already thoroughly infused with the Hawaiian aesthetic. Surfers were wearing hibiscus-print shirts and *leis*, ukuleles were being strummed gently beneath improvised beach shacks made of dried grass and palm leaves. The air was positively fragrant with *aloha*. It was common knowledge that the sport had been brought over from the Islands at the turn of the century by the likes of George Freeth and Duke Kahanamoku. However, it was the relatively gentle, rolling waves of Waikiki on Oahu's south shore that were perceived as the epitome of Hawaiian surf culture. The sight of Makaha's fifteen-foot wall sparked something deep in the hearts of the new generation who were looking for a bigger challenge than the waves of California.

By the winter of 1954, a tight cadre of Californian men (and a few women) had made Makaha their home, joined by a revolving roster of visiting mainlanders. The crew included Pat Curren, Fred Van Dyke, Ricky Grigg, Mike Stang, Mickey Muñoz, who made it their mission ▶▶

BIG-WAVE PIONEERS

The crew on the day Waimea was finally ridden, in December 1957, included Greg Noll, Mickey Muñoz, Bob Bermel and Mike Stang.

◀◀ to take the art of big-wave riding as far as they could. They were mentored by older surfers, including Downing, Trent and Froiseth, who had spent much of the previous decade living and surfing at Makaha, creating

the mould of the resourceful, simple-living wave-devotee, at one with the ocean.

Days and nights on end in this highly charged surf utopia encouraged an *esprit de corps*, unique in the history of surfing. 'We were like the pilgrim fathers,' says Muñoz, 'the first group of Californians to live in Hawaii and dedicate themselves to surfing.' What galvanised this tightly knit group further was the inherent danger and intensity of their daily existence. Surfboards didn't have leashes, there were no lifeguards, no floatation devices and precious few medical facilities on land. If you wiped out in heavy water, you were alone.

Meanwhile, about fifteen miles across the headland from Makaha was the North Shore. Completely rural and relatively cut off from the rest of Oahu by a massive acreage of taro and pineapple fields, this seven-mile stretch of coastline is shrouded in myth and legend and contains a greater concentration of world-class big-wave spots than anywhere else on the planet. At its epicentre is Waimea Bay. Waves only begin to break here once the swell is so big it closes out the remainder of the North Shore. The land overlooking Waimea is an ancient place of burial and sacrifice – for Hawaiians it was an area shrouded in taboo. For visiting surfers in the fifties, however, it was the loss of Dickey Cross that hammered home the message that Waimea should not or could not be surfed. Surfing Sunset Beach in the winter of 1943, seventeen-year-old Cross and friend Woody Brown were caught by a rapidly building storm swell in failing light. Unable to catch a wave in at Sunset, the pair decided to paddle up the coast to the deeper water of Waimea, where they hoped to be able to paddle in to safety. Caught by a massive 30-foot closeout set way out the back at Waimea, the two surfers lost their boards. Woody Brown was eventually washed up on the beach, minus his shorts, but alive. Cross was never seen again.

By October 1957 the North Shore was populated by a greater number of surfers, many of them transplants from the early days at Makaha. Still, the Waimea taboo held strong. 'We would look at Waimea and think: well, it looks like a rideable wave,' recalls Mickey Muñoz.

But it took a long while for the crew to be convinced that the Bay was anything but a killer. Greg Noll was one of the first to break the taboo. 'At some point, you had to think, to hell with it,' he said. So, with Mike Stang, Mickey Muñoz, Pat Curren, Dale Cannon, Fred Van Dyke, Harry Church, Bing Copeland and Bob Burbell, they paddled out into Waimea's four-storey maw. 'I remember paddling out to the line-up with my balls in my stomach. I felt like at any moment, the water would open up and something would eat me alive,' Noll recalls. He was first to catch a wave. 'I turned, made the drop, and I thought, shit, I'm alive!' That was the opening of the floodgates. Noll and company had shown that Waimea was rideable, and with his very potent blend of hard-charging bravery, a personality that thrived on confrontation, and publicity-generating endeavour, soon Noll was the figurehead of big-wave surfing.

Since that momentous day, the North Shore of the Hawaiian Islands has been the breeding ground for generations of surfers who have gone on to scour the world seeking the ultimate big wave.

Big-wave acolytes Les Arndt, Mickey Muñoz and Ron Hodge were in the vanguard of surfers who explored the North Shore in the late fifties.

WHICH BOARD?

PART ONE

5.25"

The fish
Easy on the eye, but relatively difficult to manoeuvre, the classic fish is an iconic piece of surfboard design.

The original fish design was pioneered at the end of the sixties by La Jolla surfer and shaper Steve Lis, and was honed in subsequent years by Oceanside shaper-guru Skip Frye. Traditionally never longer than six feet, and featuring a stubby, curved template with twin keels (with a fin on each) that form a large 'swallow' tail, the fish was originally designed to be ridden on the knees in hollow, steep surf. Today, a fish is usually ridden standing-up and often in average beachbreak waves, as well as faster, crisper pointbreaks and reefs.

The rationale of the fish design is that loss of flotation through a decrease in overall board length is compensated for by increased volume (the classic fish is usually shaped from a longboard blank and remains almost as thick and as wide as a longboard). The fish's twin keels act as 'double pintails' allowing for dynamic, explosive turning whilst retaining volume for easy wave-catching. The experience of riding a fish is similar to riding a very fast, very loose-trucked skateboard in the water. It is not, however, the board for the surfin' dilettante.

21"

2.5"

5'10"

This Skip Frye creation is one of the most refined of all surfboard designs.

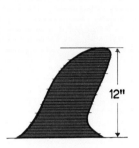

12"

The longboard
Until the late sixties all surfboards were longboards. Ideal for easy wave-catching and smooth-flowing, style-conscious manoeuvres they epitomised the Californian surf dream.

Longboards, in their purest form, are more than nine feet in length and feature a single fin over nine inches long and 'soft' rounded rails. In contemporary designs, however, you'll find a huge variety of fin configurations and rail set-ups. The perennial popularity of the longboard can be attributed to its superior floatation and stability. Crucially, longboards were perfectly suited to the relatively mellow, slowly breaking waves of California and were the vectors of the first surf boom, in the fifties. During the seventies, longboards fell out of favour with the advent of shorter, skinnier, thinner boards.

During the mid-eighties, however, with older surfers alienated by the physically demanding shortboard, a backlash was stirring. By the beginning of the nineties a full-blown 'retro' movement was in full swing. Today, longboards have once again become a fixture in line-ups all over the world. Longboards catch waves much more easily than most shortboards and can provide a fun surf experience when the waves are far from perfect. But, perhaps most importantly, the enduring appeal of these classic designs is that they enable even average surfers easy access to 'the glide' – that feeling of exalted, flowing weightlessness – which is one of surfing's peak experiences.

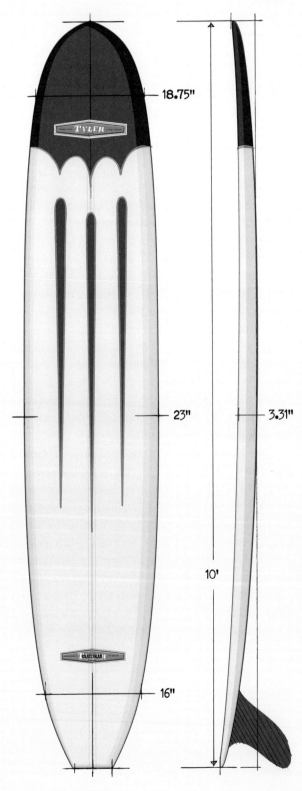

18.75"

23"

3.31"

10'

16"

Tyler Hatzikian's 'craftsman noserider' is a classic longboard built in 2005.

JOHN SEVERSON

John Severson is the man who created surf media. No other individual has been so instrumental in spreading the surfing creed.

A creative polymath from early childhood, John Severson was born in Pasadena in 1933 and moved with his family to San Clemente soon after. As a schoolboy he edited the school newspaper, scribbled imaginative cartoons and began painting and taking photographs. The focal points of life at San Clemente were, and remain, the pier and the beach, and by the time he was eighteen, Severson was fully part of the scene. Drafted into the US Army he found himself in Hawaii in the spring of 1957. By this time he was a highly skilled surfer and had learnt to work the angles, engineering for himself a role as head of the army surf team, with orders to train every afternoon. Painting and drawing between bouts of less glamorous army duty, he was also able to shoot moving images of the action at Makaha during the winter of 1957–8. The footage became the first Severson film: *Surf.* Enlisting the help of fellow surfer Fred Van Dyke, he toured the movie around California in 1958, narrating live to sell-out crowds at weekends. *Surf Fever*, released in 1960, had higher production values and increasingly sophisticated editing and sound techniques. The timing was perfect; it hit the streets just as *Gidget* arrived in mainstream cinemas across the US and just as light, foam-cored surfboards were making surfing much more accessible to the rank-and-file.

Severson's state-of-the-art films were always accompanied by an equally eye-catching poster complete with a hand-cut, Severson typeface.

Surfer magazine, Severson's most famous and perhaps most influential creation, had a relatively inauspicious beginning. The first issue arrived in the shape of a programme to accompany *Surf Fever*. To the surprise of almost everyone involved, the demand for the pamphlet far outstripped supply, and soon it was obvious that the rapidly expanding constituency of the newly stoked would be more than willing to part with $1.25 for a regular magazine. Within months Severson launched *The Surfer Quarterly*. This quickly became *Surfer Bi-monthly* and then plain old *Surfer*. Early editions of the magazine were largely written and edited by the boss himself and contained many of his drawings

Surfer magazine (*left*) was originally titled *The Surfer Quarterly*. Its contents and cover designs reflected the rapidly changing values of the sixties.

The Surfer (*below*), Severson's first magazine was produced to accompany his 1960 film, *Surf Fever*.

Pacific Vibrations was the high point in the crossover between surf and hippy culture. Rick Griffin's artwork reflected this perfectly.

and photographs. Although others were quick to catch the drift and produce rival publications, *Surfer* established itself at the heart of surf culture and certainly lived up to its tag-line as 'the bible of the sport'. It retained this position right through the sixties and well into the seventies, evolving from a wholesome, reverent organ of the longboard era into the clarion of the drug-saturated, consciousness-expanded lifestyle with the advent of the shortboard revolution. Along the way, Severson employed true surf visionaries, from writer-publishers such as Steve Pezman and Drew Kampion to artists and designers such as Rick Griffin and John Van Hamersveld, as well as leading lensmen including Ron Stoner, Jeff Divine and Art Brewer. Severson returned to film with his 1970 offering *Pacific Vibrations*, a colour-saturated testament to surfing, packaged with a funky counter-cultural

vibe and a driving soundtrack featuring Cream and Ry Cooder. The film's tag-line was 'like Woodstock on a wave' and it was probably the most sophisticated surf movie of the era.

In 1972, Severson sold his interest in the magazine and moved with his young family to Maui. With the pressures of magazine publishing behind him, he was able to explore fully his passion for painting. The colourful oils, acrylics and drawings he has produced since have fleshed out a highly commercial body of work that has ensured a lasting legacy of the Severson vision.

In an early issue of *Surfer* Severson memorably stated that 'in this crowded world, the surfer can still seek and find the perfect day, the perfect wave, and be alone with the surf and his thoughts.' No one has better expressed the timeless transcendence of the surfing act.

TECHNIQUE TWO

THE TAKE-OFF

The opening move of the ride is the most critical.

The take-off is the opening section of the ride, when the surfer moves from paddling to riding down the face of a wave.

The take-off is defined as the period between a surfer taking his or her hands off the rails or deck of a surfboard and standing in the riding position. When riding shortboards, the take-off is always a single, quick, fluid movement. Longboard riders, however, may stay in the prone position, with back arched and head up, until after the wave has opened up. At this point they leap to their feet, and the critical first turn is made.

Take-offs can be smooth and relaxed (in gently breaking, smaller waves), or can be extremely dangerous with little margin for error (in top-to-bottom breaking, fast, hollow waves). In either instance, the key to a successful take-off is to commit early and remain relaxed. When eyeing a potential wave for a take-off you should be aware of its position, the direction in which it will break and where you are in the line-up in relation to other surfers as well as the wave itself.

The development of tow-in surfing in the early 1990s saw riders being towed into huge, previously unrideable waves by jet-skis while standing – doing away with the take-off altogether in this highly specialised form of surfing. However, for the vast majority of surfers, the take-off is the crucial opening phase of the ride itself.

Ⓐ *Hands on the rails*

Place your hands on the rails or the deck of the board and arch your back. When you feel the wave lifting behind you and the board falling beneath you, it's time to go.

Ⓑ *Popping up*

In one quick and smooth movement, bring your knees towards your chest and pop to your feet. When moving into the riding position, don't stare at your feet. Look down the line of the breaking wave.

Ⓒ *Riding position*

Feet should be shoulder-width apart and flat on the deck of the surfboard before initiating the first turn. Arms and shoulders should stay relaxed and your core strong and rooted through your legs and feet.

See also

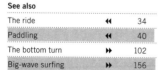

fig. II:
Take-Off

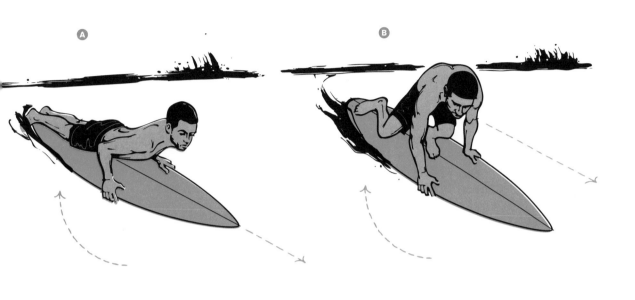

THE SURF T-SHIRT

In the early sixties Larry Gordon and Floyd Smith were among the first board shapers to screen print their company logo onto T-shirts.

The little-known story buried in the history of street fashion is that the first branded T-shirts bore the names of California surfboard shapers.

The Second World War created the T-shirt as an ubiquitous item of cheap, convenient and comfortable apparel. Cotton T-shirts were part of a GI's uniform, and they were often emblazoned with the name of the unit. In the immediate post-war years, surplus cotton tees, originally produced for the military, became widely available. As the buttoned-up forties gave way to the rock-and-roll inspired fifties, youth culture adopted the T-shirt as its standard-issue garment. When Marlon Brando draped himself over his motorcycle in a white tee in *The Wild One*, and then James Dean emoted the angst of a generation in *Rebel Without a Cause*, the humble T-shirt's image was sealed.

Surf culture took the T-shirt to another level of cool when, at the beginning of the sixties, surfboard-shaping entrepreneurs came up with the idea of screen printing the logos that appeared on their surfboards on to the T-shirts of their hottest riders. It may have been Californian legends Gordon and Smith or pocket battleship and power surfer of the longboard era, Dewey Weber, who fully popularised the idea, but either way, it worked. The best riders in the local area not only got a surfboard, but also got branded T-shirts to go with it. Soon a cult of aspiration was created around a look consisting of Mexican-made, tyre-soled huarache sandals, jeans or surf shorts and a branded T-shirt. The surfer became the cleaner-cut equivalent of the

"BING BOARDS NATURALLY"
BING SURFBOARDS/1820 PACIFIC COAST HIGHWAY HERMOSA BEACH, CALIF./FR. 2-1248 & NOW IN WHITTIER/511 EAST WHITTIER BLVD./ WHITTIER, CALIFORNIA/696-1614

The nascent surf media provided great opportunities for the young surf brands. This Bing ad appeared in *Surfer* magazine in 1963.

The famous Gordon and Smith logo was first printed
on to local boardriders' T-shirts in 1961.

Harbour Surfboards, created by Rich Harbour of Seal
Beach, California, has been in business since 1962.

One of the most aspirational brands of sixties surfing
was created by Malibu surfing legend, Lance Carson.

Hotdog surfing pioneer, Dewey Weber, is a contender, along
with Gordon and Smith, for producing the first surf T-shirt.

land-lubbing biker and grease-ridden hot rodder. They
were cool, they were stoked and they were wearing the
right T-shirts.

The classic surf T-shirt has its logo printed on the
left breast, often on a less-than-functional pocket; and
a larger logo or illustration on the back. All through the
sixties, surf teams, competitions and clubs issued their
own branded T-shirts. T-shirts from organisations such
as La Jolla's Windansea Surf Club and competitions such
as Hawaii's Duke Invitational became particularly prized
and sought-after items of material surf culture. In an age
of ubiquitous branding and commercialism, T-shirts as
political or aesthetic agitprop are perennially fashionable.
The surf T-shirt manages to hold its own and, for many
people the world over, continues to symbolise the surfing
lifestyle and the personal freedom that goes with it.

WHICH TYPE OF WAVE?

BEACHBREAK

Beachbreak at Gwithian, North Cornwall

The term 'beachbreak' refers to any surf break where waves break over a sand or a gravel beach. It is by far the most common form of wave on the surfing planet.

Beachbreaks are generally thought of as inferior to reefbreaks or pointbreaks. This is because the shifting sands of a beachbreak generally produce less consistent, less shapely waves than the other type of spots. Despite this widespread snobbery, beachbreaks are the staple of most surfers' daily diet and have nurtured some of the most competitive, highly adaptable surfers on the planet. Learning to score waves on a 'consistently inconsistent' beachbreak is perhaps the best training you can have as a surfer. To surf a beachbreak well, you must learn to read those shifting sands and identify how the ebb and flow of tide and wind affects them. You must also become adept at negotiating the riptides, currents and crowds that a popular breachbreak will typically produce. Unlike reef and pointbreaks, beachbreaks often have no set take-off area, and in bigger waves the white water and lack of a clear 'channel' free of current can make paddling out very strenuous and technically difficult.

Beachbreak waves usually form short, quick rides in either direction but they can change their nature or even disappear altogether as swell, tide and season alter the texture of the sands. Very often, sandbars that form consistently shaped waves during the summer months can be swept aside by the first powerful storms of autumn and winter. More solid, hard-packed sandbars may replace them, or featureless areas may appear that can produce no rideable waves whatsoever. With the rare exceptions of Mexico's Puerto Escondido and the spots up and down the beaches in the Hossegor region of southwest France, beachbreaks are usually best in small to medium swell, as the shape, power and consistency of the sandbars upon which the waves are formed often fail when subject to the more tempestuous forces of bigger swells.

As beachbreaks are generally perceived to offer fewer obvious hazards than reefs or points, they often attract beginners. While it is true that the sandy bottoms of beachbreaks produce a more forgiving environment in which to catch your first rides, don't get too cocky. In the right conditions, a beachbreak can offer a genuine challenge to the most experienced and skilled of surfers.

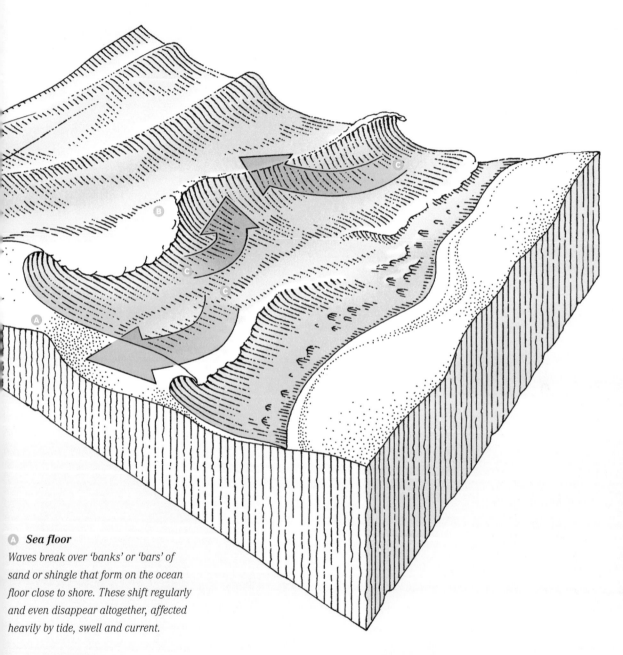

A Sea floor

Waves break over 'banks' or 'bars' of sand or shingle that form on the ocean floor close to shore. These shift regularly and even disappear altogether, affected heavily by tide, swell and current.

B Breaking wave

Peaks form over the shallowest point of these sandbars, usually creating relatively short, dynamic waves, which can break in either direction.

C Currents

Energy escapes back out to sea directly through the beachbreak in a series of 'rips' or currents, which can adversely affect surf conditions.

RON STONER

Photographer Ron Stoner's achingly beautiful, tragically truncated body of work captured in Kodachrome the soul of surfing's golden age.

Ron Stoner, who was born in 1945, grew up during surfing's first boomtime in California's San Diego and Los Angeles counties. He quickly rose through the sparse ranks of surf photographers who were beginning to ply their trade in early magazines such as *Surfing Illustrated*. It was John Severson at *Surfer* magazine, however, who gave the San Clemente kid his most important break in 1963. Gaining possession of *Surfer*'s expensive in-house telescopic lens along with, for the time, an unheard of $500 monthly retainer as staff photographer, Stoner's work quickly became the gold standard and helped establish the magazine's perennial market dominance. He specialised not only in capturing the tonal range of the surf experience, but in evoking the less-recognised but eternally beautiful moments of a surfer's existence – the fall of light behind a wave when looking to shore, or seemingly conjuring up the whiff of ozone from a feathering lip at dawn.

Towards the end of the sixties the psychedelic era began to take hold of surf culture and Stoner soon fell under its spell. The evolving, relatively laid-back aesthetic of the longboard era went through a series of rapid evolutionary leaps. Old values and ways of looking at surfing were being turned on their head as shapers chopped three feet

Ron Stoner's imagery is saturated in the gorgeous glow of California's greatest surfing moments, the visual counterpart to Brian Wilson's music. Here, companionship, forged in an evening go-out, is captured perfectly.

THE VISION

off their boards and experimented with far-out designs. Drugs, madness and mayhem formed a constant texture of Stoner's everyday life. Whether or not his heavy drug use was a contributory factor in his mysterious disappearance in the mid-seventies has been grounds for intense speculation. That aside, Stoner's true legacy is to have made photographs that provoke in surfers across the decades an emotional, almost physical, response.

MIKI DORA

Date of birth: 11 August 1936
(died 3 January 2002)
Place of birth: Budapest, Hungary
Defining wave: Malibu

He was Miki of Malibu, the Dark Knight, the Black Prince. He was everything you wanted him to be and nothing at all you could have expected. But most of all he was Miki Dora – and surfing has been in his thrall for fifty years.

It's quite a simple story really. Miklos Szandor Dora was the son of a Hungarian immigrant who first took his boy to learn to surf at San Onofre in 1940. Gard Chapin – top Californian surfer of the forties – who married Dora's mother when the boy was six years old, nurtured Dora's prodigious talent in his biological father's absence. The rebellious teenager, dropping out of military boarding school under the influence of the angry, authoritarian surfer stepfather, began to frequent Malibu, Rincon, Windansea and other surf spots up and down the California coast. By his twentieth birthday Malibu was Dora's preferred dominion and he was soon crowned king.

Dora's status in the water was based on his effortless elegance and superb sense of trim – the ability to tap the power source of the wave and stay locked in tight to its breaking curl. Look at photos of him surfing and you can spot an unmistakable gracefulness of movement – the dropped shoulders, the crooked back leg, the relaxed hands. They didn't call him

Da Cat for nothing. Though his turns, cutbacks and nose rides were templated on those of the other top Californian surfers of the day, Dora's style had a unique repertoire of syncopated shifts of weight, arched back boogies and hip shuffles. Dora's surfing was new, outrageously assertive and tapped into the spirit of the times. And though Dora was a loner, never lived on the beach and was never completely part of the Malibu beach scene, it was this scene that nurtured the Miki Dora myth.

Conveniently located just over the hill from the sprawling tracts of the San Fernando Valley, Malibu quickly drew every wannabe and poseur from Simi Valley to Thousand Oaks. They descended on the beaches around the pier in their thousands to taste the surfing lifestyle. Dora hated the 'valley kooks' and 'football-punchy swingers' who would turn up to the beach and clog the arteries of Malibu's waves, but rented out boards to them and charged them for surf lessons all the same. He was disgusted when Hollywood camera crews showed up at the beach but was soon performing as a surf stand-in for the series of teenage flicks that helped generate the first surfing boom. Complex and contradictory, Dora was the perfect, wave-riding, outlaw enigma.

All through the sixties he was a constant, aggressive presence at Malibu, threading his way through the burgeoning crowds, often launching his board into other surfers on his wave, barging and shoving others out of the way. Impenetrable first-person rants and interviews with Dora appeared in surf magazines about the state of Malibu's crowded surf and the world in general. He polarised opinion – you either dig the gospel according to Dora or you think he's a sick criminal and should be banned from the beach.

In 1970 a warrant was issued for Dora's arrest for credit card and cheque fraud. He took flight – escaping the law but also the ascendancy of an acid-fuelled counter-culture and shortboard revolution that had begun to make the Dora attitude and style of surfing look a bit of a relic. The odyssey lasted thirty years and included various stints in jail in at least two countries and brief trips back to the States. The adventure was funded by a series of scams, tricks, larceny and luck – as well as the endless kindness of strangers, admirers and Dora obsessives. Now and then Dora was sighted and sent dispatches to the surf media whilst scouring the planet for lonely right-hand pointbreaks. He surfed Angola, Namibia, Brazil and Argentina – and a host of other nameless surfing outposts. Losing the remaining scraps that were his worldy goods in a fire at a house overlooking Jeffrey's Bay, South Africa, he made his way to the wave-rich coasts of southwest France. Right up to the end a series of bewitched benefactors paid the man a retainer: all they wanted in return was for Dora to simply be Dora. In a poignant, unlikely final scene, Miki Dora spent his last days reunited with his natural father at his house in Montecito, California. He died in early January 2002, and with him an era, an ethos and a trickster talent surf culture is unlikely to see again.

Dora's surf style was an unmistakable combination of classic grace and hipster boogie – a mirror image of the beguiling image he cultivated on land.

SURF TRAVEL ESSENTIALS

For a far-flung trip, there's some kit that you just can't do without. Here's a handy guide.

1 Quiver Be realistic and travel light. Choose two or, at most, three versatile boards.

2 Wax Select the appropriate texture and stickiness for where you're bound – hard wax for warmer waters, soft for milder and cold waters.

3 Leashes If you've brought along an eclectic quiver of boards, take a variety of different lengths and thicknesses. Take spares – leashes do break, especially in heavy water.

4 Ding repair kit Filler, fibreglass cloth and resin are must-haves. A tool with a file is also indispensible. Protect the items in your repair kit with your life.

5 Rash vests If you're heading to the Tropics, take a variety of rash vests or light cotton tees that you can wear in the water to prevent nipple rash.

6 Wetsuits If you're travelling to cooler waters, it's best to take two wetties: one can dry out while you're in the water. Pulling on a cold, wet sheath of neoprene isn't much fun.

7 Boardshorts Bring proper, technically constructed boardies. Fashion victims who ignore the practical aspects of boardshort design are doomed to suffer endless chaffing on the insides of the thighs.

8 Boots If you're planning to surf tropical reef, include booties to prevent nasty lacerations.

9 Spare fin screws, plates and fixings Bring as many as will fit in your bag! Try finding your single screw and plate in a fetid jungle camp whilst addled with whatever concoction the local Kahuna has supplied.

10 Sunblock When you're out in the sun, apply, apply, apply. Choose one that has an SPF of at least 15. And don't forget to pack a hat.

11 Reading material Bring some food for your head, for when the waves are flat, or if you just fancy some downtime.

12 First-aid kit Pack anti-malarials, antiseptic creams, plasters, bandages and painkillers.

13 Mosquito coils You know that feeling of trying to sleep when the little buggers are running sorties around you. These will help.

14 Gaffer/duct tape Repeat the mantra: 'If it can be fixed by tape, then it shall be fixed by tape.' This is a universal truth for the way of the surfer.

15 Vaseline Essential for all the chaffs and scrapes that will afflict your body.

16 Gerber Leatherman The best multitool on the market, bar none. Buy one.

17 Compass You just never know. Boats sink. People get lost in jungles and deserts. So swot up on your survival techniques.

18 Surfboard straps Have you seen the way they drive in Indo? Never trust a native bungee chord.

19 Waterproof digital camera You'll regret it if you don't document at least some of the watery delights for which you're travelling halfway around the world.

20 Wind-up torch The best bit of kit ever invented for seat-of-the-pants travel. Apart from...

21 Wind-up radio Stay in touch with the football scores and listen to *Desert Island Discs*, no matter where you are. Eco-friendly too.

22 iPod A little bit of technological excellence that you won't want to leave behind.

23 Phrasebook Make the effort to learn some local lingo; not everyone understands dudish.

RICK GRIFFIN

Rick Griffin's art coupled the disparate scenes of surfing, art and rock and roll. Over three decades, his work closely shadowed the turbulent times around him.

Born in 1944, at Palos Verdes, California, Griffin was part of the generation of wartime babyboomers who grew up at a time of unprecedented American economic affluence and cultural influence. Ensconced early on in the booming beach culture around him, as a mid-teen Griffin would make nickels and dimes drawing characters on T-shirts for punters on the beaches of the South Bay. After scoring some design work for Hermosa-based Greg Noll, sixteen-year-old Griffin was introduced to John Severson. The surf media pioneer hired him and within a couple of years Griffin had become one of the earliest stars of surf culture, creating 'Murphy the Surfer' for *Surfer* magazine. Murphy, a perpetually stoked, tow-headed avatar of the Californian gremmie was an embodiment of Severson's ideal consumer. The goofball adventures of this archetypal innocent of the surf created a fervent following and helped sell the magazine to the expanding rank and file of the surfing masses.

Hitching a lift north to San Francisco in late 1963, Griffin was involved in an extremely serious road traffic accident which left him hospitalised and scarred horribly across his left eye. The pretty beach boy's symmetry disappeared overnight, to be replaced by a raffish eye-patch and goatee beard. The youthful surf artist was developing into a fully fledged beat bohemian. In 1965,

Throughout the sixties, Griffin designed ads for various surf brands, including Greg Noll Surfboards.

Murphy was killed off and replaced with the first of the 'Griffin-Stoner adventures'. Co-authored by Severson, these gonzo-like surf-toon escapades featured Griffin and surfer's staff lensman Ron Stoner. The strip followed their outrageous escapades chasing women and waves, and was pitched in a carnivalesque tone full of homespun hokum. Now fully signed up to the tripped-out psychedelic movement, Griffin collaborated with some of the most influential artists of the era. He created posters for the Fillmore concerts of Hendrix and Jefferson Airplane as well as cover art for Jackson Browne, The Eagles and the Grateful Dead. Centred in the whacked-out streets of San Francisco's Haight-Ashbury district, he became deeply committed to what he and his contemporaries saw as a spiritual revolution motored by LSD. The art he was making at this time is among the totems of the period. Back in Dana Point, meanwhile, John Severson had become all too aware of the drug references that were peppered throughout the Griffin-Stoner adventures, and the

THE VISION

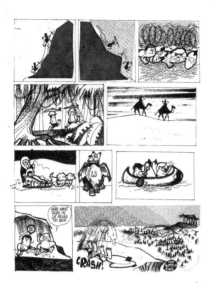

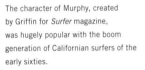

The character of Murphy, created by Griffin for *Surfer* magazine, was hugely popular with the boom generation of Californian surfers of the early sixties.

Tales From the Tube, a psychedelic comic showcasing classic Griffin characters, first appeared as an insert in a 1972 issue of *Surfer* magazine.

relatively buttoned-up, golf-playing publisher had become increasingly worried about the sensibilities of sensitive advertisers. The collaboration temporarily came to an end.

However, with editor Drew Kampion at the helm, *Surfer* magazine had become, along with *Rolling Stone* (its logo designed by Griffin), one of the meeting points of the counter-culture. By 1969 Severson had loosened up, and Griffin returned to the *Surfer* magazine roster. Griffin's work during this period was full of tripped-out drug references, insider signs, nods to Native American wisdom and barely veiled admonitions to tune in, turn on and drop out. When Severson sought to promote the surfing version of the psychedelic revolution on film in his 1970 work, *Pacific Vibrations*, Griffin was the obvious choice of artist to create its graphic identity.

As the seventies got underway, Griffin created the posters for MacGillivray and Freeman's *Five Summer Stories* and other classics, as well as *Tales from the Tube*, a twenty-page comic that he produced with the legendary Robert Crumb and other members of the San Francisco art undergound. His collaboration with Crumb and the Zap collective of comic-book artists, which had begun after a chance meeting on Haight-Ashbury, carried on well into the 1980s.

When he died in 1991, at the helm of his Harley, Griffin left a body of work that mirrored America as it moved from the gee-whiz innocence of the late fifties to the counter-culture and beyond. All the while, Griffin continued to surf, never moving too far away from the culture that gave him his most enduring inspiration.

SURF SPOT

MUNDAKA

The beautifully foiled sandbar at the mouth of the river Mundaka in the Spanish Basque Country produces one of the most intriguing and intense surf spots on the planet.

A consistent rivermouth wave is a rare gem on this surfing planet. Formed by aggregate flowing downriver to settle into point-like sandbars along the edges of estuaries, rivermouths tend to be fatally prone to the vagaries of tide, ebb and season. The sandbar in question, however, is responsible for producing the fastest, hardest-breaking left-hand barrel in Europe, and the journey through the atmospheric byways of the Basque Country to the pretty little town of Mundaka at the edge of the estuary, has become an exotic rite of passage for surfers from all over the world.

Make the trip and you'd be forgiven for thinking you might be travelling though the pages of a Hemingway novel. The people are broody and intense, and the landscape is punctuated with verdant hills and quiet towns bordered by rundown housing estates and factories. There is a thoughtful, inward-looking nature to the Basque population of northern Spain – a legacy perhaps of the political machinations of separatism that until very recently dominated the area. The region's physical nature is as spectacularly beautiful as its history is tempestuous. Inland the Picos de Europa mountain range pushes up weather systems as they roll in from the Bay of Biscay to unload the precipitation that characterises the area. The same weather systems also bring powerful swells to its coastline. The power and the glory of surfing the Basque Country all come together in the autumn at Mundaka when the summer crowds have departed and powerful swells march in from the north. ▶▶

Peacefulness and fury lie just a few
heartbeats away from each other
in the heart of the Basque Country.

SPAIN · Mundaka

SURF SPOT
MUNDAKA

◀◀ Famous for its bone-crunching and board-snapping intensity, riding a wave here is an adrenalin-charged sequence of hustle, commitment and timing. Snag a wave from the talented pack and your ideal ride here is all about the barrel. This is a barrel that doesn't quite break top to bottom, so aspiring Mundaka tuberiders must stay locked to a high line no matter how fast and steep the wave becomes as it peels into the rivermouth. At its best, rides can last for up to 300 metres along the hard-packed sandbar that sweeps into the estuary. When the swell is big and lined up from the northwest it provides three separate tube sections connected by ever-so slightly bowling, steep traverses: straightening out and outrunning the pocket of the wave's power can lead to devastating impacts. The sandbar here is rock-like and regularly holds waves of up to twelve feet – so don't go thinking that compared to surfing reef waves, this might be a cinch.

There's a stark contrast to the peacefulness and the slow pace of life across the harbour wall in the town of Mundaka itself. You'll be sipping the local cider and sampling tasty tapas one languid evening whilst watching the Friday night game of *pelota*. The next morning you might be deep into one of the most challenging situations you're ever likely to experience as a surfer.

THE SEARCH

It's not just the quality of the waves that makes Mundaka such a draw. The landscape of the Basque Country, as well as the cultural backdrop, add immeasurably to the experience.

Taking advantage of a crowd-free session, elusive Australian surfer, shaper and perennial soul-man Wayne Lynch drops into big Mundaka.

THE FERAL SURFER

The feral surfer sacrifices all worldly desires in pursuit of his obsession. He has seen the surf dream and is determined to live it, eyes wide open.

It doesn't matter how far flung, or how exotic the world of surf camps, boat charters, and all-expenses-in surf packages have become, a feral surfer got there first. The feral is the sadhu of the surf, the completely committed wave-riding survivalist who remains camped at a parasite-infested jungle camp for months on end. He is surfing's all-knowing, all-conquering Holy Fool, and every surfer who has ever travelled is deeply indebted to the tradition he has created.

The early seventies marked the ascendancy of the feral surfer, when boards had shrunk in size and new frontiers from Bali, Java and Sumatra to Latin America were being pioneered. Shorter boards meant that the powerful, tubular waves of the tropics were the high point in surfers' aspiration. When the relatively small cadre of surf explorers tamed Indonesia, there was little or no infrastructure to support tourism. Australian surfers Terry Fitzgerald, Wayne Lynch and Nat Young, as well as Hawaiian Gerry Lopez and a number of others, lived as locals, or at least made camp and made do with whatever food and drink they could beg, borrow, steal or barter.

Films such as Alby Falzon's seminal 1973 offering *Morning of the Earth* helped popularise the idea of the feral, along with dispatches such as the 1974 *Surfer* magazine cover story 'The Forgotten Island of Santosha', in which Tamarin Bay in Mauritius was showcased as the ultimate exotic surf destination. 'Santosha is not a place,' wrote writer/film-maker Larry Yates in the piece, 'but a state of mind.' Intrepid surfer writers and photographers such as Kevin Naughton and Craig Peterson scratched a living while on the road, selling stories of their travels in West Africa and Central America to various US and Australian surfing magazines, further tempting thousands of adventurous young surfers to take flight.

As the seventies turned into the eighties, packaged surf camps begun to spring up. Many pioneer ferals became owner-operators of all-inclusive surf camps and charter boats operating from the very spots they had discovered. In 1973, when hardcore Aussie ferals Tony Hinde and Mark Scanlon were shipwrecked in the Maldives en route from Sri Lanka to South Africa (along with the mad skipper and his even madder monkey), Hinde stayed, marrying a local woman, converting to Islam and surfing almost alone for at least fifteen years. In 1990, he became the founder of Atoll Adventures surfing resort in the islands and now the Maldives is indelibly inked on the surfing map. By the turn of the century, the exotic surf travel market was firmly established, and regions like the Mentawai Islands and Nias Island, once swarming with pioneering ferals, are now home to dozens of surf charter and camp operations.

Today, it is harder than ever to live the surf travel dream. But wherever the boundary of the next surf frontier, you'll find the feral there bearded, lonely and probably surfing better than anyone.

Ⓐ The beard
No designer stubble or craftily styled affectations. Have you tried getting a blade on board a charter flight these days?

Ⓑ The stance
Yoga is a great way to while away the flat spells. It keeps you loose, costs nothing, and has been known to suppress the appetite.

Ⓒ Rudimentary fishing tackle
To survive on nature's bounty alone is the best way to live. The surf camp up the point might claim to own the wave, but they can't claim the fish.

Ⓓ Mutant quiver
OK, so the original Lightning Bolt is the perfect tube-rider, but he's been experimenting with asymetrical, five-fin barrel-piercing lances fused out of the flotsam and jetsam of boat charters. Its amazing what you can do with a bit of epoxy and some duct tape.

Ⓔ Local jewellery
He's saving up for the ticket back to Sydney by selling bits of local tat.

Date of birth: 10 June 1938
Place of birth: Long Beach, California
Defining waves: Dana Point, Pipeline

PHIL EDWARDS

Phil Edwards, the clean-cut counterpoint to Miki Dora, was a pioneer of power surfing.

Phil Edwards of Oceanside, California, had spent the last few years at Dana Point, his local beach, learning to surf under the censorious gaze of the old-time riders and lifeguards who held court there. In this part of California, in the early fifties, the form was to wait for as big a wave as possible, paddle into it nonchalantly and, standing erect and noble, ride the hissing wall of white and green directly back to the beach. Then you'd simply step off, paddle back and do it all over again, preferably without so much as a hair out of place. But this was all about to change.

One sunny afternoon in 1953, during a solid summertime south swell and with a healthy crowd digging the waves from the beach, the teenage Edwards found himself locked in tight to the curl. 'Here I was, by accident,' he recounted later, 'crouched in some crazy, unconventional posture, flying along while the wave broke across my back and shoulders, in a sort of hanging, delicate balance between two worlds... A couple of minutes in the curl that day changed my life for ever.'

Although he might not have been the first to find lateral trim on a wave, it was certainly Edwards who popularised the new, dynamic way of imagining the ride. Continuing to

Chin tucked in tight, arms floating free and hips forward – Edwards skates Huntington Pier in 1964 in his own distinctive style.

ride wave after wave at speed with the rail set deep into the face, Edwards not only developed an uncanny ability before his contemporaries to find and stay in this point of power, but would shift his weight to the tail, forcing a tightly angled turn back into the heart of the wave. This new sultan of style became the young surfer to watch. Although Edwards never achieved the cult status of the Miki Dora, there are many surfers today who look at his radical style as representing the true dawn of power surfing, stripped of unnecessary stylistic adornment.

Locking into the pocket, outrunning the break and then cutting back to the curl were just a number of firsts with which Edwards is credited. He also had the first 'signature' surfboard model with Hobie and was the first surfer to complete a ride at Pipeline (his second ride was famously captured the 1961 film *Surfing Hollow Days*). Despite his achievements, Phil Edwards remains a little uncomfortable with some of the labels he's been given. In a sense he was a happy victim of timing and circumstance, growing up in a place and a period when the culture was hungry for the new. 'I was just a guy having adventures, having fun,' he told *Surfer* magazine. 'I would have been happy if surfing had stayed obscure.'

Although he may have been a reluctant hero, track down some footage of the man and you'll see why the culture eagerly embraces Edwards's dynamic style. See him locked into perfect trim completely straight backed, chest out, chin tucked in and arms relaxed. Then marvel as he cranks an explosive turn after a dramatic cross-step backwards to the tail, the nose swinging at speed as his arms fly aloft. Threading madly creative lines in the ocean, it appears as if a new kind of energy is escaping in spasms from somewhere deep inside Edwards's core. It's this style, right on the outer limits of control, that characterises power surfing.

Film-maker Bruce Brown captures Edwards riding a heavy spot between Sunset and Waimea. Brown christened the spot 'Pipeline'.

THE SURFER'S CODE

Put fifty surfers of wildly varying abilities together, from hard-charging, super-competitive alpha males to timorous beginners, and the results are potentially explosive. Fortunately, a series of basic rules have evolved, that, if observed, can maintain peace and order in the planet's crowded line-ups.

❶ Surf at spots that match your ability and attitude

It's common sense: if you are new to surfing, you'll want to stick to beginner-friendly spots. If you're a highly skilled surfer, and your idea of heaven is reeling, inside-out barrels and glory moments caught on film, don't bother with a spot popular with newbies. You'll end up feeling frustrated. And remember to steer clear of hyper-competitive spots if you are happy with a few mellow waves.

❷ Respect the atmosphere of the line-up

Closely related to the above, don't expect that just because you are a laid-back intermediate longboarder who needs only a couple of soft slides each session to stay stoked, that everyone shares your ethos. The atmosphere at any given surf spot can change day-to-day and even hour-by-hour depending on a complex nexus of personalities, conditions and unknowable factors. If you can't deal with the way the line-up feels, then you should consider whether it's in your best interests to paddle in and leave it for a couple of hours, or to seek out a spot that better suits your temperament.

❸ Don't drop in or snake other surfers

'Dropping in' and 'snaking' are the cardinal surfing sins and can ruin a surf session. The basic rule to observe is that the surfer nearest the peak of the breaking wave has right of way. You should never take off on a wave that is already being ridden by another surfer. Snaking is an even worse offence: the snake sees that the surfer nearest the critical point of the wave has priority, but paddles either in front of or behind the unsuspecting rider, catching the wave at the last moment.

❹ Don't paddle in the way of surfers who are up and riding

When paddling out, you should always try to avoid the line of the breaking wave. You can do this either by paddling the long way around, outside of the main path of riding surfers, or by taking the more strenuous route inside and through the whitewater. Common sense dictates that a riding surfer (apart from the few psychopaths of the tribe), will try their hardest to avoid any paddling surfers.

5 Take turns and take your time

A basic rule of thumb is that a person who has been waiting the longest (as long as he or she is holding the correct position in the line-up, of course) has priority over the next wave of a set. In practice, however, paddling speed, wave knowledge, skill level, or simple physical presence can mean that wave count is rarely equal or democratic. Even so, this shouldn't stop everyone having their turn. A natural rhythm always exists out there. The secret is to recognise and respect it.

6 Always help a fellow surfer in distress

Dedicated medical services are rarely available where surfers are riding waves. Boards can cause concussion and gouge the eyes, fins can cut arteries, and leashes can break, leaving surfers stranded without a board. If someone is in trouble, surfers should group together and help the injured surfer to the beach as quickly and as safely as possible.

7 Whether travelling near or far, respect the local surfers

Each surf spot has its own set of secondary, unwritten rules. The only way to approach a new surf spot is with an open, confident and friendly attitude. Don't be afraid to ask questions and closely observe what's going on in the line-up. If you knowingly break the rules, don't be surprised if the locals become intimidating.

8 Relax, have fun and enjoy your waves

When you surf, nothing should matter but the wave and the ride. Focus on the waves but bear others in mind; give other surfers around you respect and encouragement; approach the surf with an open mind and an open heart, and you will be enriched at more than just the physical level. An encounter with a wave that may have travelled thousands of miles to greet you can instill a sense of profound wellbeing. Just one perfect ride could change your life. The secret is to let it happen.

TECHNIQUE THREE

THE BOTTOM TURN

The bottom turn is the most important turn in surfing. Its main function is to transfer energy released on take-off – or from a turn at the top of a wave – to the rest of the ride.

You draw a bottom turn along the trough of the wave by leaning into the wave's face, placing your board on the edge of its inside rail. If done correctly, this angles you back up the face, and generates speed and power that you can bring to the wave's subsequent sections.

Between the late sixties and the late seventies, the bottom turn was the manoeuvre by which surfers were judged – leading surfers such as Barry Kanaiaupuni, Jeff Hakman and Nat Young were known particularly for their explosive, stylish interpretation of the manoeuvre. The lighter, thinner boards that arrived, however, in the late eighties and early nineties were more suited to dynamic moves up and over the lip of the wave rather than to long, drawn-out bottom turns. As a consequence, the aesthetically appealing manoeuvre lost much of its prestige. It remains, however, a timeless signature of surf style.

A good bottom turn equals good surfing

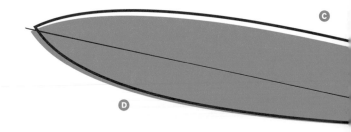

fig.III: Bottom Turn

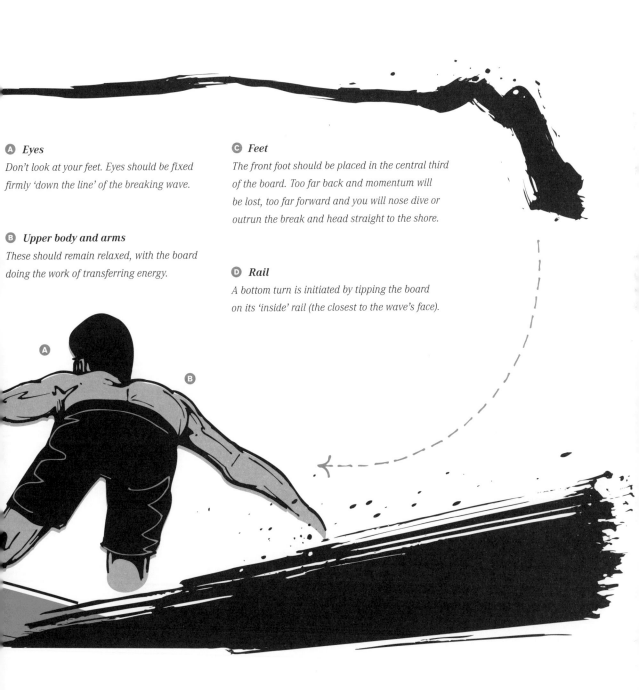

Ⓐ Eyes

Don't look at your feet. Eyes should be fixed firmly 'down the line' of the breaking wave.

Ⓑ Upper body and arms

These should remain relaxed, with the board doing the work of transferring energy.

Ⓒ Feet

The front foot should be placed in the central third of the board. Too far back and momentum will be lost, too far forward and you will nose dive or outrun the break and head straight to the shore.

Ⓓ Rail

A bottom turn is initiated by tipping the board on its 'inside' rail (the closest to the wave's face).

THE HISTORY OF THE WETSUIT

The design and technological evolution of wetsuits over the last fifty years have extended the boundaries of the surfing planet.

Santa Cruz surfer Jack O'Neill, (*left*) pioneered the development of the wetsuit in the 1950s. Cold-water surfing has never been the same since.

The wetsuit is the marketeer's dream. Read the body language and hair to make a call on which decade this O'Neill campaign was launched. Answer over the page.

In the pre-war years, surfing in cold water was not much fun. Hardy brethren would huddle around a fire, sipping on hits of rum and whisky while gingerly eyeing up the freezing winter sets. They'd pick their moment with a little Dutch courage, to pull on the woollen jersey and the thermal pants and to run to the shore, knee-paddling out for a quick, breathtaking bump and grind. Duck dives and wipeouts – anything that kept the surfer submerged – were to be avoided at all costs. Elegant, dry-haired paddle-outs and nonchalant, stylish kick-outs not only demonstrated surfing prowess for a generation, but were essential techniques a surfer could use to stay relatively dry and warm.

Hugh Bradner, a physicist working at the University of California, Berkeley in the early forties, is widely credited with coming up with the concept central to the success of the wetsuit: namely that it doesn't have to be watertight to keep the wearer warm. Bradner's research was commissioned by the US Navy in order to find a way to keep military divers in the water longer and to keep them fighting fit and flexible. Bradner realised that by using various types of rubber, PVC and other materials, a suit could achieve thermal insulation from the many tiny bubbles of air trapped in its material. Water could saturate the suit and the bubbles of water would heat up between the swimmer's skin and the suit's exterior surface.

When the Navy officially declassified the technology in 1951 it led to a flood of experimentation. San Francisco-based surfer and window-salesman Jack O'Neill was the first person, however, to adapt the concept fully to the needs of the cold-water surfers of central California. O'Neill quickly realised that a more flexible version of the Navy wetsuit would mean more water time for the wearer, and would consequently represent an incredibly saleable product. After several failed attempts to find the perfect material, the eureka moment came, legend has it, in 1952 on board an ancient Douglas DC-3 airliner. Pulling back the carpets on the aisle of the plane, O'Neill noticed an interesting rubber-like substance. It turned out to be an industrially produced material called neoprene.

O'Neill made a bulk order and stitched some of it together into a head-to-toe suit and went for a surf. It worked. A few years later and a hundred miles south of the new O'Neill surf shop at Santa Cruz, Bob Meistrell struck his own seam of gold in the relatively warm waters of Manhattan Beach, Los Angeles, with a substance known as G-231, a form of nitrogen-blown neoprene that could be found in the gaskets of car headlights. 'The material allowed us to make a much more surf-friendly suit than existed anywhere else at the time,' he recounted later. 'We improved freedom of movement manifold. It was a landmark discovery.' ▸▸

Surf Culture

THE HISTORY OF THE WETSUIT

◀◀   Since these pioneering days, the goal has always been to achieve greater lightness, flexibility, warmth, comfort and durability. A seemingly endless variety of cuts, colour combinations, zip-systems, seam configurations and even suits with no zips and seams have come onto the market. In the eighties, along with most things in that much-derided decade, wetsuits were turned out in horribly lurid colours. It took the rise of the retro movement to get the industry to start thinking again about the science as well as the style. Black material, of course, absorbed the sun's heat and helped keep the surfer warm. It also looked way cooler than tangerine.

In the nineties and into the twenty-first century, wetsuits have become incredibly light and efficient. Most modern suits can allow a surfer to stay in the water for hours on end, even in the most frigid of sea temperatures. Fully hooded and booted outfits with six-millimetre layers of neoprene have helped surfers take on the most extreme environments, allowing waves to be ridden in the Antarctic as well as the most northerly regions of Alaska. Today, the average surfer outside the tropics only ever truly needs a summer suit between two and three millimetres thick and a 'steamer' for the winter months between three and five millimetres. Exciting new innovations include battery-powered integral heating systems, water-repellent outer skins – and there's even a rumour that the iPod-compatible hooded wetsuit is only an integrated circuit away from production.

* The dude and chick on the preceding page featured in an O'Neill campaign from the early seventies.

During the eighties, there was one outright winner in the battle between style and substance.

Modern wetsuit technology has enabled surfers to colonise the planet's coldest seas, including those around Iceland.

LOCAL CONDITIONS

Favourable local tides and wind conditions are an essential part of the mix in the creation – or destruction – of the surfer's perfect day.

Every surf spot is an immensely complex convergence of environmental influences. Winds, tides and swell form an intricate equation that determines the surf conditions at any given moment. Over time, surfers build up an instinctive archive of environmental knowledge. Of course, it's relatively easy to be intimate with your local beach – you'll recognise its many moods as if it were a close friend. The real gift is the ability to transpose this knowledge to other spots, even those you haven't surfed before.

Tides are the rhythmic rise and fall of water levels caused by the gravitational influences of the sun and the moon on the earth. Although tide levels and timings are predictable years in advance, the hydrodynamics of tidal ebb and flow affect wave conditions in a huge variety of ways in different parts of the world. In the British Isles, for example, tidal range is one of the planet's most extreme, with the difference between low and high water levels reaching as much as 18 metres. This means that a surf spot may disappear at low tide, but appear again at mid-high tide as height and flow of water reaches a particular reef or sandbar. It is also common for very high tides to 'shut down' a given surf spot because of backwash from

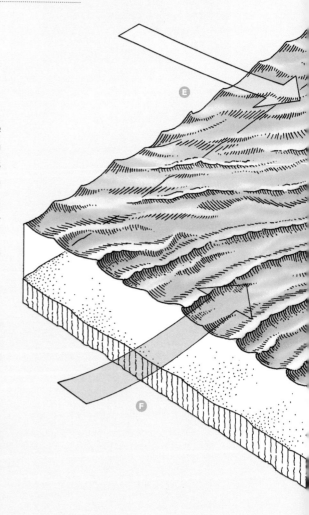

See also

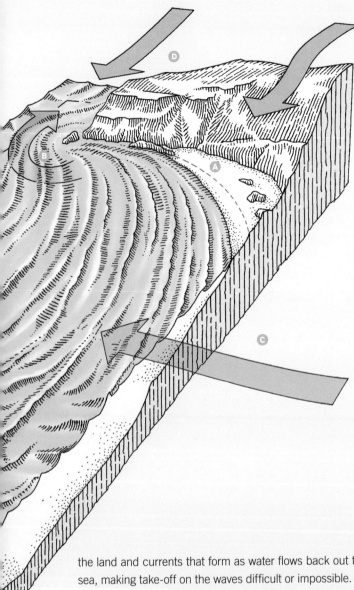

A High tide

At higher stages of the tide, as shown here, waves form as they interact with the rocky outcrops and sandbars at the foot of the headland. At lower stages of the tide the breaking waves will be more exposed to a Northerly wind.

B Currents

Waves will be affected by backwash from these rocks, and currents will form as water escapes back out to sea.

C Easterly wind (offshore)

Light winds blowing directly from shore toward the sea 'clean up' and groom the surf, holding up the faces of the waves and creating ideal waves.

D Northerly wind (cross-shore)

A wind from the North means that waves in the lee of the headland are protected from the effects of the wind, especially at high tide. Waves further down the beach, unprotected by the headland, are likely to be choppier.

E Westerly wind (onshore)

Wind blowing directly from sea to shore always adversely affects wave quality, causing peaks to crumble, except when these winds are extremely light.

F Southerly wind (cross/sideshore)

Winds blowing parallel to the land tend to crumble the peaks of waves and chop up their faces. A slight swing in wind direction can create either a clement improvement or cause conditions to deteriorate further.

the land and currents that form as water flows back out to sea, making take-off on the waves difficult or impossible.

Wind is equally important in producing good surf conditions. Light offshores (winds blowing softly from the shore) are ideal as they tend to hold up the faces of the waves and groom them into smooth, clearly defined lines. Onshore winds, on the other hand, crumble waves' faces into seething walls of whitewater, good only for running straight to shore. On any given day, winds predicted by meteorologists are affected by the topography of the surf spot: headlands and cliffs can afford protection, for example, whereas wide-open beaches are more more exposed to the negative effects of wind. How these local conditions interact with swell and tide produce the ever-fluid rhythm of a surfing day.

THE LEASH

The invention of the surf leash, tethering board to rider, polarised surfers. Depending on your perspective, it either spoiled or saved surf culture.

A hardcore of surfers continues to rail against the leash, as this sticker at Rincon, California, makes plain.

In 1970, Pat O'Neill, Santa Cruz surfer and son of surf entrepreneur, Jack, came up with the idea of attaching a length of surgical tubing to the surfboard and securing the other end, via a cuff, to the surfer's leg. Before this, if you fell off your board it was inevitably washed to shore without you. In those pre-leash days, every time you wiped out and lost your board it involved a hefty ocean swim.

The rise of the leash in the seventies had a dramatic impact: a new generation of surfers could now access waves without needing great skill and stamina in the water. Competent riders could attempt waves previously considered out of bounds because of the danger of boards breaking on the rocks after a wipeout, while highly skilled surfers could catch more waves during each session. Leashes can also be credited with facilitating increasingly radical manoeuvres. Leash-wearing surfers began to experiment with new moves, safe in the knowledge that they could fall off, recover their boards immediately, and quickly paddle back out to try the move again. Throughout the early-to-mid-seventies, however, the leash stirred up considerable controversy among many surfers and provoked a plethora of anti-leash slogans such as 'leashes are for dogs', and widespread diatribes in the surf media. 'In the good old days', the hardcore mantra went, 'kooks swam, surfers surfed.'

Initially, leashes were attached to the board with a loop built in to the board's fibreglass or through a small hole drilled in the fin. Since the early eighties, most contemporary surfboards have included a leash 'plug' set into the foam on the board's deck. The plug contains a bracket of metal around which a loop of nylon cord is tied. Big-wave 'guns', ridden in extremely powerful surf, often include two leash plugs as a fail-safe mechanism.

At their best, leashes can save lives – remaining attached to a floatation device in the shape of your surfboard can prove vital in big waves. At their worst, leashes can get caught on underwater reefs and put the surfer at risk of drowning (there are only a few ocurrences of this happening). A more common complaint is that leashes can be relied upon a little too heavily as they encourage unskilled surfers to go for waves they can't make and allow riders to bail their surfboards in critical situations, endangering other surfers.

Leash recoil is another hazard. Jack O'Neill lost his eye in 1971 using an early version of his son's invention, when the board he was riding sprung back and gouged out his eye.

However unglamorous, the leash is one of the staples of a surfer's kit. Leashes come in different lengths and thicknesses according to the board you're riding and which kind of wave you're surfing. Generally, the bigger the board, the thicker and longer the leash you'll need. Longboarders who use leashes (many don't, especially in smaller waves) attach the cuff of the leash just below the knee rather than the ankle (this helps with delicate board-walking manoeuvres).

The sale of leashes has brought welcome revenue to the surf industry. They have helped to prevent far fewer accidents than they have caused and have allowed people with only moderate levels of fitness to experience the joy of surfing. Perhaps we should, after all, celebrate one of the great democratising influences in modern surf culture.

The leash, otherwise known by its detractors as the 'kook cord' as well as a host of other epithets, enjoys near ubiquity on the surfing planet.

_____ " TRULY

BIG
WAVES
AREN'T MEASURED IN
INCREMENTS

OF FEET.

THEY
ARE MEASURED IN
INCREMENTS
OF
FEAR."

Buzzy Trent

THE SURF SHOP

A secular chapel for wave-riding devotees, the surf shop has a central place in the life of every truly committed surfer.

Ever since Jack O'Neill's legendary shop opened in San Francisco in 1952, surf shops have played an integral role in the development of surf culture.

Jack O'Neill opened the very first 'surf shop', selling boards and wetsuits, from a beachside garage.

The surf shop is where the disparate strands of surfing come together. It's where surfers have traditionally gathered to order and buy boards, to swap gossip, to trade banter, to work out the skinny on who's who and what's what. The classic surf shop is where surf fashion, fad and influence have been negotiated day to day, session by session.

Now that retail is moving rapidly online and the surf clan is a globally flung diaspora, surf shops remain one of the culture's touchstones.

The first surf shops were simply backyard board-building operations. Irate parents of young surfers, sick of their homes being crammed with half-built and broken boards, would force their offspring to store and tend to their boards in low-rent garages and pier-side shacks. Through the word-of-mouth marketing of early surf culture, board-makers were true artisans, hand building custom orders and experimenting with designs, materials and hand-wrought craftsmanship in a way that would make today's fetishists of all things organic and 'locally sourced' rejoice.

Dale Velzy is generally recognised as one of the earliest board-building entrepeneurs. In 1950 he opened a Velzy Surfboards shop in LA's Manhattan Beach at around the same time that surfer-shapers such as Hobie Alter, Greg Noll and Bing Copeland were running their own low-rent board shacks. Though it was a legitimate business enterprise, Velzy's operation was a seat-of-the-pants affair which took hundreds of custom orders a week despite chaotic or non-existent book-keeping and depended on a roster of eager kids and nubile chicks that would come to worship at the Velzy altar. Working with shaping genius Hap Jacobs, Velzy became the dominant board builder in California during the fifties, and his light-hearted scams and money-generating strokes of genius crossed with generosity, energy and vision, became legend. 'Velzy is the most wonderful, sweet-hearted person,' recalls North Shore pioneer and Velzy acolyte Mickey Muñoz, 'and whenever he'd scam it was never malicious … he gave us kids jobs, gave us money, gave us surfboards, and took us surfing to places we'd never been before …' ▶▶

Design-focused stores, such as Mollusk *(right)* in New York, have re-created the intimacy of the early local surf shops.

Surf giant Quiksilver's state-of-the-art store (*below*) in Anglet, France, with its 700 square metres of surfing merchandise, lies at the other end of the scale to the boutique shop.

THE SURF SHOP

◀◀   While Velzy's shop was incredibly influential, it was essentially a factory outlet for his board-building operation. Jack O'Neill, wetsuit pioneer and figurehead of Northern California's early surf scene, can lay claim to the first genuine article, when he opened the Surf Shop in San Francisco in 1952. You could buy wetsuits as well as surfboards in O'Neill's shop (he opened a second store in Santz Cruz in 1959).

As surf culture developed, the stock of surf shops became much broader with T-shirts, stickers, trunks and a whole range of surf-related products to entice the rapidly growing rank and file. The explosion of surfing commerce in the decades since has seen surf shops spring up everywhere from Dubai to Central London, each marketing the surf dream. Some surf shops, such as Rich Harbour's tiny store in Seal Beach, California, retain the same shaping bays out back that they've been using since the fifties. At the other end of the scale, huge retail outlets such as Ron Jon's surf shop in Florida's Cocoa Beach is a huge hypermarket of extreme sports, selling everything from rollerblades to remote control surfing dolls. Big players also include major brands, such as Quiksilver, which have franchised shops across the planet, selling exclusively branded boards and apparel.

There is a current new wave of retail outlets that sell the majority of their products online to an increasingly global clientele, but still retain the ethos of the underground surf outlet. Enterprises such as Mollusk, which has stores in California as well as New York, and Loose-Fit, based in Britain's surf-synched southwest, sell a diverse range of surfboard designs from all over the world, alongside a broad array of fashion items, books, DVDs and other products. Surf shops have always been where the commercial aspects of surfing (aka 'the industry') has touched down and nestled with the punters on the streets and on the beach. Today, however, you can order a custom displacement hull from California, or a limestone-based neoprene full suit from Japan, no matter which surfing backwater you happen to find yourself in. At one time, a surfer's choices were limited to the availability of equipment and designs from your local store. Now, the world of surf design is only a click away. As as result, there's never been a more interesting time to be a surfer.

CLASSIC SURF WAGON
VW TRANSPORTER

Surf Culture

The Volkswagen Transporter is one of the culture's best-known icons and remains by far the most popular surf wagon on the planet.

Whether it's a lowered, chopped-and-cropped, split-screen '65 T1 campervan or a bio-diesel burning T5 Sportline kombi fresh from the factory, Volkswagen's iconic workhorse has been a feature in beach car parks ever since its launch in 1950. The Transporter's super-reliable, rear-mounted, air-cooled engine was a revolution in post-war European design and engineering. Placing the power plant below decks and between the rear wheels freed up an acreage of interior cabin space – and in the early years it was cheap, too. These factors combined to make the Transporter a practical and affordable home-on-wheels for travellers on the hippy trail, as well as a legion of committed surfers who were determined to seek out uncrowded waves outside their native shores. Although it sold well over a million units between 1965 and 1975, nowadays even beat-up examples of the early T1 or T2 are sought after as classic restoration projects. The VW Transporter is continually charged with counter-cultural kudos as its resale value increases. There can be few committed surfers on the planet who haven't considered going into debt to secure a pristine example.

A *Guy is stoked with his bus*

It's a 1969 Type 2 Transporter he picked up from a mate (who didn't manage to avoid the draft) at Mullumbimby, New South Wales. Guy's escaped the draft and his chick, Cherry, has finally discovered the joys of free love.

B *The paraphernalia of mind-expansion*

Cherry and Guy were fascinated by the piece in Tracks magazine on the organic cultivation of fungi. The bong does the job, but unless they find some psilocybin soon they'll never discover the innermost limits of pure fun.

C *Cherry wears a lot of cheesecloth*

She's thinking of travelling to India. Guy's not sure, though. There's no surf on the Ganges, is there? Cherry thinks that Terry Fitzgerald is a total spunk.

D *Lightning Bolt pintails*

Guy bought a quiver back from Hawaii last January, as well as a black eye and a hatred of spam and pineapple.

BUTCH VAN ARTSDALEN

Date of birth: 31 January 1941
(died 18 July 1979)
Place of birth: Virginia, USA
Defining waves: Pipeline, Windansea

Pioneer tube rider and brawling legend of Windansea Surf Club, Butch Van Artsdalen was a swashbuckling sixties anti-hero who conquered the heaviest waves in the world.

Butch Van Artsdalen was of the generation of surfers who started out when men were men and boards were made of wood – a member of the generation that faded tragically, unfairly and wastefully in the era when those surfboards became lightweight slivers of fibreglass and foam. Born in 1941, he began surfing at the age of fifteen at the beaches of La Jolla, California. He cut his teeth at the tough-brawling, hard-partying, heavy-surfing Windansea Surf Club before heading out to the Islands and being welcomed as a *haole* soulmate by the locals. Butch stories abound in surf culture. There was the time when, pulling in to Pipeline on his longboard, he tucked his brawn in tighter to the curl than anyone ever before, with the five-star élite of Hawaiian surfing as witnesses. At that moment he became the first ever 'Mr Pipeline'. There was another time when, on a booze-addled jaunt to Tijuana, he gathered bail money for a group of incarcerated San Diego surfers, only to disappear, drinking the funds. On yet another occasion he dragged an eighteen-year-old kid off the reef at Pipeline, resuscitating him for twenty minutes or so against all odds, not giving up until the barely alive kid puked into his mouth and was taken to an attendant ambulance. Butch cracked a beer, lent on his lifeguard tower and lit a cigarette, smiling.

According to those who knew him, Butch Van Artsdalen was contradictory soul: an easy-smiling, supreme athlete who looked out for (and frequently saved) the hapless tourists who put themselves in grave danger on the North Shore. He was also a chronic, dangerous alcoholic who could fight, surf and drink with equal dedication and commitment. It would be the death of him.

But the stories of Butch Van Artsdalen are secondary to the undeniable brilliance of his switch-foot style and pioneering tube rides. Though not unique in his ability to surf with either his left or right foot forward, Butch could switch stances in the most critical of situations: at the foot of a bottom turn at Pipe or kicking out of a close-out set in mid-air at Haleiwa. His visceral, baseball catcher's crouch enabled him to ride out the deadliest of situations in the barrel, his gorilla-like presence apparently defying the laws of physics. Butch would take off deeper and later than anyone before on the big, heavy, relatively crude surfboards of the early sixties, and was probably the first surfer to wire the art of the tube.

In the late sixties, when the cultural changes sweeping through society were beginning to be reflected within surf culture, Butch became a lifeguard at Ehukai Beach. According to the man who succeeded him as Mr Pipeline, Gerry Lopez, he probably got more people out of trouble at Pipe than anyone before or since. By the early seventies, however, he felt alienated from a culture that frowned on fighting, binge drinking and longboards – the three things that most defined the man's identity. In his final few years he rarely paddled out and was drinking heavily, although he continued to save lives up and down the North Shore. 'You can have the surfing,' he told Lopez on the sand at Sunset Beach after swimming though the tumultuous Sunset shorebreak to rescue Lopez's board, 'I just do rescue work.'

The potency of Butch Van Artsdalen's story is one that is echoed in John Milius's 1978 movie *Big Wednesday*. To carry on surfing through the physical, social and cultural changes of a lifetime is an achievement in itself, but not one that all surfers – even the best of them – manage to pull off. When he died in the summer of 1979, aged thirty-eight, huge memorial services were held simultaneously at Ehukai and at his erstwhile home at La Jolla. After the service at Ehukai, the gathered crowd paddled out and, in a time-honoured ceremony, scattered his ashes at the Pipeline peak.

Van Artsdalen's muscular style, seen here at Pipeline in 1965, captured the imagination of the fledgling surf media.

SURF TRAVEL TIPS

To surf is to travel. And to travel to the other side of the planet with a bunch of surfboards and a headful of dizzying expectations can be a major hassle. Come with us and pick up a few handy hints to keep stress levels to a minimum.

❶ Packing

One of the worst-case scenarios is arriving on an Indonesian island with perfect waves the temperature of bathwater ... to find your boards in pieces. To avoid this nightmare, pick your travel quiver carefully. Smaller, lighter boards are naturally best for travel. If you're a die-hard longboarder, light, factory-built epoxy boards are more resilient than traditionally made logs. If you must take that precious original Skip Frye ten-footer or similar, bubble wrap and duct tape can go some way to provide reassurance. The downside is that all baggage handlers have a vendetta against surfers and their boards. Building a sticky, cushioned coffin which adds yet more kilos will make them hate you even more. Glassed-on fins are very susceptible to snapping in transit, so, where possible, remove all fins before packing. Never, ever take a hacky sack with you.

❷ The airport

Call in advance to make sure you will even be able to get your boards on the plane. Many airlines have specific charges and regulations about taking surfboards on board.

Heightened security makes the process more tortuous than ever. Never, ever joke about the contents of your board bags: airport security do not do humour. Costs associated with checking surfboards may be unavoidable these days, but use your head. If you don't ask, you don't get. A good tip is to avoid wearing the garb of contemporary surfer cliché: hoodie, flip-flops, boardshorts and permanently attached shades. Try adopting, instead, the Mike Hynson/Robert August technique as used in *The Endless Summer*: don a smart suit and a crisp tie. Why not throw a heavily waxed parting into the mix? This will wrong-foot the process-fascist counter clerk and charm trolley dolleys of either gender the world over. If you've insisted on bringing a hacky sack with you, never play at the airport.

③ On the plane

Under no circumstances should you try to spot your surf-boards being loaded by baggage handlers on the tarmac. Inevitably, this will provoke a rush of impotent rage and paranoia. The blue-collared bag-jockey is also likely to play up to your worst fears if he spots you gesticulating wildly at him from the porthole. Relax, flirt with the flight attendants and feign the cool resignation of the seasoned surf traveller even if your insides are leaping at every boogie and shake of the aircraft's tensile steel. Never conduct the usual hand-jiving, jargon-heavy descriptions of the endless barrels you're expecting to encounter at your destination. This will wind up your fellow travellers and you'll look like a fool. Don't overindulge in the free booze. Landing at your destination with a heavy transfer ahead of you, feeling hungover and dehydrated is a recipe for disaster. And never play hacky sack in the aisle, even if you're heading all the way to Easter Island.

④ The transfer

If your boards are covered in dings on arrival, don't freak out. Forget about attempting to organise compensation with the local office of the airline. You can repair your dings when you arrive at your final destination. If you've arranged local transport in advance, then so much the better. If not, choose your ride carefully. Taxi drivers of the developing world correctly look at you as the over-privileged hedonist that you are, and automatically presume that you have money to burn. They know you have a hangover from hell (unless you've followed the advice above) and will also charge you extra for strapping your boards to the roof. And that's another good tip: bring your own straps with you. Try finding a hardware store in Padang or Colombo at five in the morning ...

⑤ The surf camp

OK, so you've made it deep into the reef-side jungle camp more or less in one piece and with boards in workable condition. As the taxi/bus/boat/tuk-tuk/rickshaw approaches the entrance to the camp, enjoy the feeling of discovery, of the heroic and eternal search for timeless waves. Make the most of this fleeting moment before it dawns on you that there's a bunch of crew here from your home town, that what looked like a five-star chalet with 'gourmet local seafood' on the website is actually a scorpion-infested, malarial pit of bong-hit-induced paranoia and that the right hander's been mushy as hell since the locals started fishing on the reef with hand grenades after the rebel uprising was quelled. And hold on a minute ... could it be that the huge yacht anchored out in the bay is the floating home of twelve of the hottest sponsored groms this side of Coolangatta? Get out that hacky sack. You're going to need it after all.

TECHNIQUE FOUR

THE TOP TURN

The top turn is the manoeuvre used to change direction at the top of a wave.

The ability to make a successful re-entry into the power source of a wave via a good top turn is an essential skill for the surfer. As in any surfboard manoeuvre, timing is essential in the execution of a good top turn. You make a top turn at the top of the wave by hitting the lip with the bottom of your board and setting the outside rail into the wave's face. If done correctly, the top turn transfers the wave's energy to board and rider, and harnesses speed for your descent. A top turn can come in a variety of forms, and can also be known as an 'off the top', 'off the lip', a 're-entry', a 'snap' or a 'rebound'. In its most dynamic, lip-smacking manifestation, the top turn, when combined with a strong bottom turn, has become an ubiquitous point-scorer in professional surfing. Champion surfers of the eighties and nineties are well-known for their spectacular mastery of the manoeuvre. Tom Curren, Martin Potter and Mark Occhilupo became bywords for water-displacing, spray-inducing off-the-tops.

The lipsmacking top turn is a signature of stylish performance surfing.

Ⓐ

fig.IV: Top Turn

Ⓐ Rail

Initiate the top turn by shifting your weight onto the 'outside' rail (the board's outside edge that is furthest from the face of the wave). This will slow your speed.

Ⓑ Eyes

Focus your eyes on the point at the top of the wave that you're aiming to hit.

Ⓒ Feet

When you reach the top of the breaking wave, your back foot should be positioned towards the tail of the board. This will enable the nose of the board to swing quickly down towards the bottom of the wave.

Ⓓ Upper body

Let the board move with the curling lip and fall towards the bottom of the wave. Reaching forward down the line of the breaking wave with your back arm will re-distribute your weight and help project you out of the turn.

ART BREWER

Art Brewer's mastery of colour and composition is unrivalled in the world of contemporary surf photography. No one has evoked the many facets of the culture as stylishly, or exerted such influence.

Born in Laguna Beach, California, in 1951, Art Brewer first surfed at the age of twelve at San Onofre and Doheny. His first published surf photo – a tube shot of Pierre Michelle at Laguna Beach's Thalia Street – ran in a 1966 surfboard ad in *Surfer* magazine. His ascendancy as a leading surf lensman came at a critical point in surfing's evolution. By 1968, the largely self-taught photographer was hooked in tight to the newly dominant community of shortboard-riding surfers who were ripping up the waves of southern California. Sharing their lifestyle as well as their waves, Brewer successfully shot covers and editorial action for *Surfing* and *Surfer*. Building on this early success of the late sixties and early seventies, he

became a perennial favourite of the surf media. From 1975 until the end of the millennium he was *Surfer*'s senior contributor and sometime photo editor. Brewer's imposing figure and uncompromising attitude has earned him a reputation as a mercurial force to be reckoned with amongst publishers, editors and surfers. He's always combined charasmatic presence with an uncanny knowledge of how to get that special shot – whether it's through a specific lighting effect, capturing a candid situation or an offbeat composition.

The mid-to-late nineties saw one of Brewer's most creative periods, when he collaborated extensively with Japanese surfer and film-maker Takuji Masuda on *Super X Media*, an experimental Japanese and English-language magazine that took a critical, surf-infused perspective to areas as vastly disparate as post-ceasefire Sarajevo and the elusive surf and skateboard scene of Cuba. Over the last decade, with an increasingly broad range of subjects and commercial clients from outside of the surfing world, Art Brewer has staked out the boundaries of surf culture's global influence.

Munga Barry (*far left*) drops in
at Hawaii's Sunset Beach.

Larry Bertlemann (*above*), master of
understatement, marked a new breed
of surfing professional in the seventies.

Gerry Lopez, 'Mr Pipeline' (*left*),
surveys his domain.

Brewer's monochrome work memorably
captures a boat trip in the Maldives.

Released in November 1962, *Surfers' Choice* was the first great surf music album. One of the tracks, 'Misirlou Twist', famously featured in Quentin Tarantino's 1994 film, *Pulp Fiction*.

SURF MUSIC

For a brief moment in the early sixties, surf music defined American youth.

The Rendezvous Ballroom on the Balboa Peninsula in Newport Beach is heaving. It's the summer of 1961 and the surf music scene is thriving in the underground, but about to explode into the mainstream. Tow-headed kids with slick partings, Pendletons, Levis and sandals heave and twist on the floor. Chicks in three-quarter length pants and floral halternecks stomp and shake and sweat with the surfer boys and wannabes as the reverb echoes through the crowd. Dick Dale and his Del-Tones are tearing through the set. The 'king of surf guitar' himself, his Stratocaster loaded with heavy gauge strings turning blackish-blue from the intense heat he's generating, is huffing and grimacing as the notes descend and slur and bop and hiss. The crowd is being taken on a ride. It's the middle of July, the tide is high and there's been a steady southerly swell running all day. It's hot and intense in here and the crowd is calling out and responding to Dale's sonic gymnastics, and just as the guttural strands of 'Let's Go Trippin'' begin to drop, the tide breaks through the double doors at the end of the ballroom. The surf is here and the surf is good. This is the original surfer stomp.

Out in the crowd there's a kid called Dennis Wilson and his tubby brother Carl. Dennis is a drummer and a surfer. His older brother Brian is writing at home on the piano, but Dennis has managed to drag Carl out and they are digging Dick's dexterity in the twisting, damp, sweaty stomp. The brothers will get home late tonight; tomorrow, as they drift down into their dad's studio to face his wrath, they'll still be jazzed on the intensity of Dale's wrenching sound and Dennis will blather on insanely about the surf he had yesterday and the night he and Carl had. Dennis tells Brian about the water coming into the ballroom while Dick played and the kids went wild. It was just so right and so now and all the kids dig this guy the most. He tells Brian he should write a song about surfing. Somewhere over the horizon that morning John Lennon is listening to an Elvis Presley record on his auntie's single-speaker gramophone and dreaming of getting out of suburban Liverpool. Last night John went to the pictures to watch his hero in *Blue Hawaii* and although he had seemed to have lost his edge and gone all Hollywood, there was something about the Hula girls, the palm trees, the hint of waves and a glimpse of surfers that set John dreaming of America.

Dick Dale's legendary surfer stomps at the Rendezvous ended in Christmas 1961, and The Beach Boys, who were turned on to the surf sound that night, had a little hit that got to No. 75 in the charts called 'Surfin''.

Soon the airwaves and the dance halls of America were clogged with a legion of Dick Dale impersonators and lyricists like Brian Wilson who vocalised the beauty and the buzz of the beach life. Surf music began to branch out in two directions. On the one hand were the overtly commercial harmonic pop and cheesecake balladeering of The Beach Boys and Jan and Dean, and on the other the hard-charging instrumental sound exemplified by the likes of Dick Dale, The Chantays and The Challengers. Although surfing's hardcore far preferred the dirty sound of the surf guitar to the vocalists,

Surf Culture

album covers in both sub-genres were emblazoned with imagery that attempted to sell the surf dream as an all-inclusive rite of passage. Typically, they'd feature anti-heroic dudes and jaunty, lemon-popsicle surfer chicks in the mould of Gidget, punctuated by the odd heavy wave from Makaha. Although both had roots in the funky, lowdown R&B of Black America, the two branches of surf music were aesthetically divergent. While the balladeers constructed surfing's imagery out of a litany of catchy tunes, beautiful harmonies and pop references, the Stratocaster pilots were

Night after night, Dick Dale and his Del-tones kicked up a storm during their legendary 1961 residency at the Rendezvous Ballroom, Newport Beach.

trying to get inside the wave to etch a sonic image of sliding sideways on a rush of moving water. It took the arrival of the British Invasion in 1964, spearheaded by John Lennon and his band of mop-topped popsters, to knock surf music out of the upper reaches of the charts. But for a short, tempestuous time, Southern California had found the sound that defined itself.

Overleaf: classic surf albums 1962–63

COME SURF WITH ME

VEE JAY

AKI ALEONG and the NOBLES

STEREO

THE RISING SURF
RICHIE ALLEN AND THE PACIFIC SUR

SURFING WITH THE CHALLENGERS

TIDAL WAVE • DANCE WITH THE GUITAR MAN • SO WHAT • SATAN'S THEME
CAN'T SIT DOWN • MOON DAWG • THE VENTURES MEDLEY • SURFER'S PONY
THE TWOMP • COMIN' HOME BABY • FOOT PATTER • RAMPAGE   VAULT-101

THE SOUL SURFE
JOHNNY FOR

Johnny FORTUNE

SOUL SU
CHINES
SURFER
WILD W
SURF RI
SIBONEY

Park

SURFING IN THE COUNTRY THE BEACH BOYS
URFIN' USA

Capitol
HIGH FIDELITY

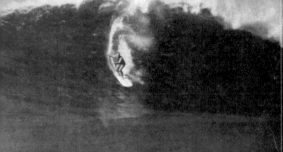

.A. · FARMER'S DAUGHTER · MISIRLOU · STOKED · LONELY SEA · SHUT DOWN
ER · HONKY TONK · LANA · SURF JAM · LET'S GO TRIPPIN' · FINDERS KEEPERS

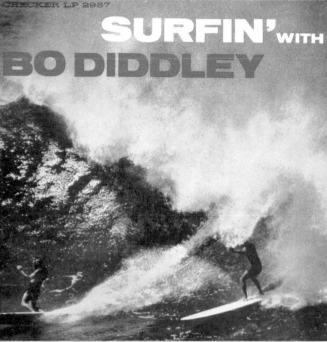

CHECKER LP 2987

SURFIN' WITH
BO DIDDLEY

nnettes BEACH PARTY

Vista
BV-331

from the
AMERICAN INTERNATIONAL FI

AT HIM NICELY / DON'T STOP NOW / PROMISE HIM ANYTHING / SECRET SURFIN' SPOT

BEACH PARTY

BEACH PARTY ■ WIPE OUT ■ CHURCH KEY ■ LATINA ■ SURFIN' TRAGEDY
DELANO SOUL BEAT ■ LET'S GO TO THE BEACH ■ SUMMERTIME IS SURFIN' TIME
THE SCAVENGER ■ SURF 'N' STOMP ■ SURFIN' WITH JIMMY ■ SURFIN' WITH VIGOR

WIPE OUT

G.S.P
RECORDS INC.

HOW TO BUILD A BOARD

Everything you wanted to know about building a surfboard but were afraid to ask.

Surfboard building remains – despite the globalisation of the economy and the increasing popularity of outsourced, machine-made 'popouts' – a cottage industry led by a few dedicated, passionate craftsmen. Shapers often work for extremely little profit, feeding years of hard-won wave-riding experience into their signature designs. They are often not only talented designers but equally skilled surfers in their own right. It's the constant innovation and sharing of experience that makes board-building such an intimate, intricate craft. To survive in an age of intense competition, many of the world's leading shapers license designs to big companies who outsource the manufacture of their boards to, say, the Far East, whilst charging a premium for a hand-crafted original from their own shaping bay.

In a truly bespoke service a customer consults with a shaper and works out everything he or she needs from a particular board, including the outline or 'planshape', fin specification, length, thickness, foil and rail and rocker profile. Everything from graphic designs to colours and other decorative details can be specified during this process. Very often, the end product is the result of a genuinely collaborative process between surfer and shaper. With luck, the surfer will experience the joy of riding a 'magic board' that perfectly suits his or her style of surfing and encapsulates the kind of alchemy that can arise from this intense sharing of surf knowledge.

What follows is a basic guide to the main elements of the surfboard building process.

ESSENTIAL MATERIALS

Polyurethane foam blank A 'blank' is a raw lump of foam in the rough shape of surfboard. Additional strength is provided by one or more strips of wood, called stringers, glued into the foam.

Fibreglass fabric A cloth, woven from glass fibres, used to seal the blank and keep it strong and watertight.

Polyester resin A liquid, which, when mixed with catalyst, forms the tough, outer shell of a surfboard.

Catalyst Also known as MEKP (methylethylkeytone peroxide).

Surface agent A styrene and wax solution that seals air out of the resin, allowing it to form a hard surface that can be sanded.

BASIC EQUIPMENT

Power planer
Preferably the iconic but difficult to find Skil 100 Power Planer.

Mini hand-planer

Handsaw

Scissors

Sandpaper

Rubber gloves

Respirator

Mixing buckets

Measuring buckets

Squeegee

Chisel

Stage one: shaping the blank

Cutting the blank

With the power planer remove the outer layer of the blank. Next, draw the shape of the board on one half of the blank, using a template ❶. (You can make your own template by tracing around an existing surfboard onto heavy card or Masonite, a type of hardboard.) Carefully, cut the shape out from the blank with a handsaw. Repeat this on the other half of the board. This will create a symmetrical surfboard shape with square edges.

Rail shaping and sanding

To turn these edges into the board's rails, plane the foam ❷ until the desired shape is achieved – hard-edged rails for quick, tight turns; soft, rounded rails for stability and drive. Next, turn the blank onto its side and run the sandpaper along the rails ❸ from tip to tail to achieve a smooth finish. Do this on both sides until the rails have the look you require. Finally, sand the deck and the bottom of the board until smooth.

After this stage, you should aim to have a perfectly shaped surfboard, but without a layer of finished fibreglass, or fins. ▶▶

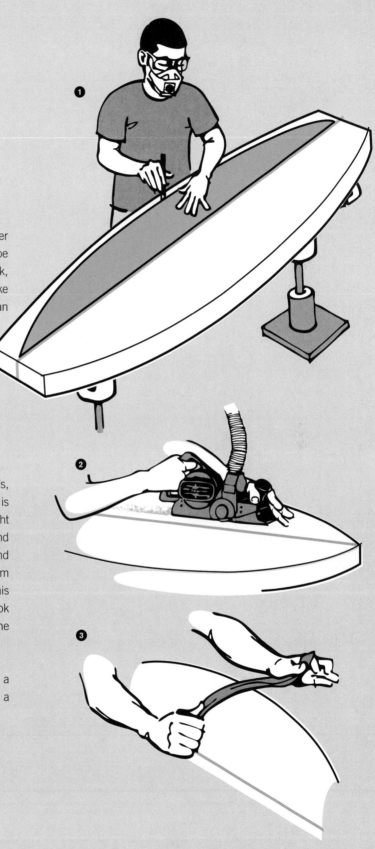

HOW TO BUILD A BOARD

◀◀ *Stage two: glassing or laminating the board*

Covering the board in cloth

Roll out the fibreglass cloth over one side of the board and, with some sharp scissors, cut the material ❹ to the shape of the board. Make sure that you have enough cloth so that the other side of the board can also be covered.

Applying the resin

Next pour out a mixture of the resin and the catalyst onto the cloth-covered board and smooth it out with your squeegee ❺. The whole surface of the board should be wet with resin. Walk around the board while the resin and catalyst mixture sets and smooth it out ❻. Repeat on the reverse side of the board. Next, apply another layer of resin, this time mixed with surface agent. This will be the layer which is sanded smooth in the finishing stage, and is also known as the hot coat. Using soft sandpaper, smooth down this final layer of resin ❼. Turn the board over and repeat the process.

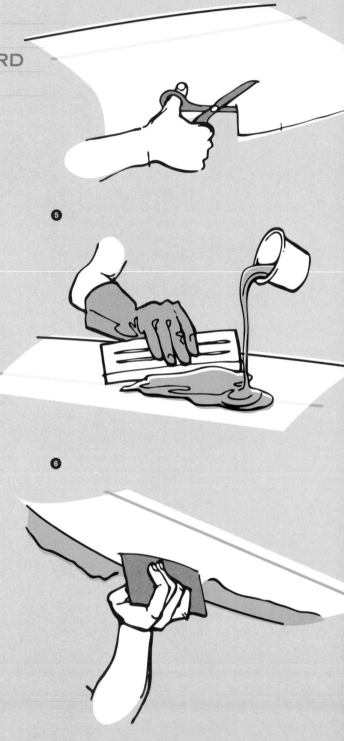

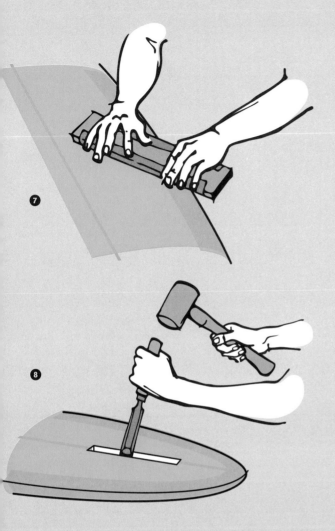

7

8

Stage three: finishing

Applying the fin box

About four inches from the tail, trace the outline of a fin box in the centre stringer of the board. Next, take a sharp chisel and cut out the fibreglass, stringer and foam from this section **8**. Then, fix the fin box into place with a mixture of resin and catalyst.

Polishing

Finally, use a buffer attachment to get the perfect finish **9** on both sides of the board.

9

NAT YOUNG

Date of birth: 14 November 1947
Place of birth: Sydney, Australia
Defining waves: Lennox Head, Angouri

In the modern era, no surfer has been as influential,
or created as much controversy, as Robert 'Nat' Young.

The thousands of spectators at San Diego's Ocean Beach didn't know what to make of it. It was October 1966, the World Surfing Championships, and California was the undisputed centre of the surfing world. Riding the nose of a surfboard was something to which every devotee of the sport aspired. The art was predicated on the long, easy-flowing lines drawn by Californian surfers on their heavy, ten-foot-long boards. Seventeen-year-old David Nuuhiwa, imperious master of the ten-second noseride, was expected to assume the crown that was rightfully his.

In the cinemas, Bruce Brown's *Endless Summer* had just exploded on screens across the country. The Vietnam War was escalating in intensity but still seen as winnable. Brian Wilson had spent most of the previous winter in the studio in Los Angeles creating his rapturously beautiful masterpiece *Pet Sounds*. To be Californian and a surfer at that precise moment was to be blessed, to be one of the chosen people. But a social and aesthetic revolution was imminent that would soon provoke trouble in this paradise.

Forming his own small, but significant, part in the stirrings of this cultural shift, a young Australian known as Robert 'Nat' Young showed up, paddled out that day and knocked Californian surfing on its head. Dropping in on his first wave in the final heat, rather than stalling and cross-stepping forward toward the nose as was to be expected, Young set his inside rail, weighted his body forward, and willed his surfboard majestically to the top of the wave, before letting it fall from the crest and resetting in front of the curl as he raced forward with great speed. 'Magic Sam', Nat's self-shaped, slightly short, wide-tailed board was rapier-thin and his lean, rangy six-foot-three frame was crouched and taut rather than pliant and yielding. Probing the fluid geometry of the wave, his body and his board seemed full of potential energy. The moves were immediate and forceful rather than flowing and relaxed. The Aussie's eyes were fixed down the line in a determined stare. Totally engaged, he had one aim alone: to tap the source of the wave's power. Rather than blending in with the wave, morphing into an extension of the ocean's grace, Young's surfing that day was an act of pure, human will. The judges were gobsmacked. By the end of the heat, Nat Young had claimed the title of World Surfing Champion.

The victory was the start of a seismic shift in the way the surf establishment looked at wave-riding. To tap the power of the wave as Young had done required a new kind of board – a board that was shorter, thinner, and with blade-like rails and dynamically angled fins. Soon, the entire surfing world had woken up to the possibilities of the powerful, committed style of wave-riding that Young had showcased. Within two years the counter-cultural revolution had taken hold. There were riots on the streets of US cities while the Tet Offensive turned the tables in South East Asia. Surfers were butchering their ten-foot longboards, recreating them in a galaxy of experimental designs while their hair grew longer and they began to reek of incense and Mary Jane. As for Brian Wilson, he was dropping into his first period of psychosis and failing to finish the greatest album that never was.

Young had been developing the style that became known as 'total involvement' back in New South Wales, along with fellow Australian Bob McTavish and Californian transplant ►►

NAT YOUNG

◄◄   George Greenough (who had designed the fin for Young's championship-winning board). McTavish was instrumental in the design process that resulted in the square-tailed, vee-bottomed boards that spread the shortboard gospel further. In 1967, he travelled with Nat to Hawaii with a quiver of eight-footers, converting North Shore surfers to the new creed. By the turn of the decade, Young had disappeared from competitive surfing, returning to his home in the Angourie area of New South Wales to farm, to surf and to appear in some of the era-defining surf films, including Alby Falzon's *Morning of the Earth* and Paul Witzig's *Evolution*. During the seventies, Young became a vocal denouncer of the establishment. 'Just by going surfing,' he famously told a surf magazine, 'we're supporting the revolution.' In his native New South Wales he eventually became a champion of local environmental politics and stood (unsuccessfully) for a seat in the state parliament. During this time he began to assert his opinions in print, and over the next twenty years published a number of books, articles and columns that represented the surfing gospel according to Nat, including *Surf Rage*, a collection of pieces on surfing violence and localism. Always unpredictable, in the eighties he became one of the leading figures of the longboard renaissance, winning five world championships, three of them back to back.

Young has been a battler, a nurturer of true surfing talent and a subscriber to the cosmic school of surf philosophy. He has also been a canny businessman who knows how to work the media and continues to polarise opinion with his unique view of the history of surfing. Now in his seventh decade, Nat Young remains a keeper of the flame of surfing authenticity. By the same force of will with which he powered to victory in 1966, he has become one of the true giants of surfing.

Nat Young charges Haleiwa, Oahu, in 1967.
His combination of power and grace enabled him to
straddle successfully the longboard and shortboard eras.

THE BARREL

Fashions change, surfing fads come and go, but the tube ride remains surfing's peak experience.

Surfers began to ride deep in the breaking curl of hollow waves towards the end of the fifties. On the big, heavy boards of that era, however, this was usually either a chance occurrence or the precursor to a spectacular and humiliating wipeout. It wasn't until the early sixties, when Californian surfer Butch Van Artsdalen and a small cohort of his contemporaries began to pull in deep behind the falling curtain of a throwing lip on Hawaii's North Shore, that 'riding the barrel' became an essential aspiration for every surfer. Tapping neatly into the consciousness-expanding ethos of that era, the tube ride became imbued with near mystical significance. By the end of the decade the barrel had become an iconic element of surf culture and those who could ride the tube had become members of an elite sub-cult. ▶▶

When you ride the tube, you engage with an environment of 'prismatic auras and spinning spectrums' (as described by Hawaiian surfer, Jock Sutherland).

THE BARREL

◀◀ Surfers subscribing to this new creed began to demand shorter, sleeker, thinner and lighter boards designed specifically for riding deep in the heart of the wave's power-source. Gerry Lopez, Pipeline's meditative tube-riding guru, consistently reached an otherworldly state of stillness while surfing deep inside Pipe's spinning vortex. The power of the tube's allure lasted throughout the seventies, and it wasn't until surfers began to reach out and over the top of the breaking wave into aerial manoeuvres that any other genre of surfing produced such fervent acolytes.

Advances in surfboard technology since the early eighties may have made the tube more accessible to surfers than ever before, but the rarity of good tube-riding conditions means that getting barrelled remains a rite of passage that only the truly committed ever negotiate. No matter how skilled or experienced a surfer you are, once you've ridden a barrel the memory of those critical, adrenalin-saturated moments remains hardwired into your cortex for the rest of your life.

The successful tube ride is all about grace and stillness when all around you is exploding into chaos.

" " IN YOUR MIND'S EYE YOU
KNOW HOW THE SCENE MUST
LOOK FROM THE BEACH.

A SMALL FIGURE
SCRATCHING UP
THE SIDE OF A
TOWERING WAVE,
MAKING IT TO THE TOP AND
GOING OVER THE OTHER SIDE,
PADDLING FOR THE NEXT ONE.
AND
SUDDENLY,
AN INSULATED, QUIET
CONFIDENCE BEGINS TO
FORM INSIDE. YOU KNOW

YOU CAN DO IT.

IT IS AS IF YOU WERE, MOMENTARILY, STANDING OUTSIDE YOURSELF, WATCHING ALL THIS, CRITICALLY, UNEMOTIONALLY, AND FEELING, VICARIOUSLY, THE TERRIBLE, TENSED

STOKED FEELING ""

BUILDING UP...

Phil Edwards

CLASSIC SURF TRIP

CALIFORNIA

*California. The word is sprinkled in stardust.
For surfers, a trip from San Francisco to Malibu
is nothing less than a pilgrimage to the the seed
bed of modern surfing as we know it.*

The five-hundred-kilometre stretch of California coastline
from San Francisco down to Malibu racks up a litany of
iconic names that evoke a golden age of freedom and
discovery in the mind of the surfer: Big Sur, Rincon, and
Malibu itself, of course. It's also the hyper-commercialised
headquarters of a surf industry whose influence is truly
global. Its prime-time, pre-packaged, brand-conscious
lifestyle represents hedonism and consumption as the
quintessential state-of-being. ▸▸

Nowhere on the planet can you experience so many of the
iconic elements of modern surf cuture. Revolving around
the alternate epicentres of San Francisco's sophisticated
metropolis (*below*) and LA's palm-fringed sprawl, modern
California's history is intertwined with that of surfing.

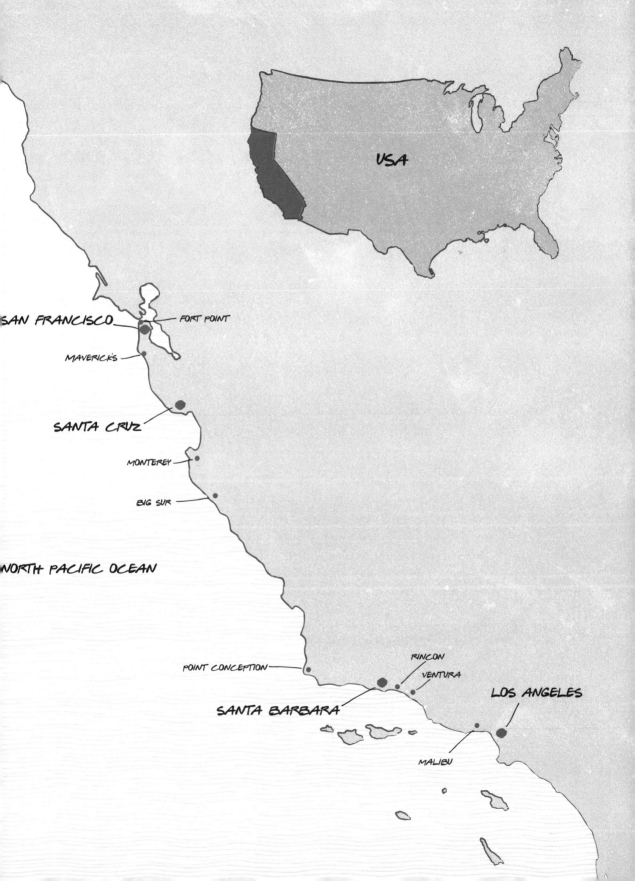

USA

SAN FRANCISCO — FORT POINT

MAVERICK'S

SANTA CRUZ

MONTEREY

BIG SUR

NORTH PACIFIC OCEAN

RINCON

POINT CONCEPTION — VENTURA

SANTA BARBARA

LOS ANGELES

MALIBU

Experience the shock and awe of Maverick's – if only with
a pair of binoculars and a heavy dose of humility.

CLASSIC SURF TRIP

CALIFORNIA

◀◀ SAN FRANCISCO TO SANTA CRUZ

San Francisco is the birthplace of the counter-culture and
the city where Jack Kerouac and the Beat generation came
of age. The city remains a haven of creativity and urban
nous, and continues to occupy a vastly different space to
Los Angeles in the mindset of the nation. The surf here, too,
is in complete contrast to that which surrounds the Angelino
sprawl. Heading south over the Golden Gate from Marin
County there's one of the most picturesque breaks in the
whole of Califorrnia at Fort Point (where surfing's own pilgrim
father Tom Blake crossed on his paddleboard in 1948). This
is a fast sucky left, loaded with the city's body boarders and
framed beautifully by the arch of the Golden Gate. It also
provides a sheltered haven when the brawny sandbanks of
Ocean Beach are blown out and overloaded. Ocean Beach
is exposed to all winds and swells and sorts out the men
from the boys. It's super-consistent and often impossibly
shifty and gnarly, but remains the draw for most city surfers.
Heading south, the beachbreaks of Pacifica curl into the
historic area of Pedro Point, where the locals were the first to
surf San Francisco's city spots at the end of the forties.

Round the headland and into San Mateo county, a
journey wouldn't be complete without at least eyeballing
Maverick's. Situated off the headland to the north of Half
Moon Bay, Maverick's, which can reach forty feet, has re-
invented California as a big-wave destination to rival Waimea
in Oahu and Peahi in Maui. If it's breaking, watch with awe.

More manageable are the spots around Santa Cruz,
a funky town heavy with post-hippy ambience crossed
with the affluent veneer of the silicon revolution. The surf
is made up of a slew of reefs, points, bluffs and beaches
that differ radically in character from one another. Steamer
Lane is the centre of the thrash-and-burn West Side
crew who take no prisoners and give no quarter in the
wave-catching stakes, and is home to some of the most
progressive, innovative surfing in the state. The succession
of reefs and points at Steamer's is counterposed with the
mellower, more relaxed rides and vibes of kelp-groomed
Pleasure Point and environs to the east and further south.
But make no mistake: when the Pacific throws long distance
groundswell at the area, the wave-focusing rocky reefs can
set a mighty challenge for any standard of surfer.

IDEAL SWELL: West-Southwest
IDEAL WINDS: East-Northeast
HIGHLIGHTS: Steamer Lane's majestic outside reefs
LOWLIGHTS: Aggro aerialists, grumpy industry types.

MONTEREY TO BIG SUR

The central coast is a beautiful, bucolic expanse of
amazing scenery and wide bays punctuated by rocky,
variegated headlands, coves and other geomorphic
features that promise much to the inquisitive surfer.
Monterey County is well served by a wide swell window
and shelter from wind. On the Monterey Peninsula a
selection of points, reefs and fickle beachbreaks keep the
locals satisfied year round. South of Monterey you hit the
fabled stretch of coast around the mouth of the Big Sur
River, a region that, despite even greater topographical
promise to the surfer, has confounded many a visiting
wave-rider. Local secrecy must be a factor here, and there
are surf spots, of course, but to get them working and
get them right, you have to put in the hours and be wise
to each spot's vagaries. Many of the spots to the south
of the Big Sur River are lethally exposed to the wind and
in tantalising view from Route 1, which in the summer

months is rammed with half of America on vacation.

Further south, down into San Luis Obispo Country, fickleness remains the name of the game, though if you're used the art of surf serendipity, the eighty-mile plus coastline full of beachbreak after beachbreak may just be your cup of tea. A good tip when visiting SLO is to recognise the importance of the dawn patrol, as the prevailing NW winds will blow out most spots by the middle of the day.

IDEAL SWELL: West-Southwest
IDEAL WIND: East-Northeast
HIGHLIGHTS: Big Sur Rivermouth's gorgeous ambience and prevailing offshores.

The waves off Hollister Ranch, to the south of Point Conception, are some of California's finest, and some of the most difficult to access.

POINT CONCEPTION TO VENTURA

The official turn of Northern California into Southern California is characterised by the switch to southern swell exposure and the privately owned Bixby/Hollister ranch. This area, at the foot of the sweeping Santa Ynez range can be accessed only by boat these days and is home to a dreamlike succession of classic spots. Cojo (where many of the surf sequences in *Big Wednesday* were filmed), is protected by Point Conception itself and is smooth and glassy more often than not. Cojo is joined in southerly succession by lefts and rights, San Augustine Reef, and the cluster of spots known as Drake's. Further south the celestial prank played upon the surf population becomes apparent. The Channel Islands, directly out in front of this stretch of coastline, block much of the southerly swell that otherwise would pummel these coastlines in the summer months. El Capitan Point looks like the ultimate right point setup, but because of these huge jags of rock out in the Santa Barbara channel, the waves here rarely reach head height as they need a west swell to negotiate the geography. Fierce locals have been known to protect the rare resource of proper waves when a more westerly swell does get through, so keep your head down if you do attempt to sample this area's delights. ▶▶

Rincon, the Queen of the Coast is the one
of the birthplaces of performance surfing.

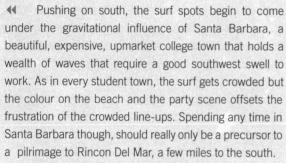

CLASSIC SURF TRIP

CALIFORNIA

◄◄ Pushing on south, the surf spots begin to come under the gravitational influence of Santa Barbara, a beautiful, expensive, upmarket college town that holds a wealth of waves that require a good southwest swell to work. As in every student town, the surf gets crowded but the colour on the beach and the party scene offsets the frustration of the crowded line-ups. Spending any time in Santa Barbara though, should really only be a precursor to a pilrimage to Rincon Del Mar, a few miles to the south.

Rincon is one of the most classic right-hand pointbreaks on the planet. Perfectly lined-up swells wrap into three distinct peaks with amazing frequency, which on the right swell, tide and wind combo can link up. The wave is composed of a number of distinct barrel sections – smooth, bowly and fast, rippable walls. This is where the style of Tom Curren was honed, where Joe Quigg's early pintailed boards were trialled, and where a young George Greenough and Bob McTavish experimented with fin designs, surf mats and kneeboard shapes before heading to the wilds of Eastern Australia to help spark the shortboard revolution. Migrants from Malibu's winter flat spells, including Miki Dora, Lance Carson, Dewey Weber, Denny Aaberg and their contemporaries, would flock here when the southerly swells of summer gave way to the colder pulses of energy from the west and northwest. The contemporary surfboard

industry's most prolific son, Al Merrick, also stars in Rincon's hall of fame, and his Channel Island Surfboards empire still resides in Santa Barbara. Rincon works in swell from ankle-high to triple overhead, but there is always a sizable, skilled crew to exploit its natural wonders. But don't let that put you off. Just to see a Rincon set sweep in from the outside indicator deep into the cove is one of the quintessential Californian surf experiences. Paddle out before dawn on the shoulders of giants, just to say you've been there.

Further south there are a number of alternative right-handers to Rincon of superb quality but less history and beauty than the Queen of the Coast herself. If hassling for a set wave with California's finest is not your bag, then spots such as Hobson's, Pitas Point, and Solimar all offer a realistic, perhaps more satisfying alternative taste of Ventura Country class. If the swell is huge, though, and you fancy tackling a spot that has its historical and contemporary chops in spades, you might want to check the spot just to the north of the city of Ventura itself, accessed through Emma Wood Country Park. Ventura Overhead breaks a couple of hundred metres offshore when big northwesterly groundswells focus on to a sharp, shallow reef. The take-off is critical, near vertical and peaky, but then fans out into a nicely shaped shoulder both ways and with more consistent walls wheeling to the right. It's like a Californian version of Hawaii's Sunset Beach in shape and, at times, intensity and consequence.

IDEAL SWELL: South-Southwest round to Northwest
IDEAL WIND: North-Northeast
HIGHLIGHTS: A set wave at Rincon
LOWLIGHTS: Flotillas of shredding students and pros at Rincon

MALIBU: THE JOURNEY AS DESTINATION

Pushing still further south along Highway 1, the road snakes eventually across LA county line, Sequit Point and on to Zuma beach, through the last vestiges of Southern California, devoid of LA's influence. Through Oxnard and the county line the population steadily increases, before you finally hit the more arid, Yucca-strewn hills that wind down past countless canyons and eventually down to Malibu. Once a dusty backwater on the Rindge Ranch and representing the exotic edges of Californian already out-there culture, today Malibu has come to epitomise the contemporary madness of upmarket surf culture. Malibu's faultlessly peeling faces form the wall upon which Californian surf style has been written. People will tell you that today the 'Bu is a nightmare. They will tell you that the crowds have destroyed the sacred ambience of the place that the native Chumash named 'surf sounds loudly'. But ignore them. Despite the pollution, the drop-ins, the funked-out crowd of wave-riders, catching a peeler from Malibu's First Point and trimming towards the pier is to step through a door into timeless tradition. Just one wave is worth the airfare.

IDEAL SWELL: *South-Southwest*
IDEAL WIND: *North-Northeast*
HIGHLIGHTS: *Perfect Malibu*
LOWLIGHTS: *Perfectly crowded Malibu*

Malibu (*below*) is the seed bed of modern surf culture. Hang heels and marvel at the timelessness of the place.

Miki Dora's influence still looms large at twenty-first-century Malibu (*right*).

In Ventura County (*above*) you'll find a hefty dose of territorialism, but quieter peaks reward the intrepid.

TECHNIQUE FIVE

THE TUBE RIDE

Riding the tube requires superlative skills, hard-won experience and a healthy dose of luck – as well as just the right kind of wave.

In the right conditions, a wave's lip will break evenly to form a throwing arc of water – a 'barrel' – through which it is possible to ride. The tube ride can be the most simple and the most difficult thing to achieve in all of surfing. In certain, extremely rare conditions, for example, a wave may be so perfect for tube-riding that all a surfer has to do is bottom turn, trim and pull into 'the green room'. In others, a heady combination of balls of steel and preternatural skill is required to achieve time in the tube. Because of this near-mystical allure, it has become the single most sought-after surf experience, with riders like Jock Sutherland and Gerry Lopez setting a zen-like template of tube-riding to which every generation of surfers has since aspired.

The basic tenet of tube-riding is all about drawing a clean line and either stalling, to slow down, or speeding up just enough to let the heart of the wave engulf you. Your goal should be to achieve a stillness in movement at the centre of a wave's churning heart. Finding this point of stillness in the middle of such powerful natural forces denotes true mastery of rail placement, speed and timing.

Ⓐ *Eyes*

Your eyes should be fixed on the escape route of the tube, otherwise known as the shoulder of the wave.

Ⓑ *Body*

The core of your body should be strong and rooted; your upper body should be relaxed.

A surfer pulls into the heart of a hollow wave.

fig. V: Tube Ride

C *Rails*

Rail placement is critical in maintaining the right speed and line through the tube.

D *Hand*

Dragging a hand in the face of the wave will slow you down, while moving into a crouching position will speed you up.

4.2

WHICH BOARD?

PART TWO

The thruster

The three-finned surfboard has enabled surfers to ride the tube deeper, to turn more radically and to take aerial manoeuvres out over the lip of the breaking wave.

A Thruster refers to a surfboard which features three fins of equal size, arranged in a triangular formation. The trailing fin is placed centrally, close to the tail of the board, while the two leading fins are situated close to the rails. This basic setup has been the preferred choice of competitive surfers for over twenty-five years, and accounts for the configuration of almost all current shortboards.

The surfing world had to wait until 1981 for the three-finned surfboard to become established, after Aussie pro Simon Anderson began to win contests riding his Thruster model. The highly competitive, six-foot-plus, 200-pound surfer from Sydney had grown increasingly frustrated by the drift he suffered when attempting fast, acutely angled turns on single- and twin-fin boards. Falling behind the smaller, lighter surfers who had learnt to ride the relatively new twin-fin designs, he began to experiment with an extra, centrally placed fin. Soon he had the new design wired. By the end of 1982 all surfers on the professional tour were riding boards with three fins. Despite the Thruster's incredible success, Anderson never claimed the patent or made much money from his revolutionary innovation.

6'3"   2.5"   18

AL MERRICK

Channel Island Surfboards' *Black Beauty*, shaped by Al Merrick, is based on the board Tom Curren used to beat Mark Occhilupo at the 1985 Bells Beach contest.

The Ride

7'

12"

21"

31"

4.13"

12'1"

19.25"

The standup paddleboard

The standup paddleboard, or 'SUP', is a modern re-invention of a method of wave-riding practised in the early 1900s by Hawaiian surfers, and is a relative newcomer to our shores.

The standup paddleboard is typically between 10 and 14 feet long, is at least 27 inches wide and at least 4 inches thick. Not to be confused with surf lifesaving-derived paddleboards that are usually paddled by hand in the kneeling or prone position, 'standups' are ridden in a parallel stance and are manoeuvred by using a long wooden, plastic or carbon-fibre paddle.

In breaking waves, standups are used in a similar style to longboards – nose rides, carves and cutbacks are all part of the vernacular. Usually ridden with a large, centrally placed single fin, SUPs grant a surfer access to large open-ocean swells and also to the smallest of breaking waves; they enable the surfer to explore difficult-to-access spots and, even when used on flat water, the paddling action can produce a useful and vigorous 'core' workout.

Maui-based innovator and supreme waterman Laird Hamilton is credited with introducing SUPs to contemporary line-ups in the early 2000s, and at time of writing they remain at the cutting edge of a new surfing boom. It remains to be seen, however, whether or not they will find a permanent place in the quiver of the average surfer.

The Surftech *Laird* SUP was one of the first and most widely available SUPs on the mass market.

BIG-WAVE SURFING

Big-wave surfing has come a long way since the pioneering days of Makaha. Tow-in surfing, where the surfer is towed into waves behind a jetski, has enabled an élite group of individuals to ride some of the planet's biggest and fastest waves.

When the surf gets big, time seems to slow down. It's a paradox because one of the unassailable truths of surfing is that bigger waves travel faster than smaller waves. Out in the water, paddling to find a peak when the surf is seriously heavy, the slowness of time is an illusion created by your heightened perceptions when all your senses are completely focused on self-preservation. It's like the moment immediately before a car crash, when it seems as if you're watching everything at one remove, and in slow motion. In a seething boil of constantly moving water, the illusion of slowness is compounded by relativity. There are no fixed positions when tide and swell and sea bottom interact to produce truly big waves.

When waves reach between 20 and 30 feet it becomes impossible to paddle into them. Despite the design of big-wave 'guns', created for paddling into the jacking monsters of Oahu's Waimea Bay, it took the introduction of the internal combustion engine to ride waves that were over 30 feet on the face – a region that had always been known as the 'unridden realm'. In the early nineties, Hawaii-based surfers Laird Hamilton and Darrick Doerner began whipping one another into waves off the North Shore of Oahu using an inflatable boat with an outboard motor and a waterski-style tow rope. Soon, they moved to Maui's wind-racked North Shore and replaced the outboard with a jetski. Boards evolved quickly as well and soon, short, heavy, stiff surfboards fitted with foot straps were the vehicles of choice.

The speed of the jetski allows tow-in surfers to ride deep in the most cavernous barrels ever seen as well as launch themselves into waves that can reach heights equivalent to a six-storey building. The tow-in surfer can also stay committed in the most extreme conditions,

with the knowledge that the jetski – the perfect rescue vehicle – is close to hand. Since Hamilton and Doerner's early successes, tow-in surfing has exploded worldwide. Each year, new big waves are 'discovered' and added to the ever-evolving roster of big-wave spots. ▶▶

Teahuphoo, a reef pass wave in Tahiti, burst into the spotlight in 1998, with waves of unparalleled power.

BIG-WAVE SURFING

◀◀   Big waves mean big business these days. Crews – usually sponsored by surf industry conglomerates, film production companies and magazines – follow huge swells around the globe hoping to capture the biggest, most spectacular ridden waves known to man. This quest for the extreme has taken the circus to Maverick's at Half Moon Bay in central California, Teahupoo in Tahiti, Todos Santos in Baja Mexico, and Cortes Bank, a reef a hundred miles off California that threw up a 65-foot monster ridden by Mike Parsons in 2001. Huge waves never ridden before have also been exposed in the Basque Country, as well as a succession of previously uncharted outer reefs off the Hawaiian Islands.

   With the take-off – the most critical part of the surf experience – taken out of the equation and the 'team' aspects of tow-in surfing at the forefront, tow-in surfing has become a sport in itself. However, it is a sport that has only been mastered by surfers of supreme skill, athleticism and fearlessness. For the riders who make up this exclusive club, tow-in surfing has rewarded them with access to places and experiences in the ocean of unrivalled grandeur.

Clockwise from top left:
Maverick's is the West Coast's best-known big-wave spot.

Dungeons, off Cape Town, which can hit 40 feet and more, is the most fearsome wave conquered to date in the southern hemisphere.

Ghost Trees is an elusive big-wave spot in Monterey Bay, California.

Waimea Bay, on Oahu's legendary North Shore, is the home of classical big-wave riding.

Todos Santos, in Baja California, has been known to reach 70 feet.

Aileens, on Ireland's west coast, was pioneered by Irish surfers Jon McCarthy and Dave Blount in the autumn of 2005.

Overleaf: A tow team contemplates the awe-inspiring sight of Jaws, off the northern shore of Maui.

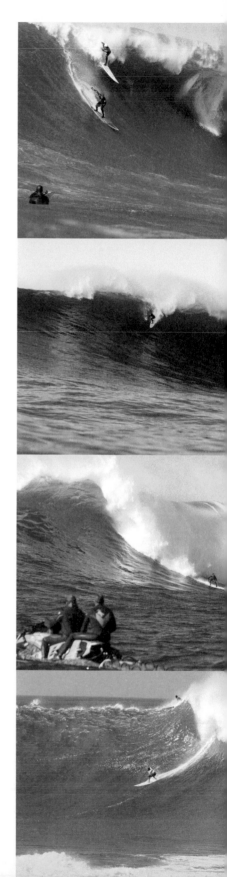

Morning of the Earth's back-to-nature ethos found its perfect embodiment in the flow of Queensland surfing legend, Michael Peterson (*left*).

CLASSIC SURF MOVIES
MORNING OF THE EARTH

Australian film-maker Alby Falzon's 1972 classic Morning of the Earth *provided the foundation myth of anti-competitive, non-commercial wave riding (otherwise known as 'soul surfing').*

Below: Falzon captured on film the beauty of Bali and the northern coast of New South Wales.

In 1970, Sydney-born Alby Falzon co-launched *Tracks* magazine. From the beginning, it was a powerful voice from the Australian surf counter-culture. Throwing non-surf related lifestyle features into an imaginatively designed editorial mix that all but completely ignored competitive surfing, *Tracks* concentrated on travel and creativity, and featured surfers that were the cream of the shortboard revolution's first generation. *Tracks* captured in words and images the hippy-surf lifestyle and was a newsprint version of the surf dream Falzon went on to evoke in *Morning of the Earth*.

Shot primarily on the northern New South Wales coast, but with a few detours, including Uluwatu in Bali as well as Queensland's Kirra and various Hawaiian spots, the film captured the 'country soul' era of Australian surfing. This was a time when surfing uncrowded waves, living simply off the land and the ocean and shaping surfboards by hand was the lifestyle of choice for the post-longboard generation. The film showed Nat Young, Michael Peterson, Terry Fitzgerald, Rusty Miller and Steven Clooney surfing spots such as Broken Head, Angourie and Lennox Head with free-flowing abandon never before documented on

THE VISION

film. The action was accompanied by a folk-rock soundtrack whose lyrics spelt out the desires of this psychedelically inspired, tuned-in cadre of surfers, alongside images of farming, wildlife and beautifully saturated sunsets. The film's popularity helped dispel the clubby machismo of the longboard era, albeit fleetingly.

The year after *Morning of the Earth*'s release, Falzon had continuing success when he collaborated with film-maker and designer George Greenough on *Crystal Voyager*, a documentary that focused on the Californian-born NSW resident's boundlessly eccentric surfing vision and introduced the world to the ridden tube.

Falzon's vision of the redemptive, spiritually charged surf experience is shot through with a romantic sense of purity. Little wonder that *Morning of the Earth* provokes a tangible ache for an era that most of us have never known.

Morning of the Earth showcased the 'sultan of speed', Terry Fitzgerald (*below*). Falzon shot some sequences with infra-red stock to create the film's distinctive look.

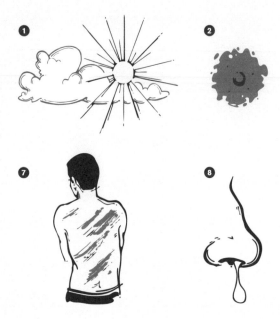

SURFING HAZARDS

A COMPENDIUM

Your soft tissues have calcified into a gnarly composite caused by repeated infections; you've been stung by jellyfish, menaced by sharks and chucked by your girlfriend. As a committed surfer, there's always a price to pay.

❶ Sunburn

Surfers spend more time at the beach than most. With prolonged exposure to the sun's UV rays comes an increased risk of skin cancer. So when you're on the beach, especially during the summer, don't stint on the sunscreen, cover up and wear a hat. Pay special attention to your nose, ears, forehead and the backs of your knees.

❷ Nipple sore

Your nipples are at constant risk of painful tenderisation caused by friction with your board, vest or wetsuit. Liberally apply Vaseline to keep things smooth.

❸ Sharks

Although shark attacks are a major source of paranoia amongst surfers, studies suggest that you are much more likely to be struck by lightning than attacked by a shark. In the unlikely event of being singled out, don't be afraid to punch back. Sharks often mistake a paddling surfer for a nice juicy sea creature and back off once they realise the scent of neoprene and polyurethane doesn't match up to their usual diet of seal, turtle and other marine life.

❹ Jellyfish

The tentacles of these simple marine invertebrates contain toxins that can kill their prey or act as a defence system. Box and Irukandji jellyfish can be found in a wide, seasonal arc in the warm waters surrounding Northern Australia and have accounted for at least seventy deaths in the last hundred years. Most jellyfish stings, however, while painful, are rarely fatal.

❺ Weaver fish

These ugly bottom-dwellers bury themselves in the sand in coastal shallows. They are about 15 cm long and contain venomous spines along their dorsal fins. If you step on one, expect a nasty sting and risk of infection. Death is extremely rare, but gangrene has been known to result if the infection is left untreated.

❻ Sea urchins

These brainless echinoderms are protected by sharp, sometimes venomous spines that can embed themselves in your flesh. If you're surfing an urchin-heavy reef, then do yourself a favour and wear booties.

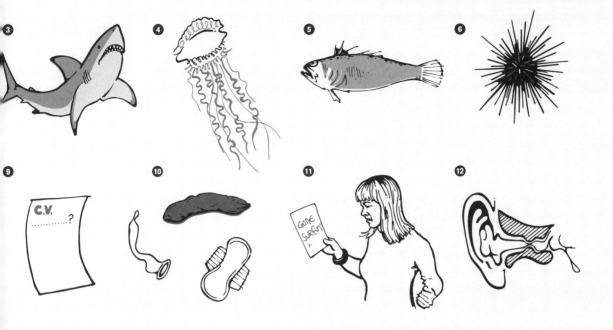

❼ Staph infection

Staph, or *Staphylococcus*, is the common name given to a clan of single-celled bacteria that can cause disease in humans and other animals. It most commonly attacks surfers through grazes caused by reef, and can lead to blood poisoning and death if the immune system doesn't mount a quick and effective response.

❽ Nose-tap syndrome

You've met up with that hot date after an evening's bump-and-grind sandbar session. As she gazes into your eyes, you take her hand in yours and reach out for that first kiss. All of a sudden a stream of snotty saline water gushes from your nostril as the sinus that's been plugging it releases. Embarrassing. And a bit gross.

❾ Surfer's CV (career void)

You've spent the last couple of decades roaming the globe looking for waves. Jobs have been merely the facilitators of plane tickets. Rejecting the ethos that life's all about balance, you find yourself, at the age of thirty-five, vacuuming a surf shop and selling beanies for a living. Meanwhile, your golf-obsessive, systems analyst kid brother buys his second holiday home in the Algarve. How the hell did that happen?

❿ Line-up lurkers

You are an intimate of society's flotsam and jetsam. Tampons, turds and condoms populate your dawn patrols. The beach looks like a fallen Eden. On the plus side, it ratchets up your commitment to environmental action.

⓫ Relationship meltdown

Your personal life is an ugly pile-up of stalled relationships. Too many times you've answered the siren song of the sea to the exclusion of all others. At dawn on a Sunday, and with a long period swell running and light breezes grooming them to perfection, your girl beckons, willing you to stay. You've chosen the simpler embrace of the ocean every time. You've tried, but going surfing with your girlfriend just isn't right…

⓬ Surfer's ear

Years of exposure to cold water and wind can cause small bony lumps to form inside your ear canal, leading to hearing loss and increased risk of ear infection. Partial deafness won't improve your chances of getting either a decent job or a girlfriend. So, if you have scored neither by the time you develop this condition, we suggest you become a wandering surf mystic and renounce the material world altogether. One barrel, after all, makes everything worthwhile!

Date of birth: 7 November 1948
Place of birth: Honolulu, Hawaii
Defining waves: Pipeline, G-Land

GERRY LOPEZ

In the late 1960s Gerry Lopez defined a new era of shortboard surfing at Hawaii's Pipeline. Effortlessly athletic and truly beautiful to watch, he is an iconic example of the 'soul surfer'.

Gerry Lopez is slight. His shoulders aren't squared off and augmented by the cartoonish *Latissimus dorsi* that characterise the physique of so many surfers. He is gentle in aspect and he smiles a lot. When threading the eye of a Pipeline barrel his arms are dropped and his feet are rooted to the deck of his surfboard, aligning his body, he is perfectly poised while the screaming cavern of water unfurls, unwraps and drains all around him. When you watch Gerry Lopez the board seems to disappear. He rides the wave, not the board. This is a man who dances with the forces of nature, rather than tries to wrestle them into submission with brute strength.

Born in Honolulu in 1948, Gerry Lopez began surfing at the age of nine, at Waikiki. He competed regularly as a teenager, winning the Hawaiian junior championships in 1966, just as Nat Young was about to arrive in the Islands as newly crowned world champion with a quiver of radically short, thin, light surfboards under his arm. Quickly adapting to the new equipment, Lopez began to concentrate on riding deeper and deeper in the tube. Where many other communards of the shortboard revolution were turning and cutting back as much as possible, Lopez remained focused on pulling in tight to the heart of the wave's power. With his yogic propensity for stillness-in-movement, the North Shore and surf culture itself was soon in Lopez's thrall. He soon became known as the one true holder of the title 'Mr Pipeline'.

Swami Vishnudevananda, founder of the Sivananda School of yoga, came to the University of Hawaii, where Lopez was studying, to lecture in 1969. 'I was a surfer-hippy.

Everyone was looking for a path to some sort of enlightenment. Yoga fitted in perfectly with my surfing lifestyle, and I've been a follower of the Swami's teachings ever since,' he told *Adrenalin* magazine in 1999. Through his interest in yoga, Lopez has become not only synonymous with tube riding and Pipeline, but also with that thread of surfing which connects Eastern philosophy and 'the church of the open sky'. ▶▶

No rider has ever been as intensely focused as Gerry Lopez, seen here in 1980 at Pipeline.

Lopez at the helm of Lightning Bolt, the hugely successful surfboard brand synonymous with seventies soul power.

GERRY LOPEZ

Lopez may be cosmically centred, but he is certainly no drop-out. Bringing his superior tube-riding knowledge to bear while channelling the tutelage of board-shaping master and psychedelic evangelist Dick Brewer, Lopez launched, in 1970, the Lightning Bolt surfboard brand. Teaming up with businessman Jack Shipley, the partnership marketed sleek, beautifully finished surfboards apparently imbued with the Lopez Zen-like approach. Lightning Bolts were soon ubiquitous wherever barrels could be found in the surfing world and the company became one of the most successful brands of the seventies. But it wasn't only in his business acumen that Lopez scotched the soul-surfing stereotype. He continued to surf competitively throughout the seventies, and was heavily involved in the surf media and the industry at every level.

Helping to pioneer many of Indonesia's barrel-rich surf spots throughout the seventies and early eighties, Lopez continued to ride tubes with sublime prowess when most surfers of his generation had either stopped surfing altogether or had deployed their energies elsewhere. 'My practising of yoga has enabled my surfing to stay at a level that would have been impossible without it,' he said. Lopez played himself in John Milius's 1978 surfing blockbuster *Big Wednesday*. Given that the film was about the coming of the shortboard age, it was an inspired piece of casting.

Moving to Maui in the 1990s, Lopez continued to shape and market surfboards under his own name (he had sold his stake in Lightning Bolt in 1980). He provided boards, significantly, to the first generation of tow-in surfers that rode Peahi on the island's North Shore. After a trip to Oregon in 1992, Lopez first sampled the delights of snowboarding. Instantly hooked, Lopez moved to the ski town of Bend, Oregon, where he started a successful snowboard company with his wife (an Oregon local).

Whether it's surfing liquid walls of water or frozen oceans in the mountains, Gerry Lopez continues to demonstrate the kinds of dedication to the ride that would be admirable in a surfer half his age. 'My style has evolved through a deeper and deeper understanding of the music I'm trying to dance to. Snowboarding made me appreciate the surf even more than I did already. Snow and waves are two of the most unbelievable wonders of nature with deep and hidden meanings just waiting to be discovered by true believers. I believe.'

'Mr Pipeline' displays the kind of poise and nonchalance that gained him his crown.

A secret reefbreak in the southwest of England

REEFBREAK

A reefbreak is a surf spot whose waves are produced by an abrupt change in the level of the sea floor, usually formed by a permanent formation of rock, coral or lava.

Reefbreaks are able to produce waves of hugely varying character, from soft, gently rolling peaks, perfect for traditional longboarding, to the deadly, hollow barrels of Peahi in Maui. The three distinct reefs at Pipeline on the North Shore of Oahu produce the most legendary and well-documented reef surf in the world and remain the gold standard of the adrenalin-saturated school of surfing.

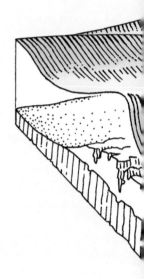

Generally, only the solid topography of reefs can deal with the huge forces that produce rideable waves of real consequence and in these sorts of conditions reef surf is the most hazardous form of wave-riding, too. Not only can sharp, solid rock and lava reefs break boards, bones and the egos of even the most famous surf star, the living, breathing coral reefs of the tropics can cause scrapes and cuts which can easily become infected. There is also the added danger when surfing reef-waves, of getting your leash caught on the reef during a hold-down, though this is rare. You tend to find rocky reefs on the coastlines of mountainous land masses, while coral reefs and 'reef passes' fringe the islands of Micronesia and other outposts of the Southern Pacific and the Indian Ocean. In areas of wide tidal range, such as Britain, reef spots may be completely unrideable at certain stages of the tide. Despite their challenging nature, however, reefbreak waves are sought after because of their power, shape and consistency.

Ⓐ *Lines of swell*

Lines of swell travelling from deep water are 'focused' by outer reefs, magnifying their size and power.

Ⓑ *The reef*

Waves break on a permanent reef of rock, coral or lava. The lines of swell are forced to slow suddenly on the reef. The lip of the wave is thrown forward to complete the internal circular movement of the water and form barrelling waves.

Ⓒ *Rips*

Strong currents often form as the water seeks to escape from shore via a 'channel' of deeper water in or around the reef.

THE AERIAL REVOLUTION

Dean Harrington, with a frontside air at Triggs, South Australia, demonstrates the aerialist's approach to the close-out section.

With increasingly light, dynamic surfboards and the cross-fertilisation between skate and surf culture, it was inevitable that mainstream surfing would sooner or later reach out and over the lip.

In the mid-seventies, rubber-jointed, afroed Hawaiian surfer Larry Bertlemann began to release his fins from the wave's face during his signature top turns. It was a natural progression from transferring the torque-heavy turns that had been honed while skateboarding banks and bowls. Bertlemann was at the vanguard of a scene that began to feed back skating manoeuvres into the mother culture, launching off the top of the wave and attempting to land back on the wave's face to complete the ride.

'Larryials' as Bertlemann's experimental airs became known, intiated a crossover movement that is now deeply embedded in mainstream surfing. By the eighties and with the advent of the dynamically turning and endlessly forgiving Thruster, the aerial movement formed a thrash-and-burn sub-cult within the culture, and was a renegade counterpoint to the tripped-out, tube-focused vibe of the seventies. Tattooed California chargers Christian Fletcher and Matt Archibold were the parent-scaring poster boys of the aerial movement and embodied the punkish ethos of that period.

Frowned upon at first by acolytes of the power-surfing era, embodied by mainstream superstars such as Tom Curren, Tom Carroll and Mark Occhilupo, it took a new school of superstars – Kelly Slater, Shane Dorian and Rob Machado – to integrate aerials into the power and flow of a functionally ridden, point-scoring wave. Taylor Steele's 1990 movie *Momentum* was the herald of this new dawn, and all throughout the nineties, even dedicated soul men and power surfers could be seen reaching out and busting airs over close-outs and sections.

Towards the end of the century, the heavily marketed crossover between surf culture, skateboarding and snowboarding had cemented the aerial's role as the spectacular touchstone of boardsports, and rising stars such as Australian surfers Oscar 'Ozzie' Wright and Taj Burrow were known particularly for the way they integrated dynamic airs into increasingly powerful waves. Early in 2008, South African surfer Jordy Smith, known for performing airs of previously unimaginable complexity in the most powerful waves in the world, is rumoured to have secured the biggest sponsorship deal ever for a WCT tour rookie, and surf and skate brand Volcom is advertising a $10,000 dollar prize for the surfer who completes the first genuine skateboarding-style 'kickflip'. It's only a matter of time until surfing's world champion is a true master of the air.

HOW TO BE A
GREENER SURFER

Surfers don't necessarily have a greater responsibility to the environment than anyone else. But, as someone who has chosen such an elemental pursuit, you'll experience the depletion of nature's gifts more keenly than most. Here are ten ways in which you can make a difference.

❶ Leave nothing but footprints

One of the great things about surfing is that in itself it doesn't deplete and it doesn't create. Make sure you hold true to this basic truth. Leave no traces of your presence at the beach. This includes wax residues, wax wrappers, discarded leashes and dead wetsuits, as well as any food and drink you bring. And clean up other people's mess too. If everyone did so, you'd paddle out at a pristine beach every time.

❷ Take nothing but memories

Be mindful of the local environment. In other words, don't park the wagon amongst fragile dunes and don't build camp fires where there are delicate local flora. If you're going to fish and gather crabs, mussels and other crustaceans, make sure you don't take the young. If it's not an adult, then throw it back.

❸ Consume less

One of the joys of the surf lifestyle is that you don't need to buy tonnes of stuff. All you need is a board, a leash and something to wear in the water. Sure, all products have their natural lifespan – in the water things deteriorate pretty quickly – and every surfer, of course, loves to try new boards. But with a little care, attention and timely repair, your wetsuit can last a decade and your quiver of boards even longer. Repair that seam and fix that ding!

❹ Consume ethically

Toxic chemicals and non-recyclable materials are part of the make-up of the modern surfboard, as well as wetsuits, leashes, surfwax and almost every other item of surfing paraphernalia. Slowly, though, the surf industry has been forced to wake up and smell the fumes. Seek out companies that actually give a damn. There are an increasing number of surfboard builders that use natural processes and sustainably grown timbers, hemps and other materials in their production. Clean waxes and sustainably produced wetsuits and other apparel are coming on to the market thick and fast. Look for the back story of the products you buy. Ask questions. Demand answers.

❺ Use technology wisely

Use the internet to make predictions accurately and to cut down on the fuel you burn for your fix of waves. Gone are the days of pure guesswork or instinctive local knowledge in surf prediction. It's pointless driving miles for a surf if you're a beginner and it's howling onshore and triple overhead. On the other hand, for the cynical salt perhaps a two-foot, offshore Sunday right in the middle of summer is best avoided.

❻ Use cleaner fuel

Surfers drive a lot. So it's a no-brainer for surfers to favour low-emitting, frugal engines over weighty gas-guzzlers. You'll need an affordable, spacious wagon, but make sure your vehicle is mechanically up to scratch and you'll improve cost-efficiency as well as the quality of the atmosphere.

❼ Stay aware, stay stoked

All over the planet, classic surf spots are being threatened by reckless, profit-driven coastal development. The story of the famous Peak at Bundoran in County Donegal, Ireland, is a classic example of how surfer power prevailed to save a surf spot. A powerful lobby of developers proposed a harbour project that threatened one of Europe's better reef breaks. The local surf community organised, campaigned and made representations to the relevant authorities. At time of writing, plans for the harbour have been shelved. Help keep up the pressure to secure rare spots. Once they've gone, like extinct species, they're gone for ever.

❽ Be an activist

Support the various surfers' environmental lobbying organisations and the environmental campaigns that they run. The Surfrider Foundation is a global network of wave-riding activists that have made real differences to local environments, and every surfing nation has its local chapter, as well as their own indigenous organisation (Surfers Against Sewage in the UK, for example). As someone who spends most of your hard-earned leisure time floating around the inshore waters of the world, it is your duty to be a worthy custodian of those waters.

❾ Go organic

The extensive use of pesticides and herbicides in crops cause toxic runoff that eventually finds its way back into the ocean. Avoiding food and other products that use toxic chemicals in their production is a small but concrete way to reduce their market viability, and ultimately, their impact on the oceans.

❿ Go local

OK, so we've said elsewhere that to surf is to travel. But do you really need to jet halfway around the world every couple of months to score surf when there are countless waves you've never ridden in your own back yard? Your local beaches, reefs and points may not match up to J-Bay and Pipeline, but do you match up to Kelly Slater? From time to time we all have the irresistible urge to find new waves, but why not seek out new spots near your home? You might be surprised at what you find.

SURF TRUNKS

Surfers at Waikiki in 1913 strut their
stuff in woollen swimsuits.

*From baggies to board shorts, surf trunks have
played a major role in selling the surf dream.*

It stands to reason. In warm-water regions, surfing shorts cut around the knee make sense. Try wearing bum-hugging speedos to go surfing. Not only will you look like a sex tourist who's found an interesting way to frolic in the surf with nubile young boys, but your inner thighs will be covered in waxy abrasions from straddling your board while waiting for a wave.

Until missionaries arrived in Polynesia in the 1800s, Hawaiians rode naked in the surf. The conquering colonials, however, imposed a ban on surfing altogether, lest the scandalous act exclude the locals from the Kingdom of Heaven for ever. With the re-emergence of surfing in the early 1900s, the beach boys at Waikiki would don woollen swimsuits while they taught *haoles* to surf. Soon, members of the Outrigger Canoe Club rejected the traditional swimsuit in favour of a bare chest and long, cut-off trousers fastened by a belt high in the waist. Surfwear from the early century until the Second World War was a question of improvisation – take a look at the photographic archive of pre-war surfing and you can see Victorian-style one-pieces as well as a wide variety of 'outrigger pants' and customised trousers.

In the immediate post-war years, Californian stores were flooded with cheap military surplus gear, and surfers began to customise light cotton military trousers that had been issued for tropical duty. Usually bleached white, they were generally cut off just above the knees and worn loose and low at the hip with the lace or button fly left open. 'We're surfers', went the subliminal message, 'we don't care for your buttoned-up conventions.'

During the fifties, cash-rich Californians began to flock to Hawaii and the first commercial surfwear operation got underway at M. Nii's tailor shop in Oahu. Nii's shorts became cult objects and Greg Noll's famous jailhouse trunks became their most famous design. Soon a variety of long-legged styles with sporty stripes, Polynesian prints and bright colourways were being marketed by different manufacturers. Most were cut with a baggy style that meant that water could escape easily and help a surfer to stay loose.

At the beginning of the sixties, surf trunks were generally made of heavy cotton, with some brands using a variety of double stitching and other gimmicky adornments to differentiate their product. By the mid-sixties, man-made nylons and polyesters, which were lighter and quicker drying than cotton, came on to the market and companies began to push their product in the new, ad-hungry surf magazines. Jams were characterised by colourful prints and innovative cuts, whilst Birdwell Beach Britches and Hang Ten shorts favoured simple designs with strong block colours and colour-coded piping.

During the fifties, a surf trip to the Hawaiian Islands wasn't complete without a visit to M. Nii's to buy the famous 'Makaha drowner' trunks.

When the seventies arrived, the legendarily durable and endlessly cool Kanvas by Katins became ubiquitous, their tighter, shorter designs gracing, it seemed, every surfer photographed on the North Shore of Oahu. In the late seventies, Australian firm Quiksilver began to market their first boardshorts: simple garments with a mixture of cotton and man-made materials that heralded a new dawn for the humble surf short. They sold in their millions. By the late eighties, almost every major surf brand was jockeying for a piece of the market. In the early nineties, with Lisa Andersen at the helm of the brand's image, Roxy were the first to market shorts especially for girls, similar in design but with a less baggy cut.

Today, shorts made from hi-tech, quick-drying materials can be found in every mall and every high street of the developed world. From hip-hop styled, skate-inspired gothic camouflage to simple retro and super-size post-ironic Polynesian print, never was a lifestyle sold to so many though so little.

Overleaf: vintage styles from c.1930 and 1973

Katins International

Our customers are our only salesmen.

KANVAS BY KATIN, INC.
16250 Pacific Coast Hwy.
Surfside, California 90743
Phone (213) 592-2052

Send 50c for decal and new 1975 brochure. Dealer inquiries invited.

1) Wayne Bartholomew, *Australia* 2) Robbie Husic, *Hawaii* 3) Bruce Raymond, *Australia* 4) Paulo Proenca, *Brazil* 5) Shawn Thomson, *South Africa* 6) Jeff Crawford, *Florida* 7) Dan Merkel, *California* 8) Guess Who? 9) Tony Staples, *California* 10) Greg Loehr, *Florida* 11) Rick Rasmussen, *New York* 12) David Scibal, *New Jersey* 13) Rory Russell, *Hawaii* 14) Reno Abellira, *Hawaii* 15) Peter Townend, *Australia* 16) Mark Warren, *Australia* 17) Ian Cairns, *Australia* 18) Mike Purpus, *California*

THE EVOLUTION OF THE FIN

Fins are stabilising devices that are attached to the underside of surfboards and facilitate turning. Over the years, fins have helped to change the way that surfers ride waves.

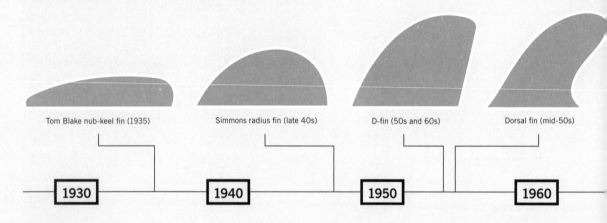

| Tom Blake nub-keel fin (1935) | Simmons radius fin (late 40s) | D-fin (50s and 60s) | Dorsal fin (mid-50s) |

| **1930** | **1940** | **1950** | **1960** |

Keel fin

Pioneer waterman Tom Blake is credited with creating the first workable fin in 1935 when he attached a speedboat keel to the tail of a surfboard. Prior to the advent of the fin, surfers would turn their boards by dipping a foot off the side of the surfboard, causing drag. Despite Blake's breakthrough, however, most surfers continued to 'slide ass', releasing the tail of the board in a less than graceful sideslip. It was another ten years before boards with fins became a feature of Californian line-ups.

Radius fins

Fin technology is all about how surfers can use the forces of physics to manipulate the way drag affects planing speed. Surfer and scientist Bob Simmons was one of the first to apply this hard-won knowledge. Crescent-shaped radius fins, usually made of a variety of woods and either glued or 'glassed' on to the rear underside of the surfboard, were used by Simmons and other shapers during the forties.

Dorsal-style fins

During the fifties, the raked, single fin, around 9-10 inches deep, had become standard. There were, of course, many variations on this theme, including the classic D-fin, with a variety of foils and profiles that would allow various degrees of hold and release in turn and trim. As the sixties took hold, fibreglass, removable versions of the shape inspired by the fin of a dolphin began to replace the wood and laminate glass-on versions of earlier years.

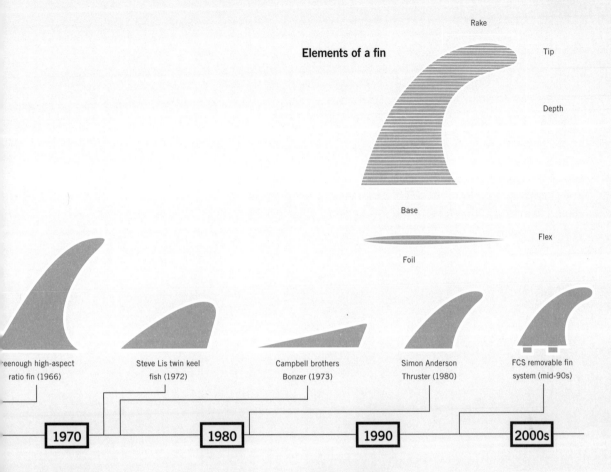

Elements of a fin

Rake

Tip

Depth

Base

Flex

Foil

reenough high-aspect
ratio fin (1966)

Steve Lis twin keel
fish (1972)

Campbell brothers
Bonzer (1973)

Simon Anderson
Thruster (1980)

FCS removable fin
system (mid-90s)

1970   1980   1990   2000s

High-aspect ratio fin

The sharply raked, narrow-based and small-tipped fin, developed by Californian design visionary George Greenough, is one of the most influential fin designs. Greenough designed the fin after closely studying the tail fin of the tuna fish. Greenough's aim was to allow turns to be made very quickly and at acute angles. Winning the 1966 World Championship on a relatively short surfboard and George Greenough-designed fin, Nat Young was quick to give credit to the fin's revolutionary design.

Seventies experimentation

During the seventies, a variety of fin shapes and configurations were tried. The twin-keeled fish designs pioneered by Steve Lis, the Campbell brothers' three-finned 'Bonzer' designs, and the quick-turning twin-fin designs (*not illustrated*), ridden by Australia's Mark Richards, were three of the most significant, providing faster and more controllable turning.

FCS Thruster fins

During the eighties, the three-finned 'Thruster' designs became ubiquitous on shortboards. In early versions, the Thruster's three-fins were glassed on, but over the last decade removable fin systems have become by far the most popular fin configuration. In the widely used three-fin system, the depth, breadth, foil and flexibility can be adjusted by the surfer as required.

The finless board

One of the most interesting movements of the last few years does away with the fin altogether. A small vanguard of highly skilled surfers, led by Australian surf polemicist Derek Hynd, has rediscovered the importance of the board's foil and rail profile in the science of turning. Seventy years of surf design may yet come full-circle with the possibility of mass-produced finless surfboards only moments away.

JEFF DIVINE

Jeff Divine has captured the resonant beauty of the relationship between surfer and wave more keenly than any other photographer.

New Year's Eve, 1968. A seventeen-year-old Jeff Divine clambers halfway down the crumbly cliff that leads to Blacks, California's premier beachbreak. Perched from the precipice he points his 400mm lens at a perfectly crystalline swell wrapping in through the submarine canyon that focuses the power of the ocean into walling, barrelling waves. Fighting the urge to put the camera back under the front seat of his car and paddle out himself, he begins shooting his friend Chris Prowse pull in to barrel after barrel. The young amateur's first published surf picture, taken from this session, appears in *Surfer* magazine.

If Ron Stoner captured the surfing moments of surfers' lives in the sixties, Divine stepped into the wayward genius's shoes for the subsequent decades. Turning his attention to the offbeat moments onshore as well as the action in the surf, he has developed one of the most finely honed photographic sensibilities in surfing. Over the last forty years he has accumulated one of the most significant picture archives in surfing history. As photo editor on *Surfer* magazine from 1981 to 1998 he presided over the key period of surfing's professional and commercial explosion. He continues to wield huge influence as photographic supremo on *The Surfer's Journal*, although

Wild-living Hawaiian surfer Montgomery 'Buttons' Kaluhiokalani throws a peace sign while paddling out at Velzyland, on the North Shore of Hawaii in 1974. Divine's photos of this period are era-defining documents.

these days as part of his job, he takes part in $40,000 commercial boat trips that can resemble a highly stressed, floating advertising agency with Bintang beers instead of Bollinger. However, the spirit of the stoked seventeen-year- old, perched on the cliff at Blacks, survives. 'Surfing is all about one man and the wave,' he says. 'He paddles out with all of his life baggage and catches one wave and it all washes off. All the commercial aspects of surfing are BS.'

BRIAN WILSON

Brian Wilson evoked wave-riding's beauty in his music more completely than any other artist.

Brian Wilson was the creative force behind The Beach Boys, the teenage family band that emerged out of Hawthorne, a couple of miles inland from the Los Angeles beach communities of Manhattan and Hermosa. After the sucess of *Surfin'* in 1961 – originally written as part of his high school music class – Brian Wilson was quick to pick up on the metaphoric potency of wave-riding. His family and management identified just as swiftly the commercial potential of publishing songs about surfing. Catching the wave of the surf obsession that gripped the West Coast and had begun to travel deep into the heart of America, Brian Wilson began to create music that expressed the California dream in all its youthful beauty – as well as its fragility.

The idea of surfing's elemental simplicity was central to the beating heart of his music. Replete with images of woodys, huarache sandals and bushy blond hairdos, the early hits of The Beach Boys were woven together with devastatingly beautiful harmonies and arrangements of a musical sophistication that easily eclipsed the efforts of other vocal surf bands such as Jan and Dean and The Surfaris. The images of untrammelled youth and fun, fun, fun that populated the songs tapped into the aesthetic of the age – and the records sold in their millions.

The music that most truly captured the beauty of the surfing lifestyle can be found in *Pet Sounds* and *Smile*, the albums Wilson was putting together after 1965 – even though they contain only a single surfing reference between them. 'Good Vibrations', the iconic single recorded during the *Pet Sounds* sessions, contains soaring, euphoria-evoking vocal harmonies that express what can only be described as sonic stoke. 'Surf's Up' is an equally ethereal and elusive composition from the *Smile* sessions whose lyrics are completely unrelated to any of the surfing platitudes that The Beach Boys purveyed in the early sixties. The words that provide the song with its title come as a culmination of wildly tangential verses and hypnotic chords that hint at surfing's talismanic qualities.

But, despite the way in which the band came to exemplify the surf lifestyle, the hard-core Californian surfers were never going to accept the music. The fact is

that the explicit surfing references in the music were little more than a function of the time and the place that Brian Wilson came of age. It's well documented that Brian never surfed, and that it was only his hard-rockin' brother, The Beach Boys' drummer Dennis Wilson, who ever paddled out. Likewise, most of the teenagers of Arkansas and Oklahoma who paid their dimes to play the music on the jukebox and surfer-stomped in the dusty drive-ins of the Midwest had probably never seen the ocean.

Though he never caught a wave, Brian Wilson understood the all-eclipsing beauty of the relationship between man and ocean and he articulated that complex, colourfully textured relationship in sound.

NOOSA

Queensland's Noosa Heads is home to a dream-like set-up of five tropical, right-hand pointbreaks.

It's a balmy Noosa morning. Here, on the other side of the world, a few hours north of Brisbane, is where your surfing dreams come together. You don't know just how good Noosa is. You have heard about the luscious set-up of this succession of right-hand pointbreaks groomed lovingly by the soft winds that blow across the headland and through the trees of the National Park. It's dawn and all but silent. You can see four figures bobbing, waiting out on the point, and an old salt towelling off, leaning against the hood of his battered Ute. He 'g'days' you and you're self-conscious as you've never surfed before but you've been devouring surf magazines for years. As you're paddling, a glint of colour flicks overhead – a flock of bright-green parakeets dive and whirl in the sky. Your heart is pounding now with the smell and the feeling and the elemental intensity of it. You're paddling, paddling, paddling, until out in front of you, on the horizon, someone hoots and spins and glides and lifts, and he's trimming right to left across the wave in front of you. The surfer passes, his back arched and his arms aloft. You duck and push the old singlefin like you've seen in the pictures and you burst out the back through a haze of rainbows. Another surfer passes on the second wave of the set, leaving you alone. Soon, another line appears on the horizon and the wave starts to break out to your front and to the right near the point. A hissing, curling, bending shoulder of green water gathers in your direction. You spin round and paddle as ▸▸

Boulder-lined Ti Tree Bay is one of five pointbreaks that wrap around Queensland's Noosa Heads.

AUSTRALIA

Noosa

SURF SPOT
NOOSA

With perfectly peeling waves, Noosa is as close to a surfing heaven-on-earth as anywhere on the planet.

◀◀ the energy fuses and rolls and begins to lift. You begin to drop and the wall begins to form to your right. You catch the eye of the surfer paddling out, the one who caught that first wave and, buoyed by his gaze, you do as you feel you should do and paddle and paddle, and soon you're riding your first wave at Noosa Heads, Queensland.

In September 1957, Hayden Kenny became the first to surf the waves that wrap around Noosa Heads. 'I turned up at the National Park and just saw these amazing waves, but I didn't know whether to paddle out or not. There was no one else around and I thought, if I wipeout and bang my head I'm stuffed. But eventually I went out, and made sure I did a big rugby tackle on my board, because to lose it was real terror.' While on the other edge of the Pacific, Dora and Edwards were hotdogging the reeling points of Malibu and Rincon, Bob McTavish, legendary shaper and harbinger of the shortboard revolution who was making boards for Hayden Kenny down the coast, chose Noosa as his home-break. 'The place was amazing and the waves were perfect. We'd cut the power cord when there was swell so we couldn't shape and go surfing at Noosa. It was superb, but it was all a bit lonely.'

'A bit lonely' doesn't really describe Noosa these days, but compared to the frenetic bump-and-grind of the rest of Eastern Australia's surfing coastline, there are great waves and relatively mellow sessions to be had if you have the time and the patience to wait. The waves at Noosa consist of a succession of five right-hand breaking point peelers; from the sometimes challenging Ti Tree way out on the Point to mind-blowingly mechanical Johnson's and First Point where the waves are perfect for honing flowing style. Unless you find

Belinda Peterson takes full advantage of Noosa's evenly tapered walls, by doing what the longboard was made for: moving to the front of the board and riding the nose.

THE **SEARCH**

anything but dredging death barrels boring, Noosa is one of the most magical right-breaking spots on the planet.

The months between December and March are the peak season, but big swells can wrap around the heads from lows out in the Pacific as late as July. Temperatures range from sweltering in the summer months to balmy in the southern winter.

In recent years, the Noosa area has become home to one of the most creative wave-riding communities in the world, and host to an eclectic mix of travelling surfers year-round who ride a variety of wave craft from traditional longboards and state-of-the-art thrusters to hulls, fishes and stand-up paddleboards. Tom Wegener, a Californian board-builder and green surfing visionary, has used the beautifully tapered Noosa walls to experiment with updated versions of ancient Hawaiian designs, and has explored the possibilities of unglassed wooden craft made from sustainable, fast-growing Palownia timber. With such an embarrassment of natural riches, the Noosa area has been through a strenuous spate of development over the last two decades. The spot does get crowded and it can be fickle as it faces north, away from the wide-open swell window that makes the rest of Australia's eastern coastline one of the planet's most consistent surfing shores. But despite these irritations, Noosa is an essential place to visit, especially if you like your boards long and your waves peeling right.

WHICH TYPE OF WAVE?

POINTBREAK

Pointbreak, Lynmouth, North Devon

A pointbreak is any surf spot where the waves form around a headland. Often with long, gracefully breaking surf, pointbreaks make up some of the world's most iconic surfing locations.

Pointbreaks can have rocky or sandy bottoms, and because of their closeness to the land can be greatly affected by shifting sands or gravel, and tidal factors. In any given area, pointbreaks form waves that all break in the same direction. The coastline of Chile, for example, is characterised by a succession of long, rocky, left-hand breaking pointbreaks, while central Morocco is, conversely, home to a great variety of right-handers. Pointbreaks are often characterised by a relatively simple paddle-out and a tight, well-defined take-off zone. They generally create long, predictable and consistently peeling waves and have consequently produced surfers renowned for their flowing, stylish surfing. The only downside to a pointbreak is that they can be infuriatingly difficult to surf for all but experts, drawing large crowds while offering only limited opportunity to catch waves from a tight peak.

The classic pointbreak – where the action is close to shore and where the surfer travels parallel to the line of the land – is perhaps the most aesthetically appealing and photogenic of all the types of surf spot. The long liquid walls they produce prove perfect for displaying self-conscious surf style. The longboard era's idea of the perfect wave was almost exclusively reserved for pointbreaks such as California's Rincon and Malibu – spots that have nurtured some of the world's greatest and most stylish surfers. But as well as creating surf history, many of contemporary surfing's high-performance arenas such as South Africa's J-Bay and the Superbank on Australia's Gold Coast are fast-breaking, powerful points. Mastering point surf remains the litmus test of style and ability.

A Lines of swell

Lines of swell 'refract' around the headland forming waves that peel along the stone, sand or rocky beach. Their lines radiate out into deeper water.

B Peaks

Waves begin to break when the lines of swell meet the shallower water close to the headland. They then taper evenly as they follow the line of the shore.

C Current

Current sweeping down the point escapes back out to sea, forming a channel around the breaking waves.

D Aggregate

Banks of stone, sand and other sediments are formed which fan out from the headland, focusing waves and refracting them toward the point.

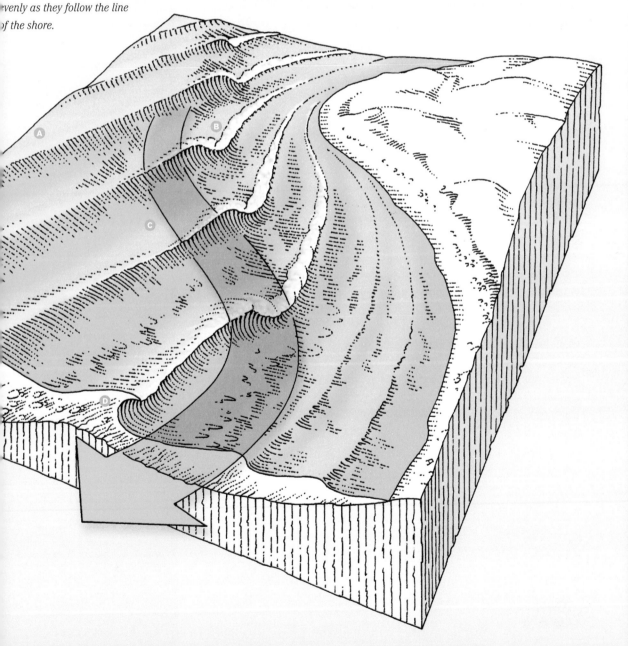

Date of birth: 1949 (died 1976)
Place of birth: Hawaii
Defining wave: Backdoor Pipeline

BUNKER SPRECKELS

The wild ride of Bunker Spreckels from the heights of a privileged Hawaiian upbringing to his drug-saturated death is a mythic tale of excess that ripples through surf culture.

Scenes From a Life

One: a bare-chested Nordic überman rests a rifle over his shoulder, tight, high-waisted trousers hugging his hips, his eyes hidden behind gold-rimmed aviators. His right hand clasps the rifled horn of the slain antelope. *Two*: a blond kid, kissed by sun and sea, hugs a stubby, disc-shaped surfboard and stares impassively into Art Brewer's lens. *Three*: a sideburned geezer in a low-necked, spacey surf T-shirt skateboards across a European city square, rocking a skin-tight, pearl-white set of flares. *Four*: a whacked-out, moustached smoker stares into the lens, this time against the backdrop of a wrecked hotel room, his expression is haunted, and now he wears leather trousers. A bullwhip and an accordion form surreal foreground props. *Five*: a quiver of strange surfboards is laid out like the spokes of a wheel in the centre of which a camp figure in a smoking jacket stands on a leopard-skin rug.

Bunker Spreckels III was born heir to a Maui sugar fortune. His great-grandfather, an early sugar-plantation oligarch, defended Hawaiian independence in the face of colonial and missionary pressure, and young Bunker was regarded as a reincarnation of a local prince by the local *kahuna*. He was taught arcane rituals and embraced by local families. Travelling back and forth from the islands to California with his family, he

Bunker, named the 'genetic space child' by Miki Dora, was one of the instigators of the shortboard revolution.

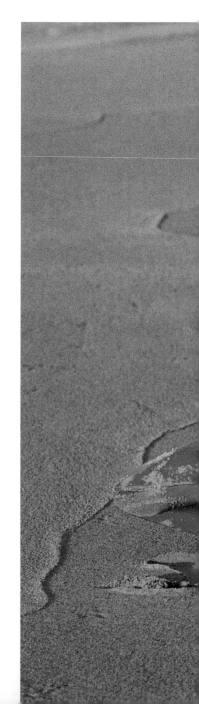

learnt to surf Waikiki and private breaks in California. In 1955, Spreckels' mother married Clark Gable – at a time when the actor was at the height of his wealth, fame and influence. With this star-spangled union, the Spreckels' family profile shot into the stratosphere.

Bunker was taught to hunt in Africa. He revelled in the Hollywood limelight in between excursions up and down the coast to Malibu and to Rincon, and, of course, trips back to the Islands for the big waves of winter. In the mid-sixties, dear little Bunker went off the rails, and his family blamed the free-wheeling crew at the 'Bu. At Malibu no one cared who Spreckels was, or who his family or his stepfather were. It was how you surfed and how you held yourself that truly mattered. In the mid- to late sixties, Spreckels took part in a series of pioneering trips to outlying surfing outposts, sprinkled with psychedelic stardust. ▶▶

BUNKER SPRECKELS

Spreckels, who was one of the first to ride Backdoor Pipeline, is seen here in 1969 on his 'Alma' board.

◀◀ Each winter, Spreckels returned to the North Shore to build and to ride some of the shortest, strangest, most radical shortboard designs ever conceived, developing, along the way, the first prototypes of the hard, down-railed surfboard. Spreckels articulated his vision by pioneering the seldom-ridden right-handers that reel off the peak at Pipeline (known these days as Backdoor). Riding prone, kneeling, crouching and straight-legged, sometimes on the same wave – Spreckels threw out the style sheet and expressed each ride in a completely original way. The elements of this new surfing vernacular included outrageous fades, speed crouches, explosive releases of energy and flowing, rail-to-rail surfing punctuated by staccato tweaks and shuffles.

As the shortboard revolution took hold, Bunker finally inherited his share of the family's fortune, estimated to be in the region of $50 million. That was when things really started to get freaky. The world truly became Bunker's chalice. Retaining a coterie of writers, artists, photographers and film-makers to follow his every move, he became the lead character in a globally unfolding docudrama with no physical or aesthetic constraints. The texture of his life becomes a madcap series of adventures involving a constant stream of glamorous females, celebrities, fast cars, outrageous costumes, drugs, drugs, drugs and alcohol. The surfer had become a composite character known as 'the player', the guiding light of an addled creativity that he funded, directed and of which he was the leading protagonist.

In 1976, Bunker Spreckels was found dead in a Paris hotel room. The coroner ruled that Spreckels died from natural causes. He was twenty-seven years old.

By the mid seventies, Spreckels – an aficionado of sex, drugs, alcohol and lethal weapons – was the lead character in a psychodrama of his own creation.

HOW TO THROW
THE PERFECT BEACH PARTY

Palm fronds sway gently in the evening breeze,
the languid chords of a slide guitar fill the air,
a mouth-watering mahi-mahi fish grills on the fire ...
You're at the perfect beach party – Hawaiian-style.

The tradition of the native Hawaiian feast – the *luau* – was created in 1819 when King Kamehameha the Second, under pressure from British and Portuguese colonists, outlawed religious and cultural traditions that dictated that nobles and commoners must eat, drink and celebrate separately. Even surfing had been subject to the same segregation. King Kamehameha's democratising decree changed all this for ever. For the first time, members of noble and commoner Hawaiian lineages would surf, feast, dance and party together.

The Lei

You can't welcome your guests, of course, without the *lei* – the traditional garland, which has come to symbolise Hawaiian culture. For the perfect *lei* you will need dental floss, some large, bold blossoms (hibiscuses or orchids are ideal), and a large needle. Take a metre of floss and tie a large knot at one end. Thread a needle with the floss and pass it through each flower's sepal (the green leafy part that protects the petals of the flower). Continue until you reach the end of the thread. As your guests arrive tie a *lei* around each of their necks.

Impress your guests by emulating this traditional hula dancer's portrayal of the sun.

Sounds

It may be impossible, alas, to create the perfect waves and sultry breezes of the islands, but a good place to start putting together the perfect Hawaiian-style beach party is to give it the right ambience. Charge your iPod with a mixture of traditional Hawaiian sounds, sprinkle it with a bit of late-period Brian Wilson, throw in a little acoustic loveliness by Jack Johnson, Oahu's most famous son, and you can't go far wrong. Some simple ukulele strumming – you only need to know a few simple chords – will finish the job.

Here's three uke chords, now form a band.

Kalua Pig

Every *luau* features grilled fish, but the heart of the traditional luau is kalua pig.

Ingredients:
one whole pig (any size)
banana leaves
salt

1. Dig a pit (*imu*) in which the pig will fit snugly. Line the bottom of the pit with smooth stones.
2. Build and start a fire in the pit and then let it burn to ashes.
3. Prepare pig. Rub pig inside and out with salt. Place extra heated stones in the cavity of pig and tie legs together.
4. Rake hot ashes and cover stones with banana leaves.
5. Lower pig into pit, cover with additional banana leaves, hot ashes and earth.
6. Roast pig for 5 hours.

Cocktail Hour

Once the food is digested, it is time for cocktails: there's nothing better for a beach party than a classic Mai Tai. The originator of the Mai Tai was Victor Bergeron, founder of the celebrated Trader Vic's restaurant chain.

Ingredients:
two parts Jamaican rum (the golden variety)
one part triple sec
juice of one fresh lime
dash of orgeat
mint

1. Pour all ingredients into a shaker.
2. Shake and pour over a tall glass full of shaved ice.
3. Garnish with sprig of fresh mint.

The Hula

Once the Mai Tais have begun to flow, it's time to rock your *hula*. There are various different kinds of Hawaiian traditional dance, ranging from the gentle gyrations of the basic *hula*, to the dramatic storytelling of the *hula ala apapa* and on to the intense bump and grind of the *hula hue*, where dancers shake it as fast as the drummer can beat time. Never *hula hue* when you should be gyrating gently. You may cause an inter-clan conflict. Local knowledge is crucial.

Love

Ocean

CLASSIC SURF MOVIES

BIG WEDNESDAY

Although it was a box-office flop on its release in 1978, Big Wednesday *has since become one of the most influential surf movies of all time.*

Director and writer John Milius's tale, which stars Jan-Michael Vincent, William Katt and Gary Busey, is told through the story of a few surfing friends who ride mellow peelers and party together in an early sixties California idyll. As the decade progresses, the Vietnam draft takes a number of the crew, and alcoholism ravages some of the others. While the war rages, those left behind stay locked into their old ways, growing older and less synched with the flow of things. At the turn of the decade, shortboards arrive with a hippy culture that few of the core crew can stomach. Drifting apart and away from the surf, the core protagonists meet again on the morning of the day-of-days (Big Wednesday itself), when the swell to end all swells arrives at their home break. On this day they will confront themselves as surfers, as friends and as human beings. The waves are eternal, goes the message, but the lives of the people who ride then are tragically, if beautifully, fleeting.

The contradictory pull of the film's formulaic structure versus its soulful surf sentiments can be traced to the vastly different CVs of its creators. John Milius grew up surfing Malibu in the early to mid-sixties, in the shadow of greats like Lance Carson and Miki Dora. He emerged with a very jockish, longboard-era style view of the world. Quickly making it big in Hollywood, his credits included penning the script for enforcer drama *Magnum Force* (1973) and co-scripting *Apocalypse Now* (1979) with its celebrated surf scene at Charlie's Point. In the latter film, the fictitiously famous surfer Corporal 'Lance Johnson', is named after leading surfer Lance Carson and *Big Wednesday*'s main protagonist Matt Johnson, played by Jan-Michael Vincent. Co-writer Denny Aaberg was, on the other hand, a mellow member of a respected surfing clan and had penned stories about the antics of Malibu surfers in various surf magazines. He had also written a tune for George Greenough's 1972 ground-breaking *Innermost Limits of Pure Fun*.

Milius assembled a stellar crew to put the movie together. Water photography was shot by George Greenough, Bud Browne and Dan Merkel, all leading protagonists of the craft, and the gorgeously executed, perfectly paced action sequences were produced by Greg MacGillivray. But despite the credibility of its creative team, the final product, with its simplistic message of everlasting friendship wrought in the waves, ended up alienating the very people whose stories it attempted to tell.

Over the years, however, the movie has unexpectedly become one of the touchstones of surf culture. One explanation may be that the surfing generation that the film originally reached out to became older, fatter and more nostalgic. Meanwhile, a whole new generation arose in the crowded waves and ached for simpler, less-crowded times – and a take on surfing that the film expressed. In fact, *Big Wednesday* was always a well-told, beautifully shot distillation of the history of Californian surf culture. Surfers were just too cynical to see this at the time of its release.

A day will come that is like no other...
and nothing that happens after will ever be the same

BIG
WEDNESDAY

starring
an A-TEAM production "BIG WEDNESDAY"
JAN-MICHAEL VINCENT · WILLIAM KATT · GARY BUSEY co-starring PATTI D'ARBANVILLE · LEE PURCELL
screenplay by JOHN MILIUS and DENNIS AABERG produced by BUZZ FEITSHANS directed by JOHN MILIUS
executive producers TAMARA ASSEYEV and ALEX ROSE surfing sequences produced by GREG MACGILLIVRAY
music by BASIL POLEDOURIS · PANAVISION · METROCOLOR® ☐☐ DOLBY · STEREO

Read the Bantam Paperback   From Warner Bros. A Warner Communications Company

780041

"BIG WEDNESDAY"

NORTH COAST CORNWALL

Travelling northwards from the ancient cragginess of Cornwall's western extremity to the Devon border, this is a surf trip full of rugged beauty.

The North Atlantic throws ceaseless swell at the British Isles and Ireland. Parts of this jagged archipelago's coastline retain the atmosphere of the wild, Celtic frontier, and countless shapely and powerful waves go unridden there. Other regions, such as the central swath of the north coast of Cornwall, are host to a mature surf culture where you'll experience scores of quality surf spots as the Atlantic articulates with countless reefs, points and beaches. The secret to a successful surf trip in these latitudes is to pick the right season (autumn or spring), the right quiver of boards (longboards and fishes as well as chip-thin thrusters) and the right trinity of wetsuits (thick, thicker and very thick).

SENNEN TO NEWQUAY

At the very toe of Cornwall, England's most westerly promontory, Sennen Cove is one of the most picturesque beaches in the whole of the British Isles. It is home to a soul-deep community of committed wave riders. The area catches more swell than any other part of the Cornwall

The essence of Cornwall can be found at Sennen Cove.

coastline. Sennen and Gwenvor light up especially at low to mid tide, and the prevailing southwesterly swell and wind nearly always give you something worthwhile to ride. Gwenvor is the place to go to escape the crowds, as access is a little more strenuous than at Sennen. This is Cornwall stripped-down to essentials. Quality waves, slanted light and a sense of being out at the edges of England.

Pushing north across the often mist-shrouded moors toward the picturesque fishing town of St Ives, you'll notice how isolated the area remains despite the UK's intensely opportunistic tourist trade. Porthmeor beach faces due west and has been known to hold quality sandbars that perfectly shape a westerly swell. St Ives' harbour wall can produce world-class pitching lefts in a big southwesterly storm, and can be protected from the wind, too. To the north of St Ives, Carbis Bay offers a convenient piece of protection, and is often much less crowded than the St Ives area. Recently emerged as one of the busiest surf spots in West Cornwall, the huge arc of sandy beach at Gwithian Towans up to the lighthouse at Godrevy point has consistently well-formed banks that can produce fun waves with easy take-offs with workable bowly sections.

If bump and grind is more your thing than the relaxed, swooping drops of Godrevy, then head to Portreath Harbour wall, a few miles to the north. On a decent swell, right-hand barrels will spit in the lee of the breakwater, perfect for bodyboarders and knee riders. A few clicks further and you'll hit the area that was once known as the Badlands, a stretch of bays and beaches that hold some of the highest quality, most contested breaks in the whole of the country. Although its fearsome reputation for localism is a bit of an anachronism these days, some of the best surfers in the country who ride here are understandably protective. Keep a firm eye on etiquette, don't hog the waves and be friendly. You'll have no problem. Porthtowan can be a heavy, powerful wave with tricky rips and solid banks that have been known to shatter boards and even the egos of visiting pros. Chapel Porth is another beautiful, secluded bay at high tide which opens out on the drop to an excellent selection of high-quality peaks. Trevaunance Cove in St Agnes is a tight, rippy peak ruled by locals and is no place for beginners, despite it being one of the prettiest little spots on this stretch of coast. Once the fix of the Badlands is complete, it's up to Perran Sands, ▶▶

The sandbars of Porthtowan (*right*) create some of the most powerful waves in Cornwall.

Carbis Bay has the beautiful backdrop of St Ives (*above*). But don't be distracted. On a good day, the spot can produce world-class waves.

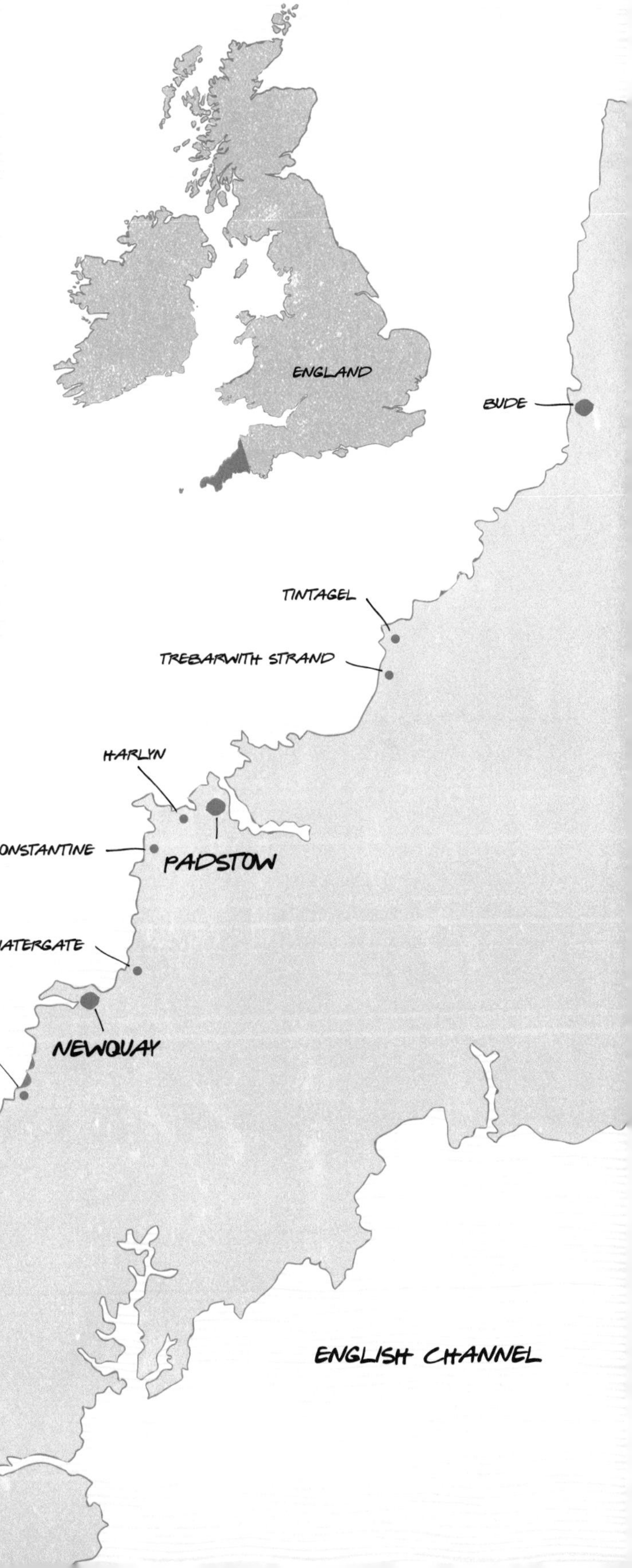

201

ENGLAND

BUDE

TINTAGEL

TREBARWITH STRAND

HARLYN

CONSTANTINE

PADSTOW

ATLANTIC OCEAN

WATERGATE

PERRANPORTH

NEWQUAY

ST AGNES

PORTHTOWAN

GODREVY

ST.IVES

ENGLISH CHANNEL

SENNEN

Low tide at Crantock can be as challenging as any on the north coast of Cornwall.

CLASSIC SURF TRIP

NORTH COAST CORNWALL

◀◀ which is a huge, arcing stretch of sand backed by dunes and a military area to the north. This northern area holds some of the most consistent banks, so a little bit of walking can often pay off in spades. Round the headland is the rippy, shifty series of peaks at Holywell Bay, which is at the southern extremity of Newquay.

If it's a good time you're after and you don't mind hustling for waves, then Surf City, UK, is a good place to base yourself. Fistral, the centrepiece of the area, is a genuinely world-class right and left on its day, and even in average conditions can throw down some tasty walls and fast, punchy peaks. More relaxed, but still powerful, particularly on low tide, is Crantock, which also benefits from a bit of protection from a variety of southwesterly to northerly winds. Newquay Bay is much more mellow than Fistral, and offers nice left handers and the odd faster right at higher tides. All in all, Newquay is the place to enjoy a varied surf platter whilst wading through the uproarious gaggles of hens and stags doing their best to drag Surf City into the gutter. They usually succeed.

Fistral (*above*), with its high-quality beachbreak, is Newquay's finest. Most of the major UK competitions are held here.

IDEAL SWELL: West-Southwest
IDEAL WIND: East-Southwest
HIGHLIGHTS: Gwenver's uncrowded beachbreak
LOWLIGHTS: Newquay in high summer

See also		
Pressure chart	◀◀	38
Beachbreak	◀◀	82
Reefbreak	◀◀	170
Pointbreak	◀◀	190
Localism	▶▶	228

WATERGATE TO BUDE

Escape the uproar by venturing just to the north of Newquay. Here you'll find Watergate Bay, a spectacular surf check that offers plenty of space. A little further north, the beaches around Constantine and Booby's Bay provide a wide selection of consistent waves with a little bit of protection thrown into the mix in the shape of Trevose Head. In a hefty swell and with a howling southwesterly, Harlyn Bay, around the headland, will be busy as it faces north and is offshore in the prevailing winds. Its quick, short drops are fun for ripping if your board of choice is

Trebarwith (*below*) redolent with Arthurian legend, is one of North Cornwall's most dramatic spots.

Tides and weather conditions (*above*) are all liable to change rapidly, making surfing in Cornwall a truly elemental experience.

Despite the popularity of surfing in Cornwall, secret spots stil exist.

six-foot long or below. There are a number of more protected spots that have not raised their heads above the parapet in this area so seek them out. Heading across the Camel River, Padstow is a haven of quality seafood, thanks to culinary icon Rick Stein. Hayle Bay to the north of Padstow and in the lee of Pentire point, is a swell magnet.

Head west of Hayle Bay and you hit the spooky, wondrously isolated stretch of North Cornwall, fragrant with legends of King Arthur. Trebarwith Strand, Tintagel, Bostacle and Bossiney Haven all hint at delectable surf possibilities, although finding the right lane to turn down for access can be a needle-in-a-haystack affair. The area has been linked with Arthurian legend for centuries and the dramatic cliffs and isolated pockets of population create an atmosphere worthy of the tales of the Celtic heroes. All around here are madly disorienting networks of lanes and footpaths, some of which lead to quiet, undisturbed surf spots. High Cliff, at over 700 feet high, looks down into the foreboding Strangles, a treacherous stretch of slab and boulder that cost many a sailor's life in the age of sail. Crackington Haven, a couple of miles further around the coast, has a fun, punchy wave, and retains a feel of mystery and discovery, despite its increasing popularity. All along this stretch, there are more intensely variegated nooks, bays, havens and beaches. Bude's beaches are consistent and busy summer spots, although it's easy to find an empty peak at spots to the north as Cornwall gives way to Devon's gentler landsape.

IDEAL SWELL: *West-Southwest*
IDEAL WIND: *East-Southwest*
HIGHLIGHTS: *Constantines consistency and N.Cornwall's secret reefs*
LOWLIGHTS: *Wind ruining the best swells*

"**I'M EXTREMELY INTERESTED IN FINDING A**

NEW WAY TO LIVE AND I THINK THAT SURFING COULD POSSIBLY BE THE ANSWER. **I FEEL THAT SURFERS REALLY HAVE A HEALTHY ATTITUDE.**

THEY'RE AGAINST THE CAPITALISTIC STYLE OF LIVING, THEY'RE MORE INVOLVED AND INTO THE OCEAN AND JUST THE WAVES, **THE WAVES MEAN EVERYTHING.**

I'M SEEKING OUT A WAY TO LIVE AND IF IT'S SURFING, THAT'S THE WAY I'LL DO IT, **I'LL BE A SURFER.** FOR THE REST OF MY LIFE. 🙶

Andy Warhol

TOM CURREN

Date of birth: 3 July 1964
Place of birth: Newport Beach, California
Defining waves: Rincon, Bell's Beach

With a blend of gracefully applied power and uncanny wave sense, Tom Curren redefined high-performance surfing during the 1980s. His natural talent set a new benchmark for other surfers.

There had been rumours that Tom Curren was on the island of Lhohifushi in the Maldives for the 2005 O'Neill Deep Blue Open. Word was that he had begun to compete again on the World Qualifying Series tour, at the age of forty-one. It was a beautiful story. Winner of three ASP World Championships, the ageing icon, born in 1964, dusts off his Merrick and qualifies the hard way – slogging through heat after heat against kids who weren't even born when he won his first title in 1985 (the others followed in 1986 and 1990). The stage would then be set for a series of heroic encounters with the current crop of superstars in the best waves in the world. An encounter with his fellow ageing gladiator and competitive nemesis Mark Occhilupo also beckoned. It would be the surfing equivalent of Ali coming out of retirement and squaring up to George Foreman.

Few of the junior pros on the qualifying tour would have realised that before his first ASP title in the mid-eighties, Americans weren't considered class competitors on the world surf stage. The early years of the ASP World Tour had been dominated by a marauding band of Aussie larrikins who had created the professional version of the sport in their own distinct image. Curren's arrival blasted a hole in that particular conceit, with his blend of graceful radicalism, poise and timing that together created a new approach to performance surfing. Tom's lineage (son of North Shore pioneer and shaper-hero Pat Curren) together with his youthful encounters with the pointbreaks around Santa Barbara, had gifted the kid a natural reservoir of surf genes and the kind of nurturing environment an ambitious surfer would die for. Regular exposure to evenly tapered, consistently breaking point surf has a tendency to encourage the sort of wave-sense and positioning that would perfectly prepare a talented surfer for competitions in high-performance rights such as South Africa's J-Bay and Victoria's Bells Beach – consistent winners of which tend eventually to be crowned world champs.

The surfing that Tom Curren demonstrated in the early eighties linked the flowing, tube-focused single-fin sensibility of the seventies with a future of vertical, lip-smacking top turns, radical re-entries and water-displacing, full-rail cutbacks – a blend of soul and power that paved the way for everything that came after. Curren's style was predicated on a bottom turn that harnessed all the speed of the drop, turning it into devastating forward projection. His solidly planted stance enabled him to release centripetal energy through his upper body and to hook turns deeper in the curl than ever before. Using an Al Merrick-shaped Thruster in competition, Curren drew the most creative lines on a wave anybody had ever seen – the peaks and troughs of which were linked by incredibly smooth transitions.

Curren's elusive nature has been analysed in countless column inches in the surf and mainstream media. Rolling Stone magazine gazed into the supposedly enigmatic heart of surfing's icon No. 1. The elements of the discourse generally include: a distant father; an evangelical mother; a rootless, bohemian childhood populated by a cast of surfing's freak talents; drug and alcohol abuse at ▶▶

TOM CURREN

A combination of radically applied power and apparently effortless style had surfers the world over in Curren's thrall.

◀◀ an early age; a teenage marriage and youthful fatherhood; a wandering adulthood finally earthed though discovery of Christian faith. A healthy dose of transcendental, otherworldy genius and shaman-like characteristics are often thrown into the mix. Others assert that the 'Tom Curren enigma' is a consequence, in part, of the inability to translate natural talent such as Curren's into conventional social interaction. But, obfuscating commentary aside, no surfer has engendered such widespread admiration and fascination in the average surfer. Even cynical, seasoned pros tended to fall silent when Curren paddled out.

Unfortunately, the great comeback of 2005 never materialised and he failed to qualify for the Dream Tour. Despite this, Curren had provided a tantalising taste to the youngsters of the style and wave sense that characterised one of the greatest surfers of the modern era.

Never afraid to push the boundaries of surfboard design, Tom Curren has always been the soul surfer's choice of world champ.

SURF WAX

Surf wax, used to create grip on the slippery decks of surfboards, occupies a humble but essential station in a surfer's life.

To outsiders, surfers appear to have a strangely intense relationship with their surfboards. Check out the way we lovingly caress the sculpted rails of a new surfboard and feel its weight in our hands. We may even smell the lamination and gaze long and lovingly into the glass as if consulting an oracle. An understanding of how the curves and concaves of a new surfboard interact with a moving wall of water is what motivates this visceral relationship. Once this partnership is forged it's time to give the board a wax job. And applying a layer of traction to the deck of a new board can take things to the next level.

The simple fact that the laminated surfaces of surfboards are slippery when wet has created a diverse industry in the production of little bars of wax – their arcane formulae are some of the most jealously guarded secrets in the surf industry. What was once a backyard operation, involving the kind of paraffin-based material that American and Australian mothers would seal jars of preserve with, has evolved into a highly partisan industry where smells, packaging and chemical credentials are all thrown into a rigorous, ever-evolving marketing mix. As wax is typically a petroleum-derived product there is a growing movement toward less toxic, more environmentally friendly products. Current formulas include a range of beeswaxes and vegetable-oil-based ingredients.

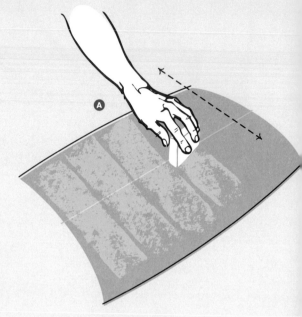

Ⓐ *The base layer*
Wax should be applied to a brand-new board in a lateral direction. It's best to use the edge of the bar.

The stakes were hiked significantly in the eighties when a series of stick-on 'traction pad' products flooded the market, threatening to make wax obsolete. The wax industry retaliated by increasing the diversity of its range and marketing different grades of stickiness. Harder, 'base-layer' compounds and different waxes for cold, cool and warmer waters became widely available. Today, the wax industry is healthier than ever, with around thirty commercial companies with global distribution in the market. The leading exponent of the unguent art remains Mr Zog's Sex Wax, a California-based brand founded by Frederick Herzog in 1972. Mrs Palmer (and her five lovely daughters) is an Australian counterpart to the Californian behemoth. Laden with risqué imagery designed to create loyalty in teenage males, surf wax has

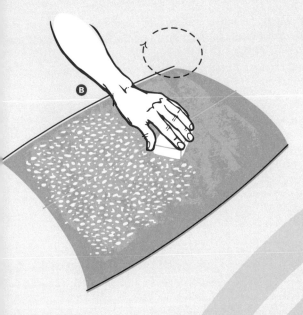

B *The top coat*
Once you've built up the base layer, a series of quicker circular movements will bring up the pleasing 'beading' effect of a classic wax job.

also been used as a weapon when applied by disgruntled locals to the windscreens of visitors' cars. It has also been the cause of numerous arguments and break-ups in surfers' relationships, thanks to the product's tendency to ruin car paintwork, upholstery and random items of clothing.

The other thing about surf wax, and something that the marketers have been incredibly clever to exploit, is that it smells damn good. Mr Zog's product comes in four different 'flavours' and manufacturers have been forced to tag on a warning that you should neither chew nor eat the stuff. But the secret to the ongoing popularity of wax over other forms of traction is that lovingly intimate moment you get when waxing a board. It's all about quality time spent with something a surfer loves.

Sex Wax is the most popular brand of surf traction on the planet. It comes in four different aromas: grape, coconut, pineapple and strawberry.

CLASSIC LONGBOARDING

Classic longboard style, with its emphasis on functional flow accentuated by varying degrees of stylistic flourish, will remain a feature in the line-ups of the world as long as there are waves to ride.

The cross-step is the stylish way to transfer weight fore and aft, by stepping one foot in front of another to form crossed legs in the shape of an x.

During the thirties and forties, surfboards were big, relatively cumbersome and heavy. A surfer had to have sufficient brawn just to lug the weighty log to the beach, and then heft it, leashless, through the shore break and out to the line-up. Ironically, in this sport for man-mountains, the elegant and subtle art of achieving perfect trim was the bedrock of surf style.

The drop-knee turn is a stylistic hangover from the days of heavy boards, which were much more difficult to turn than contemporary longboards.

Trim – staying locked for an extended period in the part of the breaking wave just ahead of the curl – was the Holy Grail for surfers immediately before and after the Second World War. Losing much of its kudos with the rise of the dynamic, trick-based 'hotdogging' style of the late fifties, the art of trim was dealt a further blow with the advent of the shortboard revolution at the end of the sixties. Hotdogging was developed primarily at the pointbreaks of California during the mid- to late fifties by surfers such as Dewey Weber, Corky Carroll and Mickey Muñoz (who were all short in stature and very light on their feet). The flashy vernacular they created included quick, repeated radical turns along with head-dips, spinners and high-camp poses such as the hunch-backed 'quasimodo' and the 'coffin ride'. Nose-riding, where a surfer rides the front third of the board and attempts to hang ten or five toes over the nose itself, bridged the classic/hotdog divide and was a surfing subcult in itself in the years immediately preceding the shortboard revolution.

Today, leading contemporary exponents of the classical art of longboarding – such as Joel Tudor, Jimmy Gamboa and Dane Peterson – can turn any wave they ride into pure gold by demonstrating the subtle, hard-won ability to tease a big, egg-railed, single-finned surfboard gracefully through a breaking wave. Fusing function with aesthetic form, good longboarding taps deeply into a tradition that, although eclipsed long ago on the pages of the magazines by the radical attack of the Thruster – remains as beautiful to witness and as difficult to achieve as it ever was.

For the nose ride, a few cross-steps forward will bring the longboarder to the front portion of the surfboard, where five or ten toes can be placed over the edge of the board.

Trim

Ⓐ Upper body
A relaxed upper body is the key to finding your point of balance. This stance will also help you to develop flowing, linked manoeuvres.

Ⓑ Legs
Legs should remain only slightly bent, and ideally no more than shoulder-width apart. A crouched position lowers the centre of gravity and will cause you to overshoot the curl, while too wide a stance will tend to result in an ugly stall.

Ⓒ Feet
To achieve trim when riding frontside (facing the wall of the breaking wave, as illustrated), you first need to lock the board into the wall of the wave by shifting your weight towards your toes.

Litmus showcased an eclectic quiver of boards and styles.
Here, Derek Hynd rides a 5'8" Skip Frye twin-keeled fish.

CLASSIC SURF MOVIES
LITMUS

Litmus *was a defining moment in surf film-making of the 1990s – it forged an open-minded vision of surfing that still burns brightly today.*

Litmus, created by Australian film-maker Andrew Kidman along with cinematographer John Frank and artist Mark Sutherland, sparked an aesthetic revolution in surf culture. Shot in Australia, South Africa, Ireland, California and Hawaii, and featuring surfboard design guru Derek Hynd and iconic surfer-shaper Wayne Lynch (as well as appearances by Tom Curren and Miki Dora), the film, released in 1996, was entirely devoid of the hard-driving, thrash-and-burn ethos of the era. *Litmus* helped shake the surfing world awake to the fact that stylish, flowing surfing didn't fade out with the advent of the tri-finned shortboard, and that the act of surfing itself is far richer than a set of saleable clichés. The film spread the gospel of what has been labelled a 'retro-progressive' school of surfing, and what was being practised by an avant-garde core soon spread all over the world. According to Kidman, 'originally cinematographer Jon Frank and I just wanted to make a film that showed how Wayne Lynch and Derek Hynd had remained surfing extremely well into their forties, and how they had achieved this through design exploration. Other things happened along the way, like the waves in Ireland. We just put the time into the subjects and the places until we felt like we'd represented them with honesty.'

The film evoked a type of surfing that had very little to do with the mainstream surf industry's marketing of the surfing way of life as elemental youth cult. If surfing was a cult, through the lens of *Litmus* it was re-imagined as one of eternal youth – accessible by an incredibly wide range of wave-riders and the hydrodynamic potential of a universe of surfboards. In addition to its creative new approach, for the first time Kidman showed the cold, powerful quality waves of Ireland to the surfing masses. He also represented the essential part that genealogy played in surfing's evolution by focusing on Terry Fitzgerald's son Joel surfing his family's ancestral coastline with a radical style that bridged the generations. With the inclusion of Frank's soft-focus, less than perfectly lit action, Mark Sutherland's anti-heroin animation *Dream*, a soundtrack by The Val Dusty Experiment (Kidman, Frank and Sutherland), and an unashamedly opinionated message, the film touched a nerve with a generation of surfers who had become alienated by the way their passion was being represented by the surf media.

Today's scene, in which surfers can ride an incredible variety of boards and, by-and-large, be respected for their choices, owes much to Kidman's exploration of the possiblilites. But the truly lasting influence of *Litmus* just might be the ambience, the elevated mood and the meditative approach that Kidman took to making a film about surfing. Ultimately, Kidman's mission was to show people the beauty that surfers are heir to. 'We weren't trying to change the world when we made *Litmus*,' Kidman asserts. 'We were just trying to show how rich what we're involved in is. We're given such a window into how the world works each time we paddle out into that fathomless force, so surely we should take that back into what we do and reflect it.'

THE VISION

Passionate and contemplative in equal measure, *Litmus* helped to ignite a new era in surf culture.

ULTIMATE SURF FOOD

In terms of energy expended, an hour's surfing is the equivalent of a six-mile run. If you want to keep the stoke going, what you eat before a session – as much as how fit you are – is vital.

Don't believe the hype of the surfer as hard-partying hedonist. Sure, surfers let loose every now and then and have been known to augment the boundless stoke of the surfing life with late nights saturated with nefarious substances. A sustained life of wave riding, however, entails looking after yourself – and being watchful of the fuel that feeds the surfing fire.

The night before the morning after
You check the chart around 5 p.m. A powerful storm is working its magic over the horizon and a new swell is about to hit. You plan a dawn patrol. Now is the time to start thinking about your energy levels. The last thing you want to be doing is waking at 5 a.m. and chowing down a hefty high-fat grease-fest, thinking that the quick hit of carbs, proteins and fats will keep you catching waves. Eat a big greasy breakfast, even two hours before a surf, and by the time you hit the water not only are you likely to feel nauseous but your body will still be expending valuable energy digesting all that food. The key is to eat a relatively low-fat, high-carb meal the night before. Complex carbohydrates such as pasta, rice and grains should be the basis of the evening meal. Avoid combining these carbs with too many saturated fats such as butter or cheese. Complex carbs release their energy gradually and sustainably, avoiding the crash and crave for sugars that a hit of fat will produce. Marathon runners swear by a big bowl of pasta the night before a race, and as you're about to take part in your own aquatic Olympiad, you should think about following their lead. Eat early in the evening, too, and aim to get to bed at a reasonable hour.

Spaghetti with chilli, garlic and oil
An Italian classic: quick, nutritious, delicious.

Ingredients (serves two)
400 g spaghetti,
1 chilli (finely chopped)
2 garlic cloves (finely chopped)
6 tbsp extra virgin olive oil
2 tbsp fresh parmesan cheese
handful of fresh parsley (finely chopped),

1. Bring a large pan of lightly salted water to the boil and add the spaghetti. Cook the pasta for one minute less than it says on the packet. Once it is cooked but still nice and firm, drain and set aside.
2. Put the oil, chilli and garlic in the pan from which you drained the pasta, and put on a very low heat. The garlic and chilli should fry gently, releasing their flavours into the oil. After two minutes, turn up the heat, return the pasta to the pan, and mix it together thoroughly with the garlic- and chilli-infused oil.
3. Serve in large bowls, covering the pasta with grated parmesan, chopped parsley, and a little salt and pepper to taste. Accompany with a fresh green salad with a simple dressing of lemon or lime, and a drop of olive oil.

The morning after the night before

We've said that you don't really want to eat a big breakfast before a big surf. In fact, it's probably best to stick to a minimal breakfast. Any intake of carbs or sugars immediately before a surf will be detrimental to your surfing. You should be fully fuelled from the night before, but if you must eat, have a banana or a bowl of porridge or muesli. A really good tip is to make a fresh smoothie which you can take down to the beach and drink right after your surf session. The natural sugars and other nutrients are perfect for quick recovery after a surf; you'll be back in the water for the second session of the day in double-quick time.

Bananaberry Smoothie

This recipe is a personal favourite that uses the secret ingredient of porridge oats to add a bit of substance for the ultimate post-surf smoothie. The idea comes from local surf guide and hardcore fisherman Derek Coili, who was inspired one cold March morning in the Scottish islands of the Outer Hebrides. You can make it the night before and refrigerate before putting it in a Thermos flask to keep it cool.

Ingredients
2 large bananas
a big handful each of strawberries,
blueberries and raspberries
200 ml apple juice
2 tbsp porridge oats
pinch of salt

❶ Throw all the ingredients into a smoothie maker.
❷ Blend until smooth.

The evening after the morning before

After your sixth hour in the water and countless waves later, it's only fair that you reward yourself with a couple of pints of Guinness and a fish and chip supper. There's no point in surfing well and with boundless energy if you can't talk story around some ale and decent grub with your fellow surfers, sharing the stoke. The blow-out will, of course, be dictated by local cuisine. In California, nothing can compete with a gargantuan burrito and a brace of ice-cold *cervecas*; in southwest France you'll be forgiven for heaving into *entrecôte* and a flagon of *vin rouge*. Either way, keep it local and keep it large. You deserve it.

THE WIPEOUT

The wipeout is one of the universals of surf culture. Everyone who has ever surfed – from Tom Curren to Tom, Dick and Harry – has fallen off their board more times than they have completed an elegant ride.

Wiping out, because of its ubiquity, has attracted the widest variety of slang terms in the whole of the surfing lexicon, from 'taking gas' to 'getting ragged'. In a major wipeout, after falling from the board, the surfer may be pitched with the lip, then tossed around in the wave's tempestous maw before being pushed below the water by the force of subsequent waves. This kind of wipeout is known as 'going over the falls'. It can result in trauma from impact, severe disorientation and, in extreme cases, drowning.

Another common scenario is for a surfer to get 'caught inside'. This happens when a paddling surfer is trapped on the beachward side of an approaching set of waves. Depending on the size and the power of the surf, getting caught inside can result in as severe a thrashing as going over the falls. Staying relaxed and not fighting the forces of nature is the key to getting through this situation. In the vast majority of cases, the surfer is pushed away from the impact zone (the point of seething whitewater where a set of sizable waves is breaking).

Although deaths by drowning are incredibly rare in surfing, when they do occur they're a reminder that paddling out into breaking waves is never without its dangers.

Unless you are prepared to take such risks, however, you'll never become a competent surfer. Once you've experienced a few of them, wipeouts become an essential part of the surf experience. It's possible, even, to learn to love the elemental intensity of going over the falls.

❶ Over the falls
If you fail to make a take-off and fall from your board, you may be pitched with the lip of the breaking wave.

❷ Back up the face
In powerful, hollow surf, you may be sucked back up the face of the breaking wave, to be pitched again. The surfer becomes like a particle of water in the wave itself.

❸ Hold-down
During a hold-down, the force of the water above can drill you towards the ocean floor. Your leash will keep you attached to your board, which may 'tombstone' at the surface.

❹ Recovery
Once you make your way to the surface, gather yourself, your board and your breath. But be prepared to take more waves on the head!

Overleaf: wipeout at Banzai Pipeline.

WHICH BOARD?

PART THREE

The boogie board

Often sneered at and derided by surfers who stand up on their boards, bodyboarding is nonetheless by far the most popular form of wave-riding on the planet.

Prone surfing on wooden bellyboards has a long history that reaches back to ancient Polynesia through to the beaches of Victorian England and beyond. The first modern bodyboard – essentially a short, wide lump of colourful foam – was created by Californian Tom Morey. Cheap, easy to produce and child-friendly, the 'Morey Boogie' board was launched in 1973. An instant hit, the product soon became available the world over and became most people's first experience of wave-riding. The boogie board has proved to be much more than a plaything. By the end of the seventies the first competitive bodyboard events were being held, and bodyboarders were venturing deep inside barrels and performing 'barrel rolls'. During the eighties and nineties, seriously committed bodyboarders began exploring the most extreme rides on the planet. Today, riders such as Mike Stewart, with a repertoire of huge aerials and intense barrels at Pipeline, have taken the sport to new heights.

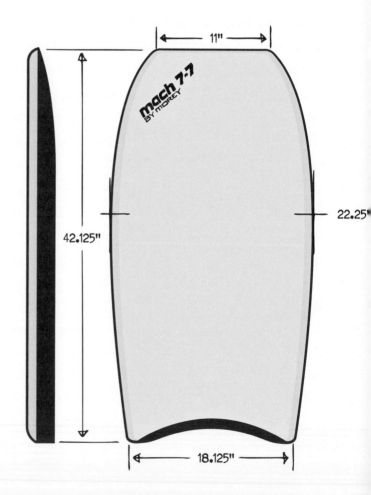

Tom Morey's boogie board has introduced more beginners to the joys of wave-riding than any other form of wavecraft.

The gun

A 'gun' is a board made for paddling into big waves; their basic shape has changed little for over forty years.

Long, spearlike and majestic, the classic big-wave surfboard is designed with two aims: gaining and maintaining forward paddling speed to catch fast-moving big waves; then achieving enough speed to 'outrun' the crashing lips of big waves. In addition to being longer than day-to-day boards, the gun has a more pronounced rocker (the curve of a surfboard from nose to tail), particularly in the forward area of the board. Most guns also have a 'drawn-in' pin tail, which enables the surfer to angle tight into the face of a big, fast wave. Early guns, shaped by George Downing and Pat Curren – pioneers of Makaha and Waimea Bay respectively – were single finned. This low-drag design was ubiquitous until Simon Anderson demonstrated the superiority of three-finned boards in 1981. The intense, life-threatening surf of the North Shore of Hawaii has dominated the design of classical big-wave surfboards and Waimea Bay remains the home of paddle-in big-wave surfing.

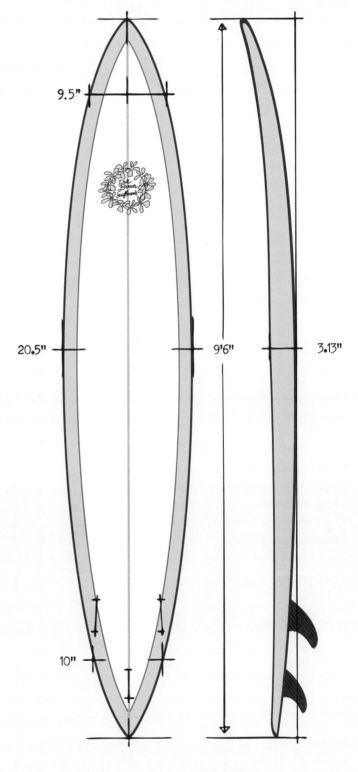

The three-finned gun, combined with lightweight epoxy construction, has taken the gun's performance to another level.

See also

Date of birth: 8 March 1969
Place of birth: New York
Defining waves: Ormond Beach

LISA ANDERSEN

Though pure commitment and talent, four-time world champion Lisa Andersen proved that surfing doesn't have to be driven by testosterone.

Lisa Andersen displaces water with a frontside snap at Pupukea, Oahu, in 1995 – the year she won the second of her four world titles.

The pressure had been building up for years. Her family had driven her crazy. Moving to Ormond Beach, Florida, from Long Island, New York, when Lisa was thirteen was supposed to have fixed everything. Sure, there was the surf. That made things a whole lot easier outside the house. But when the surf was flat or the sun went down or friends got sick or went away, there was always the home life to deal with. Her folks associated surfing with drugs and loose-living and hated the fact that she spent all her time at the beach with those stoner surfer types. Now she scribbled a note that said she was going to 'go and win the world surf championships', and hopped on a California-bound plane with a one-way ticket.

Finding herself in Huntington Beach, a new but chaotic chapter in her life began. Although Lisa was sleeping rough occasionally, she was perfectly toned from all that paddling, gorgeously blonde and full of the elemental verve that the beach life had granted her. The most important thing was that she was competing, scoring well in regional competitions each week. She cut clippings from the local press about her placings in the competitions and sent these anonymous dispatches back to her family in Florida. She didn't write anything, and she always neglected to include a return address. She just wanted them to know that she was safe and that she was making it on her own through surfing.

Lisa had a smooth but radical style that was amazing to watch. Even in the hothouse environment of Orange County, she began quickly to stand out. In 1986, she found herself travelling to the world amateur championships in Newquay, Cornwall. This was her first trip abroad, and Lisa glimpsed at this point that it might just be possible to make good on the wild promise she had made on that scribbled note back in Florida.

In 1992, having finished the tour ranked fourth in the world, she received her first sponsorship deal with Quiksilver's fledgling girls' brand, Roxy. It was immaculate timing. Women's surfing had always been marginalised, subject to toe-curling cliché, despite the achievements of top female surfers such as Joyce Hoffman, Lisa Benson, Margo Oberg, Rell Sunn, Pam Burridge and Frieda Zamba. In 1994, Lisa won the first of her four back-to-back world titles and began to pave the way for women's surfing to be taken seriously at the very highest level. Two years later, she even made it on to the cover of *Surfer* magazine. It was only the second time in its history that a woman had graced the cover. The coverline provocatively stated: 'Lisa Andersen surfs better than you.'

Roxy as a brand, with Andersen as its central character, was the spearhead of a hugely influential movement that transformed the perception of women's surfing. Although Lisa's story proved that surfing could nurture a woman's independence as well as make her look cool, the movement was from the start a hyper-commercial, girl-powered revolution wrought in pink. The mood-board of the women's surf brands remains subject to the hibiscus-laden, coconut-fragranced ideals of the beautiful, sun-kissed 'surfer girl'. There's no question, however, that the combination of Lisa Andersen's surfing mastery and the marketing of the 'Roxy girls' has helped bring an entirely new generation of women into the sport.

"WHEN I SURF

I DANCE FOR KRISHNA. "

Ted Spencer

LOCALISM

Surf territorialism, otherwise known as localism, is an ugly response to the increasing numbers of people who have been bitten by the surfing bug.

The guy was just floating there. He was a big, pale, hairy-armed German and he was precariously straddling a battered old longboard. This was 1986 at Bondi Beach: the swell was good and no one had seen a longboard here for years. The banks were perfect and all the core crew were out. There were rare barrels to be had and a heavy, testosterone-laden atmosphere was rippling through the crowd like a virus. The German guy didn't know what he was doing. Seeing the pod of young, DayGlo-clad locals start to paddle outside, he followed. He was a big dude and the huge board he was paddling gave him good hull speed. Soon he was way out in front of the pack when the set started to show. It was a sneaker, a rogue pulse of cyclone-generated energy that had formed into a menacing black line filling the horizon. He was never going to make it over the top so he should have just bailed to cut his losses. But, not knowing any better, as the first wave of the set started to feather, he continued to paddle right up into the lip of it. As the crew saw what was about to happen, there were curses as they gathered themselves to dive as deep as they could. The lip started to throw and the guy, all 200 pounds of him, ten feet of Volan-glassed log and ten inches of hatchet fin came backwards, flailing fast and deadly through the

crowd. Once the set had passed, the German guy came up to the surface, laughing, looking around at the other surfers paddling in the boiling water. But you knew the joke wasn't shared. Right on cue, as the bubbling and hissing of the impact zone had died down, a tiny young larrikin paddled up toward the German and began screaming at him. He had a great gash on his cheek where the fin had sliced him. A moment later he was joined by another guy, and then another, and soon the smile slipped off the German's face as the sharp, short blows started to rain down on his head as the pack rounded on him like piranhas. It was ugly. It was pathetic. And it's a scene that has been replicated in various versions throughout the line-ups of the world. But no fear. Because despite what anyone may think, no one can ever own a wave.

Localism is pretty simple. It's the way of being that regards waves that break in any given area to be the right of certain people to ride. It's a by-product of the transient, elusive nature of high-quality surf and the often small-minded, small-town mentality that can arise in outposts where the surf is good and the population is high. Although crowd pressure is sometimes to blame for localism, you'll also find localism alive and well in less dense areas. Some of the worst recorded examples have been documented in the remote desert areas of South Australia, where innocent surfers, as well as industry photographers and journalists, have suffered physical attacks.

Local aggro-merchants the world over justify their actions in a variety of ways. They may have grown up surfing waves in a particular area that they regard as exclusively their own. They may consider themselves the best surfers in the line-up and therefore may lay claim to

the best waves (although truly accomplished surfers are rarely known to visit harm on out-of-towners or less-skilled surfers.) The endless marketing of the surfing lifestyle is also, in part, to blame for localism. It might appear from the outside that to be a surfer all you need to do is buy the T-shirt, get a board, buy the book, and shazzam, you're a wave-rider. There is a school of thought, however, that sees surfing as a never-ending rite of initiation, presided over by a highly adept group of elders who claim the right not only to the best waves, but also the right to grant waves to the lesser ranks in the hierarchy.

Localism's excessive extremes can be avoided by abiding to the unwritten rules of the surfer's code. Don't surf waves too far beyond your ability; don't drop in; paddle in the right place and observe the natural rhythm of a line-up; talk to other surfers with a positive, inquisitive attitude, and if a vibe is so heavy that it ceases to be enjoyable, then paddle in and wait for it to change. Duke Kahanamoku, however, had the best advice of all: 'There are so many waves coming in all the time, you don't have to worry about that. Just take your time – wave come.'

WHICH TYPE OF WAVE?

RIVERMOUTH

Rivermouth break at La Ticla, Mexico

Surf spots are created in the mouths of rivers as they open into the sea by the flow of alluvial deposits from upriver. These deposits produce sandy or rocky banks along which waves break.

Similar in structure and appearance to pointbreaks, rivermouth waves often form as long, tapering walls that wrap around the head of an estuary, breaking toward the mouth of the river itself. Mundaka, in the Spanish Basque Country, is the most famous example of a high quality, powerfully breaking rivermouth wave. Mundaka is a fast and heavy wave that can represent a challenge to all comers, but not every rivermouth is a high-performance board-breaker. Because of their location at the exposed confluence of two bodies of water, rivermouths are especially affected by current and wind exposure and are often unsuitable for beginners. They can be fickle and inconsistent, their structure subject to rhythmic shifts and shut-downs caused by the ebb and flow of time and tide. Even the relatively consistent and usually solid sandbar at Mundaka deteriorated in 2005, caused, apparently, by the dredging of an adjacent reservoir. Pollution is also a frequent problem at rivermouths as waste matter and agricultural runoff is often flushed downriver to the estuary where it gathers with other deposits along the banks. Adding another black mark, they are also notoriously sharky, as many species of sea life congregate around the mouths of rivers to feed, forming perfect cruising grounds for the supreme predators of the sea. For the exploratory and adventurous surfer, however, it's the edgier elements of a rivermouth wave that make them special: a relatively rare, wild, tapering treat. With the notable exception of Mundaka, waves in the mouths of rivers can also be a great place to escape the crowds.

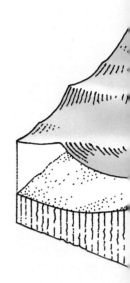

A **Deposits**

Alluvial deposits such as sand, soil, pebbles and other aggregate travel downriver, forming banks around the mouth of the river.

B **Waves**

Swells shoal on shallower water in the rivermouth. These produce waves that taper along the foiled banks.

C **Hazards**

Toxic runoff and other pollutants can collect along the banks and in the line-up, creating a challenging environment.

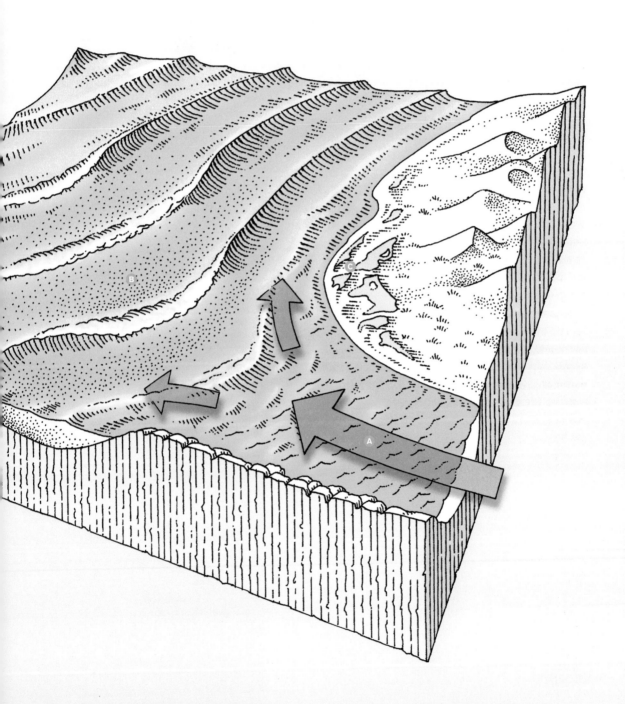

LAIRD HAMILTON

Date of birth: 2 March 1964
Place of birth: San Francisco
Defining waves: Peahi (Jaws),
Teahuphoo

Laird Hamilton's vision of the ridden realm has staked out the boundary of surfing's extremes.

Teahupoo (pronounced *cho-pu*) dwarfs the six-foot-three, 220-pound Laird Hamilton as he makes the wave on 17 August 2000. The news even made the front page of the *LA Times*.

The photographers and film-makers, assembled on a flotilla of small craft, are watching a scene drawn straight from the Old Testament. The wave appears to draw up the entire weight of the ocean. The wall of the wave and the reef part. You'd have to be a man with the stature of Moses to put yourself at the point of the wave's critical mass. Smoothly, almost casually, a figure appears in the line of sight. Laird Hamilton drops the tow rope. The rail and the fins of Laird's board dig into the wave's face. As he angles, his right leg begins to bend more and more, and his left straightens as the surface he is attempting to ride becomes steeper and the transfer of kinetic energy becomes increasingly extreme. From the bystanders' perspective it looks as if he is the point of stillness in a vortex, then, as if he is travelling backwards, the wave begins to arch and to detonate on the reef with a peeling, thunderous snap and crack and rumble. The wave is big in every dimension – it is thick, it is wide, it is deep as well as tall. Then, Laird is gone, sucked deep into an explosion of mist as the huge tube spits. The hooting flotilla is silenced, and a moment later the rider of this beast emerges – arms wide, shooting out of the mist at speed and flying out on to the shoulder to safety. Laird

Hamilton is riding if not the biggest, then most probably the heaviest, scariest and most powerful wave in history.

The wave broke at the reef pass at Teahuphoo, Tahiti, on August 17, 2000. Images of it were beamed instantly around the world's media. 'It was an extremely emotional situation. You've been gearing your life for this moment and suddenly you get the chance to experience it,' he told an interviewer in 2007. 'Riding that wave made it made it easier to do other things afterwards. It was like breaking the sound barrier or the four-minute mile,' he continued.

For Laird Hamilton, it was a definitive moment in a lifetime full of them. The first one came when he dragged surf legend Billy Hamilton up the beach to meet his mother when he was four. Laird's mum and Billy fell in love and married. Billy became little Laird's stepfather and tapped him firmly into a noble surfing lineage. A second came when he quit school on Kauai at the age of sixteen and headed back, via California, to the North Shore of Oahu, the arena his stepfather's generation had made its own. Yet another came when, in 1992, he decided to let Buzzy Kerbox tow him into a giant wave on the North Shore of Maui with a Zodiac inflatable boat – and created a new genre of big-wave riding.

His latest exploration has involved re-introducing the standup paddleboard to the world. Once again, Laird Hamilton has demonstrated that he is the creator of more visionary pushes in surfing's evolution than any other surfer of the modern era.

SURF PHOTOGRAPHY
A BRIEF INTRODUCTION

As a surf photographer, having the right kit is only part of the secret of success. An intimate understanding of the ocean – as well as of your subjects – is an essential element of the craft.

You're swimming through the shorebreak, pushing out through the spray. Your camera housing is lashed securely to your diver's belt but you check from time to time to make sure it's still there. Soon you reach the calmer water beyond the break. The surfers you are working with have been warming up while you swam out. Over the years you have developed an understanding of the way these particular surfers ride their waves. You drift to the inside, position yourself, and wait for your subject to drop in.

As well as the specialised kit (some of which is illustrated on the facing page), it takes a detailed and mature knowledge of the ocean environment to capture that all-important, elusive, frozen moment. If you're committed to taking pictures of surfing, most professionals advise that you start with the big lenses, shooting from the beach to develop an understanding of the infinitely variable, constantly changing conditions of any surf session. Shooting from the beach will also help hone your skills of composition in advance of working in the much more challenging and unforgiving environment of the ocean itself. And remember that truly experienced and successful shooters spend years building up relationships with the surfers they photograph.

Ⓐ Camera and tripod
Lenses between 400mm and 600mm are ideal for getting intimate with the action from the beach. A sturdy tripod is also essential for shore-based shooting with telephoto lenses.

Ⓑ Safety helmet
In the water, this vital piece of kit protects the head when getting up close and personal to the surfers and their boards.

Ⓒ Life preserver
The flotation jacket keeps the photographer safe and buoyant. While shooting, you want to be able to concentrate on the decisive moment rather than staying afloat.

Ⓓ Wetsuit
Many water shooters wear a wetsuit even if the water is warm. Some pros stay in the water for as long as three hours at a time, and even in the tropics, muscles start to lose their efficiency after a couple of hours.

Ⓔ Swim fins
Specialised, hard rubber fins provide extra power for speedy and efficient swimming.

Ⓕ Housing
The camera is held inside a waterproof housing, made from acrylic and fibreglass, with a rubber coating. A very high-grade glass globe on the front of the housing protects the lens.

Ⓖ Pelican Case
Fully waterproof and shockproof, the go-anywhere, indestructible Pelican Case is the industry standard. As well as holding the camera and lenses, it contains a waterproof flash (top left), tethers, multi-tool and caribiner (bottom left). The caribiner is used in conjunction with a diver's weight belt (top centre) – minus the weights – to tether the camera to the waist while the photographer swims out to where the action is.

Ⓗ Camera
Shutter speed, aperture and other controls can be operated from outside the housing. The shutter can also be triggered from the pistol grip attachment. A pole attachment can be fitted to the housing to increase the photographer's 'reach'.

Morris's muse: the wave at Solander
Point is a mutant slab of Aussie power.

BILL MORRIS

*A Sydney firefighter for the last three decades,
Bill Morris has spent his spare time capturing
the action of the heaviest waves known to man.*

Captain Cook didn't surf. Shame. Because at Solander Point, near the spot where the explorer landed in 1770 and claimed New South Wales for the English Crown, is a psycho wave that breaks over a reef at the foot of a cliff. The locals call the place 'Ours'. The only resistance Cook experienced were peaceful remonstrations by the Aboriginal population. Outsiders daring to lay claim here in the twenty-first century encounter far worse. The wave at Solander Point is presided over by the infamous collective of South Sydney surfers known as the Maroubra boys. On any given day when the spot is working in its vertebrae-compressing glory, the 'Bra boys will be policing the population with an iron fist. The porpoise-like figure of photographer Bill Morris will be at the heart of the action, capturing the charged drama as it happens. 'Ours' is Bill's favourite spot. 'It's an amazing wave to shoot. Always different. It's got it all: big tubes, dangerous rocks, heavy wipeouts. It's crazy! And it's right near my home.'

His first published surf photo, a double-page spread of Speed Reef at Indonesia's Grajagan ('G-Land'), appeared a quarter of a century ago in an obscure Australian surf magazine called *Surfing Snaps*. Since then, Bill has earned a rock-solid presence on the staff at *Surfing*, California's top-selling surf title, as well as contributing to surf magazines all over the world. Over the years he has become known as one of the best water shooters around, and his legendary swimming abilities give him an unparelleled intimacy with riders at the heart of the action. 'There is definitely something special about shooting in the surf, especially wide-angle work where you are actually swimming inside the wave with the surfer.' Getting cosy with waves like Pipeline and Solander Point takes a particular blend of superior wave knowledge, technical acumen and courage. Bill Morris has these attributes in spades.

Getting intimate in the most intense
situations is a Bill Morris speciality.
Here, Koby Abberton takes on the
tube at Solander Point.

THE VISION

The Abberton brothers are the
core of Sydney's Maroubra boys.

Speed and timing are the basis of a good cutback.

TECHNIQUE SIX

THE CUTBACK

The cutback is a turn performed on the wave's shoulder in order to return the surfer to the faster and more powerful part of the breaking wave.

Top turn initiated here

Ⓐ Upper body

As you turn, gradually rotate your upper body to the left, reaching forward with your right arm to grab the rail of your surfboard. This will help you make a smoother turn.

Ⓑ Back foot

Although you are pivoting on your back foot, the sensation should be that your front foot is guiding the nose around through 180 degrees.

fig. VI: Cutback

In the long, drawn-out 'roundhouse' version of the move, in which the surfer describes a figure of eight, as shown here, the cutback can be a beautiful-to-watch combination of form and function. The roundhouse cutback is a combination move initiated by a bottom turn, followed by a top turn that rotates the rider through 180 degrees. Although there are various manifestations of the cutback – including the longboarders' classic drop-knee version,

as well as the 360, in which the surfer rebounds off the whitewater in a full spin – the main aim of the cutback is to sustain a dynamic ride by returning to the point of power.

Cutbacks in one form or another have been around since the thirties, but the big, carving manoeuvre as we know it was pioneered by surfers such as Phil Edwards in the sixties. By the eighties a spray-slashing roundhouse was an essential move for any aspiring power surfer.

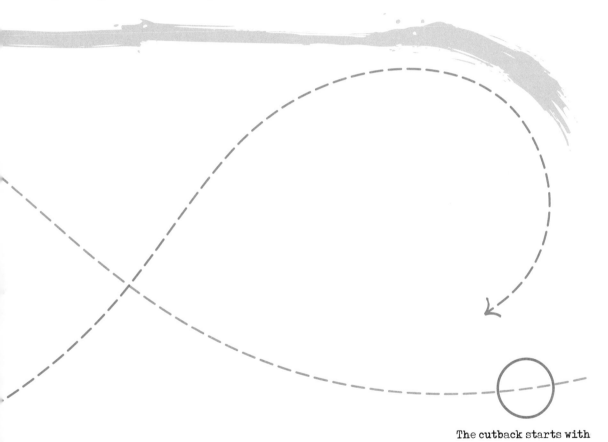

The cutback starts with a bottom turn here

Ⓒ *The nose*
If you've managed to keep enough speed, the nose will eventually turn back towards the whitewater on the inside. Keep your eyes fixed on the point you want to hit.

CLASSIC SURF TRIP
SOUTHWEST FRANCE

France's beautiful southwest coast is home to some of the best waves in Europe. A surf trip there is an object lesson in the global spread of surf culture – and an essential rite of passage for every serious European surfer.

Located at the northern extremity of the French Basque Country, Biarritz is the place where surf culture first touched down in Europe. It was 1956 and Hollywood scriptwriter and surfer Peter Viertel had been working on the set of the screen adaptation of Ernest Hemingway's *The Sun Also Rises.* After seeing the waves pushing into La Côte des Basques, he decided to send for his surfboards from California. The collision of California surf culture and the French Basque's laid-back sensibility has resulted in a rich and diverse indigenous surf scene. With the fast, hollow beachbreaks of Biarritz and Anglet, the shifting sandbars of Hossegor and the powerful reefs and points nestled close to the Spanish border at Guéthary, as a surfer it's easy to fall in love with the region. ▶▶

Few places in the world have such beautiful waves in such a civilised setting as Biarritz.

Anglet, a series of very consistent beachbreaks, north of Biarritz, can produce some fast hollow tubes.

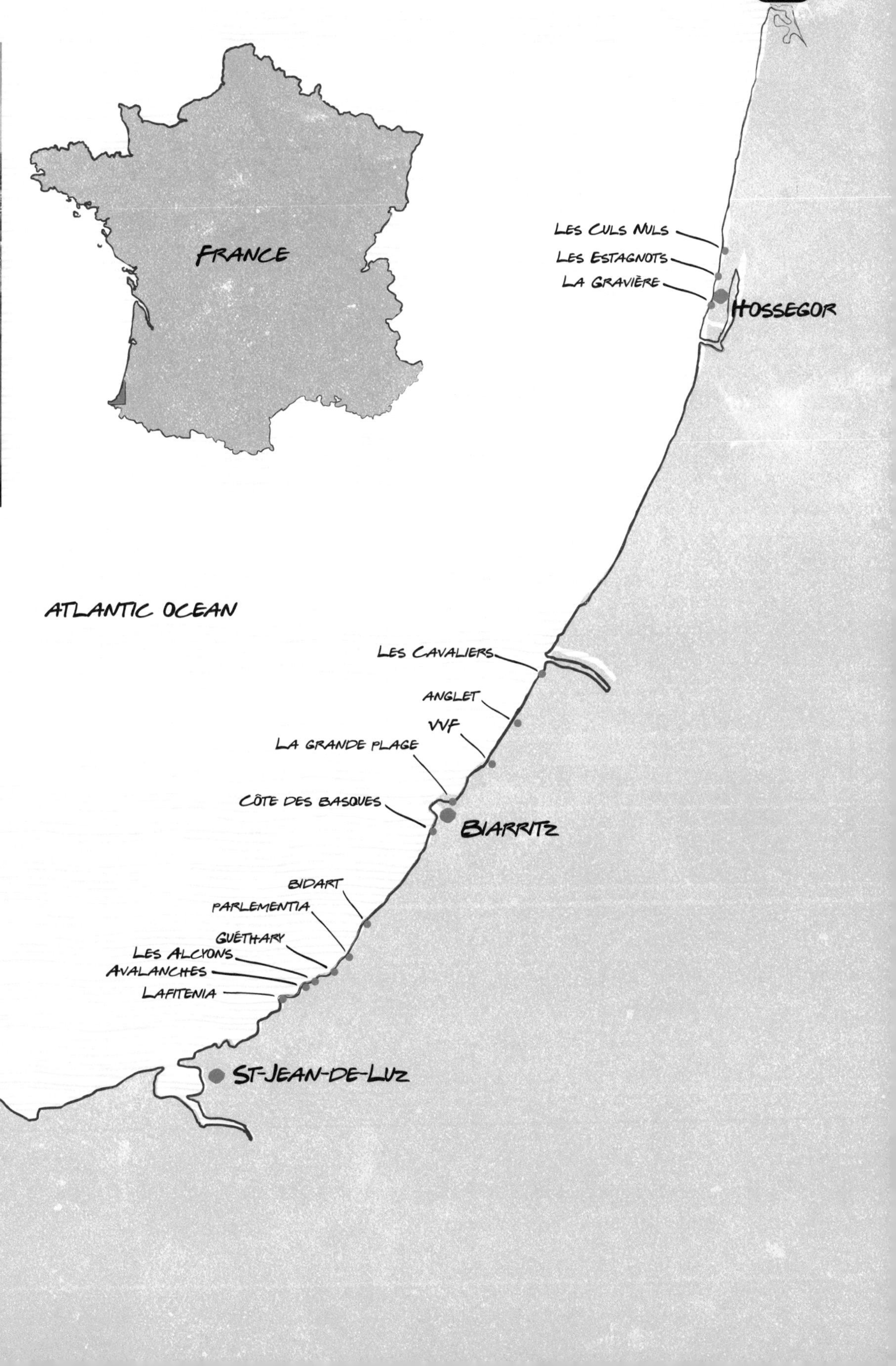

FRANCE

ATLANTIC OCEAN

LES CULS NULS
LES ESTAGNOTS
LA GRAVIÈRE

HOSSEGOR

LES CAVALIERS

ANGLET
VVF
LA GRANDE PLAGE

CÔTE DES BASQUES

BIARRITZ

BIDART
PARLEMENTIA
GUÉTHARY
LES ALCYONS
AVALANCHES
LAFITENIA

ST-JEAN-DE-LUZ

CLASSIC SURF TRIP

SOUTHWEST FRANCE

Biarritz is home to the mellow peelers of Côte des Basques (*above*) as well as hosting the Roxy Jam (*below*), Europe's premier women's surfing event.

See also

THE SEARCH

◄◄ BIARRITZ AND ANGLET

Surrounded by beaches and dotted with beautiful vistas, Biarritz is a chic, Napoleonic resort town where you can consume heartily the wine, food and atmosphere for which the region is famous. As far as surfing goes, in the heart of town there's *la grande plage* in front of the casino. This is a relatively crowded catch-all spot where groms, holiday makers and learners hustle for waves with some highly skilled locals. When there's a moderate swell running, the waves can be nice and hollow. If you're more into long, smoothly tapered walls, then pop around the headland toward Côte des Basques. This spot is home to Biarritz longboarding, and although the waves are generally slower and more mellow than the rest of the beaches in the area, when the swell is in the right direction and of fair size, the surf can have more than enough punch and form. Côte des Basques is the venue for the annual Biarritz Surf Festival as well as the Roxy Jam – two of the most prestigious surf events in Europe, which draws top surfers to Biarritz every year. Just a few minutes to the north of Biarritz itself is Anglet, a stretch of high-quality beachbreaks that includes the high-performance waves of Les Cavaliers. At the southern extremity is VVF (Very, Very Fast) – a quick, hollow bump-and-grind sandbar. Pretty much anywhere along this five-kilometre stretch of beach you'll come aross fun, fast peaks, as well as an enticing array of restaurants and bars on shore. On its day Cavaliers is a true world-class beachbreak, and often plays host to the French leg of the World Championship Tour.

IDEAL SWELL: *Northwest*
IDEAL WIND: *East*
HIGHLIGHTS: *Tubular perfection at Cavaliers*
LOWLIGHTS: *Summertime traffic and flat spells*

The breaks at Hossegor are renowned for their powerful, hollow waves. During the summer months, there's a great party atmosphere on the beaches.

HOSSEGOR

A thirty-minute drive north from Biarritz will take you to the beaches around the small town of Hossegor, where you will find some of the heaviest and most challenging beachbreaks in Europe. Every summer, hordes of European, Australian and South African surfers set up camp around the area, and enjoy a variety of conditions from mellow summer peelers to some of the most intense beachbreak action this side of Hawaii. The party scene is spectacular too, with impromptu beach gatherings fuelled by inexpensive wine and the summer ambience. La Gravière is the centrepiece of a string of infamously heavy Hossegor sandbars that can work in swells of up to fifteen feet. Les Culs Nuls and Les Estagnots are similar in power although they work better in slightly smaller swells. When the swell is running, Hossegor's highlights swarm with some of the best surfers in the world, particularly in the prime months of September and October, when the WCT tour stops between there and Mundaka on its European leg. Crowds are a real issue in summer and early autumn, but if you wander along the endless beach you're sure to find quiet, out-of-the-way peaks if you're not trying to hog the media spotlight in death barrels. Any crowd pressure is easily offset by the beauty of the beach and the relaxed atmosphere. If Europe has a place that rivals Southern California in its emphasis on the pleasure principle, then this is it.

IDEAL SWELL: *Northwest-west*
IDEAL WIND: *East*
HIGHLIGHTS: *Majestic sandbars and world-class action*
LOWLIGHTS: *If you don't like camping, there's nowhere to stay*

On its day the off-shore reef at Guéthary can produce waves that rival those of Hawaii's Sunset Beach.

GUÉTHARY

If you're not all about campfires, beach parties and spitting sandbars, then you might want to head south from Biarritz to discover the sophisticated delights of the Guéthary area. Parlementia, just to the south of Bidart, is a world-class reefbreak that sits offshore. With a bowling, deceptively makeable-looking take-off, opening up to a steep, walling section and on to more bowls and speedier runs inside, the right can be one of the longest, most enjoyable waves in the whole of France. Beware, though. This place is home to some of the most dedicated, mature and competent wave-riders, and local residents include some of the past masters of pro-surfing from around the world. It is a real wave for grown-ups, much heavier and more difficult to make than it looks from shore. Malibu legend and knight errant Miki Dora called Guéthary his home for years. Further south are the big-wave spots of Avalanches and Les Alcyons and around the headland is the crowded, right-hand pointbreak of Lafitenia. The weather down there is not as consistently sunny as up in Hossegor. There are not as many empty peaks to enjoy and the vibe is certainly not as young and hedonistic, but with a little time, patience and *politesse*, the traveller to the south of the French Basque Country will be rewarded with some of the best waves and most agreeable atmosphere anywhere on the planet.

IDEAL SWELL: *All swells as long as they're big*
IDEAL WIND: *Southeast*
HIGHLIGHTS: *Five-star waves, five-star food*
LOWLIGHTS: *Meagre scraps for beginners*

WHICH BOARD?

PART FOUR

The spoon
George Greenough's radical design paved the way for the shortboard revolution.

Although the history of knee-riding is as long as that of standup surfing, it has always been – and remains to this day – a somewhat offbeat subcult within the mainstream. In the modern era, at least, it can be traced to George Greenough's incessantly creative, visionary approach. Greenough's experimentations with short, light, dynamic surfboards culminated in his low-volume, highly flexible 'spoon' design. The original Greenough spoon, which he built in 1965 and named 'Velo', weighed just six pounds. Its tail and mid-section were composed of layers of fibreglass without a core. A small degree of buoyancy was provided by a thin core of polyurethane foam around the edge of the nose section and the rails. Although it was an extremely difficult projectile to ride and paddle, the spoon extended the possibilities of surfing, enabling Greenough to ride a wave in a series of high-frequency top-to-bottom turns. Greenough's surfing directly inspired innovators such as Bob McTavish to experiment with shorter boards that tapped into a wave's power as never before. On the spoon Greenough was able to ride waves radically and dynamically, long before the shortboard revolution would fully take hold and the rest of the surfing world caught up.

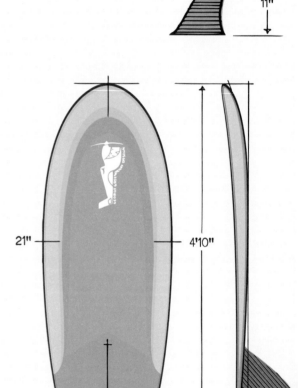

Cross-section at mid-point

See also

Very fast and responsive, but difficult to paddle and with minimal flotation, the knee-ridden spoon has always been for the specialist only.

The displacement hull
Greg Liddle's mid-length board is the culmination of fifty years of surfboard design.

Known variously as the 'hull' and the 'stubby', these user-friendly shapes in the seven-to-eight-foot range have their roots in the Californian branch of the shortboard revolution centred around Malibu from the late sixties to the mid-seventies. Greg Liddle was at the heart of this scene and, after witnessing Nat Young riding his short, stubby single-finned flyer known as 'Keyo' in 1967, he began an era of experimentation. Four decades later, the result is an incredibly fine-tuned and sophisticated surfboard whose rail profile, foil, planshape and ride characteristics draw on almost every element of surfboard design of the last fifty years. The stubby is perfect for down-the-line, smooth point surf as typified by Third Point at Malibu, enabling the rider to link a succession of dynamic turns in a radical shortboard style, but with all the flow of the longboard. The original transitional-era designs have had a direct influence on modern mid-range boards. These designs, known variously as 'eggs', 'hybrids' and 'mid-ranges' are aimed at enhancing the surf experience for everyone who chooses to ride them – not just surfers at the cutting-edge of performance.

See also

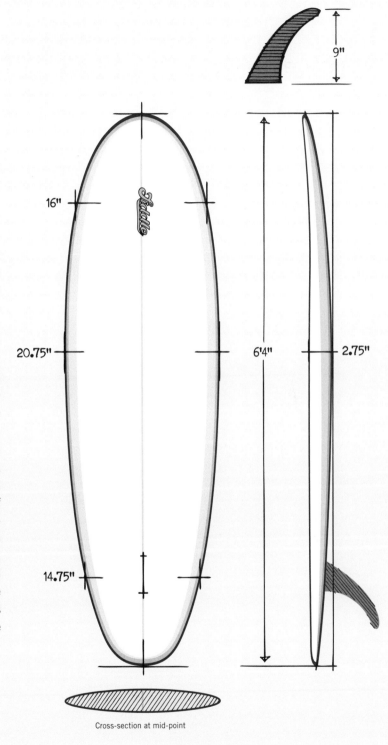

9"

16"

20.75"

6'4"

2.75"

14.75"

Cross-section at mid-point

Displacement hulls, such as the Greg Liddle model, have become increasingly popular with surfers who seek a dynamic, easy-flowing ride.

Date of birth: 19 August 1976
Place of birth: Florida
Defining waves: Cocoa Beach, Lance's Right

KELLY SLATER

Eight-times world champion Kelly Slater is the greatest competitive surfer who has ever lived, and probably the greatest surfer of all time.

Kelly Slater is a freak. The lines he draws on the ocean are like the classroom doodlings of a maths-bored, surf-stoked teenager. Inscribing inside-out, back-to front trajectories, his body contorts in a lightning-quick succession of *asanas* – yogic poses woven together at the speed of thought. When Slater's moves are captured in the pages of a magazine or on a pixelated screen, the images fail to express the power and the flow of his wave-riding. There are brilliant surfers whose signature is power and radicalism. There are enigmatic surfers whose wave-traces are characterised as subtle, sensitive, surprising or even obscure. There are a few prodigiously talented riders that achieve a combination of the two and even throw into the mix an uncanny wave knowledge and intense competitiveness. But no one combines all of these things together in one ride, on one wave, as consistently and as unmistakably as Kelly Slater.

Watch him at Jeffrey's Bay in South Africa. Speeding down the line, back knee bent, arms cast wide and loose, the forward foot teasing the wafer-thin thruster ahead of everyone's imaginations. In the blink of an eye, he goes vertical against a throwing lip, kicks his tail around and floats over the throw to revert back deep into the pocket. As J-Bay's wall opens up he digs a classic arc and launches up the face, whipping a cockatoo fan of spray higher and faster than your eye can follow ...

Kelly Slater stalls for the tube at Rifles, off Indonesia's Mentawai Islands.

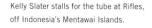

Although he might not have been motivated by the financial rewards that have inevitably come his way, Kelly Slater is by far the wealthiest professional wave-rider ever to have signed on the dotted line. He is the brand representative to end them all, winning events from the onshore dribble at Lacanau to the towering mountains of Waimea and the ferocious maw of Tahiti's Teahuphoo. His performances in Taylor Steele's era-defining 1990 video series *Momentum* launched the new school aerial movement. And almost twenty years later, gunning for his ninth world title, he still sets the standard by which all other surfers are measured.

Despite the fame and the glory Slater remains a steel-eyed enigma. His aura oscillates from the fickle mettle of surfer-boy cliché (remember his role in *Baywatch*?) to a stoic, almost regal presence. After all, he carries the weighty responsibility of being the undisputed king of the surfing world, as handed down by the likes of Duke, Blake, Edwards, Dora and Curren. Like other supreme sportsmen – Ayrton Senna, Pelé, Michael Jordan – Slater's talent has been imbued with a quasi-mystical allure. He once told an interviewer that often, when in competition, he would feel so deeply focused and 'in the zone' that he was able to will a wave to come to him. The way he has managed to win so many competitive surf heats by pulling out that last-minute nine-pointer against all odds would seem to support this. Could the Floridian really be some sort of surfing shaman? Or can he simply tap deeper into the ocean's natural rhythms than anyone else on the planet?

SURFING FITNESS

Surfing is an intensely physical activity. Learning a classic yoga sequence will help keep you fit, strong and flexible – perfectly prepared, in other words, for that precious water time.

1 *Stand with feet together, shoulder-width apart, each foot rooted on the floor.*

2 *Inhale as you sweep your arms out to the sides and up until they touch palm to palm overhead.*

3 *Exhale as you fold forward from the hips over your legs and place your hands on the floor, bending your knees if necessary.*

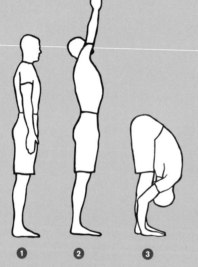

The best training for surfing, so goes the saying, is surfing itself. There is a nugget of truth in this popular mantra, because the sort of fitness you need for successful wave-riding is a very specific mix of strength, endurance, core stability and flexibility that is relatively difficult to target out of the water. Why bother with time in the gym, goes the thinking, when you can just go surfing instead and work all those elements directly? The sport, though, has grown exponentially in the last couple of decades. Men and women in their thirties, forties and beyond – many of whom hold down jobs and care for families – are forced to spend a lot of their time inland but remain passionately committed to the sport. This increasingly broad constituency needs a way to stay fit and loose so that they can make the most of their surfing.

In India, 'yoga' is the name for a philosophical and spiritual tradition developed over thousands of years, whose practices aim to bring about transformation on the deepest

4 *Inhale – come up and make your back as flat as you can, lifting on to your fingertips if necessary.*

5 *Exhale – flatten your palms and jump or step back to a plank-like position (as in a press-up).*

6 *Inhale – roll over the toes to 'upward dog' with arched back. Make sure your neck isn't hunched and keep your face forwards if it's more comfortable.*

7 *Exhale – roll back over the toes to 'downward dog'. Have your feet hip-width apart and spread your fingers wide to help you push through them. Take five long, full breaths.*

8 *Inhale – jump or step forward, back to position 4.*

9 *Exhale – fold forward, back to position 3.*

10 *Inhale – back to position 2.*

11 *Exhale – return your arms to your sides.*

level in the individual. In the West, as yoga classes have become popular everywhere from gyms to school halls, the focus has been primarily on yoga's physical postures. These poses, called *asanas* in Sanskrit (India's equivalent of Latin), may either be held or repeated several times following the rhythm of your in-breaths and out-breaths. They may also be built into flowing and often demanding sequences, as in astanga yoga.

Working up to the flowing sequence known as a 'sun salutation' is a good starting point for surf fitness. Sun salutations in various forms are an integral part of astanga yoga. By focusing the body, breath and mind in the moment,

it can promote a kind of meditative stillness in movement – exactly the kind of flowing, controlled movement a surfer needs to master to bring order to the chaos of the elements exploding around him. In the process of learning the salutation and developing the strength and flexibility to do it well, you will also develop the attributes you need for a successful, sustained surfing life.

TECHNIQUE SEVEN

THE AERIAL

Aerials are the purest product of the surf-skateboard cross-over.

An aerial, or 'air', is a high-performance manoeuvre in which a surfer launches from the lip of a wave before landing back on its face.

The air has evolved from being little more than a dramatic and stylish end to a ride to being a central element of performance surfing. There are countless variations on the basic frontside air (where the move is performed with the rider facing the wave), and airs can of course be performed backside (with the back to the wave). Most variations of aerial manoeuvres are rooted in skateboarding. In a 360 air, for example, the rider rotates in a full circle before landing back on the face of the wave. As in skateboarding, the various ways of grabbing the board in mid-air define what the air is called. A 'method' for instance, is a backside air with a one-handed grab on the outside rail, while a 'stalefish' involves a grab with the back hand on the inside rail between the rider's feet. 'Rodeos' are even possible, (when riders flip or twist upside down to revert back to the wave's face).

Highly skilled surfers are able to perform the whole gamut of aerial manouvres in big, powerful surf, and indeed many of the top pros on the World Championship Tour have a full quiver of signature airs. The majority of airs are seen, however, on less-than-perfect, onshore surf, where mushy peaks and close-out sections form 'ramps' perfect for 'boosting airs'.

B *Feet*

When you reach the target point of the lip step on the tail of the board with the back foot to help get you airborne.

D *Landing*

Once airborne you need to focus on the re-entry spot. Any part of a wave is suitable for landing except a vertical face.

The Ride

fig. VII: Aerial

A *Hands*

Bring your front knee up toward your chest and grab the rail of your board to stop the board flying off into infinity.

C *Nose*

To turn the nose of your board back toward the beach, you will need to straighten out your back leg after you've grabbed the rail.

E *Speed*

Speed is the key to performing a successful air. After driving hard off the bottom turn, you should aim as early as possible at the part of the lip from which you want to launch.

THOMAS CAMPBELL

Film-maker, painter, graphic artist, music producer and photographer – Thomas Campbell is prolific in so many media that his work is impossible to pigeonhole.

The softly spoken Santa Cruz resident came to the surf's world attention with the release of *Seedling* in 2001. Billed as a 'loggin' movie dedicated to small waves, it was the first in a projected triptych of movies in which Campbell has focused on a pod of open-minded surfers. Their choice of equipment reflects the eclectic sensibilities of the film-maker, while the surf styles on display delve deep into the history of wave-riding, re-interpreting them in a contemporary context. *Seedling,* featuring the crystalline waves of California, demonstrated Campbell's signature off-beat aesthetic,

Campbell has received critical acclaim for his art as well as his films. This mixed-media piece, one of a series of sewn works, features Joel Tudor.

including heavy colour saturations, split screen edits, unusual compositions and overexposures, as well as a dose of humour and commentary (in homage to Bruce Brown) along the way. He used a relaxing, lo-fi score that threaded scenes together with a laid-back ambience of its own. With the lightest of touches, *Seedling* came to redefine what it was to make a surf movie.

Sprout, the second episode of the triptych, picked up where *Seedling* left off. Showcasing an increasingly diverse roster of boards, exotic locations and riders, including Joel Tudor, Rob Machado, Dave Rastovich, Alex Knost, Dan Malloy, Belinda

Baggs as well as old-school legends Skip Frye and Gerry Lopez, it's all held together with a dazzling array of filmic techniques. Early tasters of *The Present*, his current project, and the final part of the trilogy, have been creating a groundswell of anticipation.

As with all the most interesting art, Campbell's work has polarised opinion. Campbell's approach, and the starting point of the movies themselves, is a fine-art perspective, whereas the vast majority of surf movies are firmly rooted in the industry and its all-encompassing commercial agendas. There are those who recognise in Campbell's work a rootlessness that defines contemporary surfing itself. Others, however, regard the artfulness of the work as an obfuscating manipulation of the medium.

The artist has been an essential part of a mini-Californian surf renaissance that has paved the way for a whole swathe of surfing film-makers, artists and photographers to expose their work to an increasingly broad audience. According to Jeff Divine, photo editor of *The Surfer's Journal*, 'Thomas has schooled everyone in a different, modern approach to capturing our sport – through film, art as well as photographic images.' Without the backing of the mainstream surf industry, Campbell has come to define surf-oriented creativity in the twenty-first century more than any other individual.

Right: Scenes from Campbell's films including *The Present* (*top left*) and *Sprout* which has been lauded as one of the most beautiful surf movies ever made.

THE SURFER'S PLAYLIST

Music can stoke the fires before a surf session or simply evoke the feelings created by wave-riding.

It might have something to do with the way that the serotonin flow induced by music acts in a similar way to the biochemical rushes induced by wave-riding. Whatever the reason, surfing and music have long been intertwined. Here's a selection of playlists which can help you get to the heart of the surf experience.

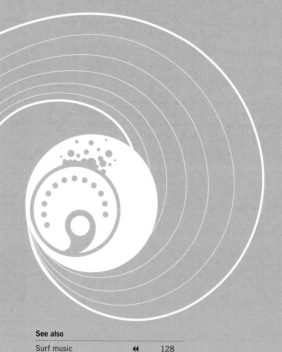

Classic surf sounds

A selection of guitar-driven music from the early sixties

'Let's Go Trippin'' Dick Dale and his Del-Tones (1963)
'Pipeline' The Chantays (1962)
'Wipe Out' The Surfaris (1963)
'Surfing Bird' The Trashmen (1964)
'Apache' The Shadows (1960)
'Miserlou' Dick Dale and his Del-Tones (1962)
'Walk Don't Run' The Ventures (1960)
'Telstar' The Tornados (1960)
'Surfer's Stomp' The Marketts (1962)
'Hawaii Five-O' The Ventures (1964)

Vocal anthems

Giving voice to the sixties surf dream

'Surfin'' The Beach Boys (1961)
'Surf City' Jan and Dean (1962)
'Surfin' Safari' The Beach Boys (1962)
'Surfer Joe' The Surfaris (1962)
'The Warmth Of The Sun' The Beach Boys (1964)
'Ride the Wild Surf' Jan and Dean (1964)
'Surfer Girl' The Beach Boys (1963)
'Catch A Wave' The Beach Boys (1963)
'Justine' Adrian and The Sunsets (1963)
'Sidewalk Surfin'' Jan and Dean (1964)

The dream's over

Evoking the culture's loss of innocence

'Surf's Up' The Beach Boys (1971)
'All Along The Watchtower' Jimi Hendrix (1968)
'Good Vibrations' The Beach Boys (1966)
'Apostrophe' Frank Zappa (1974)
'The End' The Doors (1967)
'Ride Of The Valkyries' Richard Wagner (1870)
'Heroes And Villains' The Beach Boys (1966)
'Horse With No Name' America (1971)
'Dancing Girl' Terry Callier (1973)
'My Sweet Lord' George Harrison (1972)

Liquid Groove

Surfin' the dance floor

'Let The Children Play' Santana (1977)
'There But For The Grace of God Go I' Machine (1979)
'M.U.S.I.C' D Train (1985)
'Southern Freeze' Freez (1981)
'Still A Friend Of Mine' Incognito (1994)
'London Town' Light of the World (1980)
'The Pressure' Sounds of Blackness (1992)
'Harlem River Drive' Bobbi Humphrey (1973)
'Time' Stone (1981)
'Ordinary Joe' Terry Callier (1974)

Wet chords

Jazz evocations of surf-like sensations

'The Creator Has A Master Plan' Pharoah Sanders (1968)
'Journey In Satchidananda' Alice Coltrane (1971)
'Om Mani Padme Hum' Sahib Shihab (1965)
'Stolen Moments' Oliver Nelson (1960)
'Parker's Mood' Charlie Parker (1948)
'So What' Miles Davis (1958)
'Let's Get Lost' Chet Baker (1956)
'Brother John' Yusef Lateef (1963)
'Softly As In A Morning Sunrise' John Coltrane (1962)
'Celestial Blues' Gary Bartz (1972)

Contemporary downbeat

Fuel for the flow

'Pictures' Mojave3 (1995)
'F-Stop Blues' Jack Johnson (2001)
'Love Song Of The Buzzard' Iron and Wine (2007)
'No One Knows' Asa (2007)
'Andrade' Taunuka Marya (2007)
'Silver Stallion' Cat Power (2007)
'New Romantic' Laura Marling (2007)
'The Funeral' Band of Horses (2007)
'This Is' Lizz Wright (2007)
'Every Step' Tawiah (2008)

JOEL TUDOR

Date of birth: 23 January 1976
Place of birth: San Diego, California
Defining waves: Windansea, Pipeline

Joel Tudor is a true surfing alchemist. He has an uncanny ability to accentuate any wave's form and bring out its beauty.

Watch Joel Tudor in jbrother's film *Longer*. The soundtrack is Errol Garner's velvet-soft piano classic, 'Play Misty For Me', and the wave is a knee-high California beachbreak, the perfect setting to demonstrate the longboarder's art. There's a perfectly weighted grace in the surfer's movement that's wired to the pace and the rhythm of the wave. He switch-foots, cross-steps, hangs heels and ten toes, pulling drop-knee cutbacks all the way to the beach. The whole gamut of classical wave-riding technique is threaded together with an ease of movement that belies its difficulty. Watch very closely the infinitesimal adjustments of weight and the complex, precise footwork. Always slightly off the beat and unexpected, Joel improvises on a signature move the way a jazz musician takes a standard phrase and re-invents it as a universe of textures.

Cut now to a screaming barrel in Tavarua, Fiji. Joel drops straight to the bottom of the wave on a diamond-tailed six-foot-eight single fin before leaning deep into a bottom turn and drawing an unbroken line back up the face, perfectly describing the beauty of the barrel's form, before disappearing deep behind the falling curtain of water.

Joel has been immersed in surfing history from an early age. When he was twelve he was introduced to Nat Young in the parking lot at Cardiff Reef, San Diego County, by shaper Donald Takayama; three years later the Aussie legend hooked Tudor up with Oxbow. As part of the Oxbow team they toured the world surfing the best waves with the best surfers that had ever lived. Nat Young became a definitive era-straddling master to a supernaturally talented apprentice.

Although there is much more to Joel Tudor's surfing than traditional longboarding, his name is synonymous with the nine-foot-plus renaissance that took over the surfing planet in the 1990s. The seventies and eighties had seen surfboards shrinking in length and volume, so much so that many surfers and would-be surfers became alienated by the equipment that was available in the average surf shop. On the wafer-thin, extreme-rockered Thrusters of the late eighties and early nineties, if you didn't possess the natural abilities of a Kelly Slater or were a competent athlete but weighed over 170 lbs, you could forget about becoming a serious surfer. Surfers all over the world began to realise this and there was a stirring underground movement amongst a small cadre of shapers, who began to resurrect interest in pre-1980 surfboard design. When photographs of a teenage Joel Tudor riding longboards with real style began to appear in the surf media, they opened people's eyes to the simple fact that big boards provide access to the glide much more easily than shortboards. They also seduced a generation of old timers back to the sport from which they had felt excluded after the shortboard revolution. The re-emergence of longboards was ideal for having fun in less-than-perfect waves, and connected beautifully with the emerging retro movement in surf fashion. Longboards proved perfect for sustaining the ongoing stoke of surfing for mere mortals – and were certainly good for business.

By the end of the nineties, whether he liked it or not, Joel Tudor had become the coolest surfer in the world and the poster-boy for a 'retro-progressive' school of surfing that unearthed designs previously regarded as outmoded. Tudor's classically proportioned 'Takayama Model-T' became the bestselling signature board in the history of surfing. And thanks, in part, to his influence, fishes, bonzers, beak-nosed single fins and all manner of hybrid designs returned to line-ups the world over.

After finally winning the Longboard World Championship in 1998 (despite a frustrating reluctance on behalf of ASP judges to accept his hard-to-pigeonhole style), Tudor has only sporadically competed, preferring to sit in the shadows of contemporary surfing's limelight, and taking up Brazilian martial arts competitively. His influence, however, cannot be overemphasised. By synthesising all the surf styles of the modern era, he has helped to free up twenty-first-century surfers to follow their own path, free of dogma.

Joel Tudor demonstrates his preternatural grace and economy of movement in jbrother's 2002 film *Longer*.

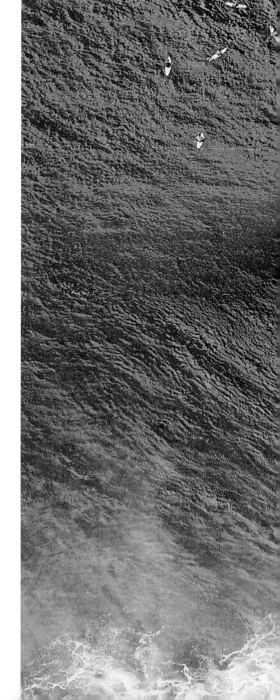

SURF SPOT

BANZAI PIPELINE

A bewitching combination of elements makes Banzai Pipeline the most photographed, and perhaps the most challenging, wave in the world.

Situated smack in the middle of the cradle of surf culture, otherwise known as the North Shore of the Hawaiian island of Oahu, Banzai Beach faces the breadth and depth of thousands of square kilometres of Pacific Ocean. Incredibly powerful swells fetch over long distances from storms crossing the Pacific, particularly between the months of November and February each year. There is no continental shelf around the Hawaiian Islands, so when the swells hit the North Shore they hit hard, out of deep water. This is big-wave season in Hawaii, and the reefs off Banzai Beach are the main arenas.

Pipeline actually consists of three separate reefs, each of which produces intense tubular waves, depending on size and swell direction. The main arena is first reef, which is situated shaka-throwing distance from the beach. This breaks most often and with terrifying force, and produces short, intense rides on waves up to ten feet. The first reef surf experience is a near-vertical drop directly toward the beach, followed by an insanely critical bottom turn. If the drop is survived and trim achieved, then it's another few seconds of one of the fastest, hollowest, deepest barrels on the planet before the surfer is spat out on to the shoulder. Second reef, a little further out, feathers at about fifteen to twenty feet before re-forming on first reef. Third reef is for big-wave hellmen only. It breaks much further out and is very rarely surfed. ▶▶

When the swell approaches from the north-northwest, an intense right-hander, known as Backdoor, forms off Pipeline's peak.

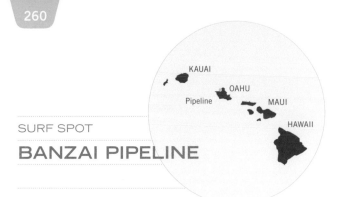

SURF SPOT
BANZAI PIPELINE

◀◀   Such is Pipeline's fearsome reputation that it remained unsurfed until 1961 when Phil Edwards, the Californian pioneer of performance-surfing, broke the taboo – a feat captured by film-maker Bruce Brown and cut into his short film *Surfing Hollow Days*. The wave's intensity soon produced the kind of arena where reputations were made and quickly broken. Californian charger of Windansea Surf Club fame, Butch Van Artsdalen, was the first to earn the hallowed moniker 'Mr Pipeline'. Butch's hard longboard charging was superseded with the arrival of the shortboard revolution, epitomised by the transcendental poise and positioning of talented master Gerry Lopez. During the eighties, local superstar Derek Ho took deep-tube riding to new levels, while eight-times world champ Kelly Slater has taken the art of surfing Pipe backside further than the pioneers could ever have imagined.

Pipeline remains a brutally unforgiving arena full of testosterone-tweaked aspirants to the limelight of surf culture. It's the barrel against which all others are judged.

Pipeline's reefs lie close to the beach, creating one of the sport's most dramatic and crowd-pleasing arenas.

Tom Curren displays grace under pressure at Backdoor Pipeline.

"PERHAPS, AS SOME HAVE ARGUED, THE WAVE IS THE FUNDAMENTAL FORM OF THE UNIVERSE AND EVERYTHING IS WAVES, WAVE AFTER MIGHTY WAVE, RISING AND FALLING FOR EVER AND EVER.

BUT,
IN ANOTHER WAY,
THE WAVE IS NOTHING,
A GHOST, AN
EMPTY,
       EVANESCENT
             ARCHITECTURE.

"

Andy Martin

GLOSSARY

Aerial A skateboard-influenced surf manoeuvre in which the surfer launches from the top of the wave.

A-frame The appearance of a peak that has a left-breaking wave and a right-breaking wave forming on either side of it.

Aloha Hawaiian term for the spirit of love, compassion and kinship, used also as a generalised greeting.

Barrel The hollow part of a breaking wave.

Beachbreak Any surf spot where waves break on to a beach.

Big wave A wave that is around three metres or more from crest to trough.

Bottom turn Any turn performed at the bottom of a wave.

Bowl A wave or a section of a wave that bends or slopes making it appear concave.

Close-out 1) A wave that breaks at the same time across its entire length. 2) The end section of a peeling wave when the curl folds over to form a surge of whitewater.

Crest The leading edge of a breaking wave.

Curl The curved, breaking part of a wave.

Cutback One-hundred-and-eighty degree turn, usually performed on a wave's shoulder.

Dawn patrol A surfer's search for uncrowded waves at first light.

Deck The upward-facing surface of a surfboard, on which a surfer stands.

Ding Any damage to a surfboard.

Down-rail A sharply angled outside edge of a surfboard, usually found on shortboards.

Drop in 1) Opening manoeuvre made down the face of the wave, directly after take-off. 2) To take off on a wave that someone else is already riding.

Duck dive Technique in which the surfer pushes the nose of the surfboard down and through the face of an approaching wave, while paddling out.

Egg Surfboard with a rounded shape, invented in the early seventies.

Face The unbroken part of a wave, or its measurable surface from trough to crest.

Fetch The area of the sea where waves are generated and form lines of swell.

Fin Stabilising device fitted to the bottom of surfboards.

Foil The relative thickness of a board from nose to tail.

Gnarly Surf slang for heavy, chaotic or dangerous surf conditions.

Grom Term for a young surfer.

Groundswell A set of waves formed by an offshore storm as opposed to localised 'wind swell'.

Gun A surfboard designed specifically for big waves.

Hang ten Iconic longboard move where the surfer places both feet over the tip of the nose, so that his toes hang over the edge.

Haole (pron. 'howlie') Hawaiian term for a non-Hawaiian (literal translation is 'person without the breath of life').

Hold-down A potentially dangerous occurrence when the surfer is pushed under the surface of the water by waves breaking above.

Hotdogging Trick-based surf style, usually associated with the period between the late fifties and the late sixties.

Hybrid A type of surfboard whose design takes elements from longboards as well as shortboards.

Kick-out A stylish way to end a ride, in which the surfer flicks the nose of the surfboard over the lip to ride out of the wave before it closes out on top of him.

Kook Derogatory term for a beginner, or unskilled surfer.

Leash A cord used to tether surfers to their boards.

Left A wave breaking from left to right, as seen from the beach.

Line-up The area, near the peak, where surfers wait to catch a wave, or the area in which waves are breaking.

Lip Surfer's term for the crest of a wave.

Localism Surf territorialism manifesting itself as antipathy towards visiting surfers by those who live locally to a particular surf spot.

Log Slang term for longboard.

Longboard A full-nosed surfboard over nine feet in length.

Nose ride Riding the front third of the surfboard.

Nose The front third of a surfboard.

Off-the-lip A dynamic turn at the top of the wave, where a surfer rebounds from the wave's lip and continues riding on the wave's face.

Outside The area on the seaward side of the breaking waves. Also known as 'out back'.

Overhead Term used to describe a sizeable wave (between five and six feet on the face) whose crest is 'over the head' of the average surfer.

Paddle out The act of getting out to the line-up.

Peak 1) The place at which a wave begins to break and from where a wave should be caught. 2) A type of wave with a pronounced central portion, either side of which is a sloping, peeling face.

Peeling Describes a wave which breaks gradually and evenly from either right to left, or left to right. Great for surfing.

Performance surfing High-energy style of riding, based on performing a quick succession of dynamic turns and other manoeuvres.

Plank 1) Crudely designed surfboard dating from the early twentieth century. 2) Slang term for a longboard.

Pocket The most powerful part of a breaking wave generally where the wave's face is the steepest and fastest moving.

Pointbreak Any surf spot where the waves peel around a rocky promontory or headland.

Popout Term, often derogatory, for any mass-produced surfboard.

Power surfing Style of surfing that puts hard, carving turns and big, spectacular moves to the forefront.

Radical Perennially popular term used to describe spectacular, aggressive, difficult or dangerous surf manoeuvres.

Rail The outside edge of a surfboard.

Reefbreak Any surf spot where waves break over a submerged outcrop, usually formed by a line of rock, lava or coral.

Retro-progressive Neologism from the turn of the millennium coined to describe a widespread movement in which surfers and surf-inspired artists and photographers explored the possibilities of designs previously considered to be outmoded.

Right A wave breaking from right to left, as seen from the beach.

Rip 1) Current formed by water escaping back out to sea. 2) To surf aggressively and radically.

Rocker The degree of curve in a surfboard from nose to tail.

Roundhouse A full figure-of-eight cutback.

Section Part of a wave, as in 'tube section' or 'close-out section'.

Set A group of waves that is approaching the line-up. Usually created by a groundswell, and forming one after another, sets are punctuated by lulls.

Shaka Universal surf gesture and salute performed by sticking out the little finger and the thumb, tucking in the middle fingers into the palm, and shaking the hand from side to side.

Shaper A surfboard builder who sculpts the shape of a surfboard. Some shapers also laminate and 'finish' the surfboard.

Shortboard A lightweight surfboard usually between 5 and 7 feet in length.

Shoulder The sloping portion of a wave, found directly on either side of the peak.

Soul surfing Generic term used to describe the non-competitive, contemplative approach to surfing and surf culture.

Stoke The feeling of euphoria stimulated by surfing.

Surf wax Sticky substance which is rubbed on the deck of a surfboard to provide traction.

Swell 1) Waves that are produced by inshore wind or offshore storms. 2) An unbroken wave or set of waves.

Switch-foot To ride, or the ability to ride, a surfboard with either foot forward.

Tail The rear third of a surfboard.

Take-off The point at the beginning of a ride when a surfer pops to his or her feet and drops into a wave.

Template The outline shape of a surfboard when viewed from above. Also known as 'planshape'.

Thruster Term for a surfboard with three fins of equal size, one placed centrally, the other two positioned forward of the central fin and close to each rail.

Tombstoning Term for when a surfboard comes to the surface nose-first, after a wipe-out, to form the appearance of a tombstone, while the surfer is held down underwater by the force of the breaking waves.

Top turn Any turn performed at the top of a breaking wave, on, or near, the crest.

Tow-in surfing A form of surfing in which the rider is pulled behind a jetski or other personal watercraft and then launched into a big, unbroken wave.

Tube Another term for a barrel.

Wall A near vertical, unfurling face of a peeling wave.

Waterman An aquatic athlete, accomplished in all ocean-related activities including swimming, fishing and diving as well as surfing.

Whitewater The foam left after a wave has broken.

Wipeout Falling off a surfboard.

INSPIRATIONS

THE SURFING PLANET

Surf Science: An Introduction to Waves for Surfing
Tony Butt (Alison Hodge Publishing, 2002)
Originally commissioned as a textbook for the oceanography course at Plymouth University, this detailed little book has everything you wanted to know about meteorology, bathymetry and more for surfers. A perfect piece of pop-sci for anyone interested in the ocean.

The Book of Waves: Form and Beauty of the Ocean
Drew Kampion (Arpel Graphics, 1989)
Part photo book, part surf science start-up, part philosophical meditation on the nature of waves. Unmissable.

www.magicseaweed.com Easy-to-navigate surf forecasting portal based in the UK, with increasingly rich content.

www.surfline.com The mama and papa of global surf forecasting, with deep, rich and broad content.

The Ride

The Surfboard: Art, Style, Stoke
Ben Marcus (Voyageur Press, 2007)
A beautifully presented and comprehensive photo-led survey of a century of surfboard design.

www.swaylocks.com Indispensable online resource for anyone interested in surfboards and surfboard design.

www.harboursurfboards.com Online home of Rich Harbour, one of the most revered shapers in California. Tonnes of great information on surfboard design and construction.

www.tylersurfboards.com Post-modern gliders and sliders from the hot-rodding craftsman of twenty-first-century surfboards, Tyler Hatzikian.

www.cisurfboards.com Web-based hub of Al Merrick's Channel Island Surfboards, the centre of California's performance surfing design.

www.mandalacustomshapes.com State-of-the-art surfboards crafted by San Francisco's Manuel Caro.

THE VISION

Ether: The Collected Works of Andrew Kidman 1986–2007 (Consafos Press, 2007)
Two decades of surf-related creativity in print from the creator of Litmus.

Leroy Grannis: Surf Photography of the 1960s and 1970s
Jim Heimann (ed.) (Taschen, 2006)
Beautiful tome presenting some of the master's finest photographs with exquisite reproduction.

Photo/Stoner: The Rise, Fall, and Mysterious Disappearance of Surfing's Greatest Photographer
Matt Warshaw (Chronicle, 2006)
Essential not only for Ron Stoner's achingly beautiful photographs, but for Warshaw's well-told story of a wayward genius who communicated the heart of surfing's golden age.

Ron Church: California to Hawaii 1960 to 1965
Brad Barrett and Steve Pezman
(T. Adler Books, 2007)
Photobook documenting surfing's first modern boom by one of surf photography's pioneers.

Heart & Torch – Rick Griffin's Transcendence
Doug Havery, Greg Escalante and Jacaeber Kastor (Gingko Press, 2007)
A rich, comprehensive review of the artist's best work.

Masters of Surf Photography
(*Surfer's Journal*, 2001)
Definitive series of monographs, including those featuring Art Brewer and Jeff Divine.

Surf Movie Tonite! Surf Movie Poster Art, 1957–2004
Matt Warshaw (Chronicle Books, 2005)
More superb surf movie collectibles from Mr Warshaw.

Surf Legends

Nat's Nat and That's That: A Surfing Legend
Nat Young (Nymboida Press, 1998)
Authoritative surfing autobiography from the man who sparked the shortboard revolution at the end of the sixties, as well as the longboard renaissance two decades later.

Dora Lives: The Authorized Story of Miki Dora
Drew Kampion and C. R. Stecyk
(T. Adler Books, 2005)
Get inside the nine lives of Da Cat with this Stecyk/Kampion collaboration. With a wealth of rarely seen pictures, this book takes you to an intimate place with the Malibu legend.

Bunker Spreckels: Surfing's Divine Prince of Decadence
C. R. Stecyk (Taschen, 2007)
A superb documentation of one of the most interesting characters in the history of surf culture. Incredible candid photos from the master of surf lifestyle, Art Brewer.

Pipe Dreams: A Surfer's Journey Kelly Slater
(HarperCollins, 2004)
A candid account, written with Jason Borte, of the life of the world's greatest surfer.

Tom Blake: The Uncommon Journey of a Pioneer Waterman Gary Lynch, Malcolm Gault-Williams, William K. Hoopes
(Croul Family Foundation, 2001)
The definitive study of the life of visionary surfer Tom Blake.

You Should Have Been Here an Hour Ago
Phil Edwards (Harper and Row, 1967)
Fascinating but long out-of-print memoir from the master stylist and pioneer of performance surfing.

Bustin' Down the Door Wayne 'Rabbit' Bartholomew (Harper, 1996) Hyperbolic but entertaining autobiography of the legendary Aussie tube rider and North Shore infiltrator.

www.legendarysurfers.com Malcolm Gault-Williams's unmatched online resource of information on notable watermen and -women of the past 100 years.

THE SEARCH

World Stormrider Guide
Antony Colas
(Low Pressure Publishing, 2000)
The original global guide to places and surfing spaces.

Surfing Britain,
Surfing the World, Surfing Europe
Chris Nelson and Demi Taylor (Footprint Handbooks, 2004, 2005, 2008)
Extremely detailed, entertainingly presented information on when and where to surf from the Cornwall-based duo.

California
Bank Wright (Mountain and Sea Publishing, 1973)
A duotone classic with a homespun feel. Incredibly detailed breakdown of the entire California coast from Crescent City to the Tijuana Sloughs. Only slightly out of date, despite the fact that it's in its fourth decade of print.

Surf Nation
Alex Wade (Simon & Schuster, 2007)
A great account of the state of surfing and surf culture in Britain and Ireland.

www.wannasurf.com A global and comprehensive guide to a myriad of surf spots, but be careful not to rely on the user-generated content and try to ignore the hateful banter of the forums.

www.wavehunters.com US-based high-end dream surf adventures: boat charters, island experiences. The packaged surf dream for those with the disposable.

www.surftravel.com.au Australian-based pioneers of the boat charter surf vacation, South-East Asia specialists.

Surf Culture

www.loose-fit.co.uk The world's first carbon-zero surf shop and stockists of great boards, art, clothing and books from all over the surfing planet.

www.mollusksurfshop.com Mini-chain of beautifully realised boutique-style surfshops that stock everything from Greg Liddle hulls to Thomas Campbell artworks and everything in between.

www.surfresearch.com.au Brilliantly informed online journal of surf culture from an Australian perspective.

www.switch-foot.com Drawing together of surf-oriented creativity from Australia. A unique flavour of the soulful side of Aussie surfing.

INSPIRATIONS

General

The Encyclopedia of Surfing
Matt Warshaw (Harcourt, 2003)
Without question the most comprehensive and detailed work to date on surfing and surf culture from the rigorous Californian surf editor, historian and writer. This is a behemoth work of reference that takes in everything from 'A-frame' to 'Mr Zog'. A sublime inspiration for *The Book of Surfing*.

Stoked: A History of Surf Culture
Drew Kampion (Evergreen, 1997)
A wonderful trawl through the annals of the culture from one of the most influential of all surf writers. Drew edited *Surfer* magazine in the tempestuous years of 1968–72, and the breadth and depth of his knowledge and contacts book shows. Great pictures too.

Surf Culture: An Art History of Surfing
C. R. Stecyk (Gingko, 2002)
Published to accompany a major exhibition at California's Laguna Art Museum, this combines Stecyk's offbeat hipster authority with David Carson's highly influential graphic aesthetic. A collectors' piece and the most extensive examination of surfing's impact on mainstream popular culture to date.

The Surfinary: A Dictionary of Surfing Terms and Surf Speak
Trevor Cralle (Tenspeed Press, 1991)
Entertaining illustrated lexicon of Dudish.

We Approach Our Martinis with Such High Expectations
Jamie Brisick (Consafos Press, 2002)
A life-affirming lyrical journey by the globe-trotting Californian surfer.

Super X Media Combine
Takuji Masuda (ed.)
(First Point Productions, 2003)
A compilation of the best moments of Super X Media, Masuda's ambitious collective project that takes a surf culture perspective to global events and issues.

Stealing the Wave
Andy Martin (Bloomsbury, 2007)
Brilliantly readable and creative account of the epic rivalry between big-wave riders Ken Bradshaw and Mark Foo.

A Selection of Surf Magazines

Pacific Longboarder (Australia)
Class pictures and classical surfing from the southern hemisphere. Essential reading for the man of surfing substance.

Surfing (US)
Dispatches from the belly of California's surf beast.

Surfer (US)
John Severson's creation and the bible of the sport.

The Surfer's Journal (US)
Perennial surf sage Steve Pezman publishes and steers this graceful and beautifully produced periodical. A magazine for grown-up surfers.

The Surfer's Path (UK and US)
Environmentally friendly bi-monthly focusing on surf travel, co-edited by Drew Kampion and Alex Dick-Read. The *Path* has evolved into one of the most open-minded surf publications on the planet, focusing on every type of wave riding, as long as it's got soul.

Australian Surfing Life (Australia)
ASL is the glossy magazine of the Australian surf establishment. Classic straight-ahead surf fodder from Down Under.

Tracks (Australia)
Originally a missive from the Australian surf counterculture and once published and edited by Alby Falzon and John Witzig, *Tracks* is more mainstream now, but still retains a whiff of the leftfield for edgier ocker watermen.

Stab (Australia)
Self-consciously reprobate and stylishly irreverent, *Stab* is the surfin' *GQ* with a gonzo twist, courtesy of editorial head honcho Derek Reilly's rapier wit.

Huck (UK)
True cross-over magazine between the worlds of surf, skate and snowboarding, *Huck* is all about the people leading the global cult of those who slide sideways.

Carve (UK)
Straight-ahead surf mag fodder straight outta Newquay, England.

Wavelength (UK)
Longest surviving UK surf magazine with its roots deep in the Cornish earth.

Zig Zag (SA)
South Africa's premier surf magazine comes with that nation's characteristic stripped-down focus on powerful waves and a radical approach. The leading voice of South African surf culture for over thirty years.

How to Choose Your First Board

The main question you should ask yourself the first time you go surfing is: has the board enough volume and floatation to facilitate easy paddling? The board you choose is very much dependent on your size, weight and fitness. Beginners who are below six feet tall, relatively light and fit should be able to paddle well on a mid-range board, about seven to eight feet in length, with around 21 inches of width at its widest point and around 3 inches in thickness. There are obviously many different shapes to choose in this range, but the wider and rounder is its nose, the more stable and beginner-friendly the board will be.

If you're a little taller and heavier, over six feet and over 170 lbs, then it's probably best to start off with a basic longboard. Longboards are usually between nine and ten feet long. Most longboards (apart from the light, thin, high-performance variety) should have enough volume to float anyone up to around 220 lbs. Bigger boards are available if you weigh more than this.

It also is worth considering using a relatively cheap, pop-out such as a 'soft top' variety. These are designed without hard edges to prevent injury to yourself and other surfers when starting out. They are popular in board rental shops and surf schools, and you can often pick them up very cheap at the end of the summer surf school season.

Most surfers buy a new board every couple of years, as even the most modern, high-tech designs are prone to dings, scrapes and other types of wear and tear. As a beginner it doesn't make sense to spend a lot of money on a brand-new, handcrafted board, as your first board will be the one you drop, scrape, ding and generally treat the worst. As your surfing improves, you will get the feel for what sort of board might be the one to step up to. Talk to other surfers, if possible borrow their boards and pay attention to how your riding is progressing and how different equipment affects the way you ride a wave. Many surfers say the perfect board finds them, rather than the other way round.

Some Beginner-friendly Waves Around the British Isles

North Devon
Saunton Sands, near Braunton: miles of peaks and slow-breaking, forgiving surf.

North Cornwall
Widemouth Bay, near Bude: plenty of room to spread out.
Newquay Bay: mellow peelers in the shelter of the headland.

West Cornwall
Godrevy and Gwithian Towans: miles of relaxed rights and lefts.

South Cornwall
Perranuthnoe: great longboard wave.

South Wales
Caswell Bay: picturesque small wave on the south of the Gower Peninsula.

West Wales
Whitesands Bay: manageable peelers in the far west of Pembrokeshire.

Northeast
Saltburn-by-the-Sea: soft peaks perfect for that first wave, near Middlesborough.

Scotland
Pease Bay: the focal point of surfing on the east coast of Scotland, between Edinburgh and Berwick.

Republic of Ireland
Lahinch: a popular beach in the heart of the local surf community.

Northern Ireland
West Strand, Portrush: striking coastal views deliver a backdrop for uncrowded and forgiving lefts and rights.

INDEX

ACKNOWLEDGEMENTS

I would like to thank Caroline Harris for inspiring the book with her zen-like arrow of logic; Clive Wilson for helping to make it all happen (we've been talking about it for long enough); artists Nick Radford, Gary Hincks, Ross Imms and Alex Rowse, for giving the book its unique visual identity; Doug Young at Transworld for commissioning it and his team for nurturing it with a beautifully light hand.

Most of all, thanks to Lucy, Gabe, Jude and Grace Fordham. And to Patricia Ann Fordham for teaching me how to love.

Because of you, everything makes sense.

Michael Fordham

For all their invaluable help with this project, Dogstar/September would like to thank the following:

Art Brewer, Thomas Campbell, Jeff Divine, Andrew Kidman, Vince Medeiros, Moonwalker (Neil Armstrong), Bill Morris, Mickey Muñoz, David Pu'u, Andrew Shield and Mickey Smith.

Thanks also to:

Wayne Barnes, John Blair, Scott Brearton (www.surfwarez.com), Tony Butt, Tod Clayton, Bing Copeland, Chris Gentile, Peter Gowland, Jim Heimann, jbrother, Renee Linton, Chris Mannell, Alex Mercl, Martin Morrison, The Reel Poster Gallery, Shirley Richards, Lori Rick, Kate Ruggiero, Robert Schmidt, Roger Sharp, Brett Simundson, Sharon Turner, Hannah White, Nat Young, Zog.

CREDITS

The publisher would like to thank the following for their kind permission to reproduce their photographs:

© **Jakue Andikoetxea/3Sesenta** 92–95; © **Associated Press** 70–71; © **Bishop Museum** 32, 33; © **Art Brewer** 126–127, 169, 192–195, 256; © **Bruce Brown Films, LLC** 42, 43 (bottom), 99; © **Thomas Campbell** 252–253; © **Ron Church** 20–21, 98; © **Bing Copeland** 80 (bottom); © **John Blair** 128, 130–131; © **Sylvain Cazenave** 240–243; © **Sean Davey** 64 (bottom), 65 (bottom); © **Jeff Divine** 6, 16–17, 106–107, 166–168, 182–183, 208, 209, 224–225, 280–281; © **Epes/A-Frame** 250; © **Alby Falzon** 138, 162–163; © **Ed Fladung** 230; © **Jeff Flindt/ NewSport/Corbis** 220–221; © **Hector Garcia** 64 (top); © **Gordon & Smith, Surfboards, Inc.** 80 (top); © **Peter Gowland** 87–88; © **LeRoy Grannis**, courtesy of M+B (www.mbfala.com) 54–55; © **Hodgson/A-Frame** 238; © **D.Hump/A-Frame** 78; © **Griffin Ink** 90–91; © **Ryan Heywood** 186–187; © **Hulton Archive/Getty Images** 178; © **Ross Imms** 110; © **jbrother** 257; © **Katin, Inc.** 179; © **Andrew Kidman** 214–215; © **Alex Laurel** 4–5, 278–279; © **MacGillivray-Freeman Films** 43 (top), 44–45; © **Al Mackinnon** 2–3, 159 (top), 286–287; © **Greg Martin** 82, 111, 170, 190, 200, 201 (bottom); © **Tom McBride** 177; © **Tim McKenna** 232–233; © **Mollusk Surf Shop** 115, 117; © **Moonwalker** 102, 188–189, 212–213, 284–285; © **Juliana Morais** 246; © **Bill Morris** 236–237, 246–247; © **Mickey Muñoz** 72–73, 120; © **Tim Nunn** 201 (top), 202, 203 © **O'Neill, Inc.** 104–105, 114; © **Michael Ochs Archives/Getty Images** 129; © **PhotoRussi.com** 258–261; © **Fred Pompermayer** 148, 156–157, 158 (top), 158 (bottom), 159 (bottom);

© **Davidpuu.com** 1, 26–29, 40, 146, 149, 151, 160–161, 277, 282–283, 288; © **Quiksilver, Inc.** 116; © **Gregory Rabejac** 243; © **Andrew Shield** 62, 65 (top), 66–67; © **David Simms** 207; © **Mickey Smith** 10, 30, 140–143, 152, 158 (centre left), 173; © **Ron Stoner/Primedia** 84–85; © **Warner Bros. Entertainment Inc.** 199; © **Steve Wilkings** 138–139; © **John Witzig** 137.

Every care has been taken to trace copyright holders. However, if there have been unintentional omissions or failure to trace copyright holders, we apologise and will, if informed, endeavour to make corrections in any future edition.

Illustration credits:

Gary Hincks
18-19, 31, 47–51, 68–69, 82–83, 108–109, 170–171, 190–191, 230–231

Infomen/Carlos Coelho and Aman Khana 36–37, 118–119, 234

Nick Radford
22–23, 34–35, 40–41, 74–75, 79, 89, 97, 102–103, 124–125, 132–135, 152–153, 154–155, 164–165, 180–181, 196–197, 210–211, 213, 218–219, 222–223, 238–239, 244–245, 250–251

All other illustrations by A-Side Studio.

Photographs at the front of the book:
1 David Hopkins, California Gold Coast.
© David Pu'u
2–3 Bag Pipe, North Shore, Scotland.
© Al Mackinnon
4–5 Eric Rebiere, Mentawai Islands.
© Alex Laurel
6 (title page) Gerry Lopez, Pipeline, Oahu.
© Jeff Divine

Photographs at the back of the book:
277 Mary Osborne,
Ventura County, California
© David Pu'u
278–279 Fredo Robin, Mentawai Islands.
© Alex Laurel
280–281 North Shore, Oahu.
© Jeff Divine
282–283 Coast Highway,
LA County, California.
© David Pu'u
284–285 Ventura County, California
© Moonwalker
286–287 Rick Willmett, Bag Pipe,
North Shore, Scotland.
© Al Mackinnon
288 Rusty Keaulana, Makaha, Oahu.
© David Pu'u

© Marc Wilson

ABOUT THE AUTHOR

MICHAEL FORDHAM first surfed in Australia as a teenager. Realizing that he was not the next Tom Curren, he became a writer and journalist, and, in 1997, he launched *adrenalin*, an acclaimed quarterly magazine on the culture of surfing, skating, and snowboarding. His passion for the history, culture, and practice of wave-riding has taken him from the pointbreaks of El Salvador to the barbed-wire beaches of the Gaza Strip, and quite a few places in between. He lives and writes, and surfs most often, on the west coast of England.

*it***books**

Originally published in Great Britain in 2008 by Bantam Press, an imprint of Transworld Publishers.

THE BOOK OF SURFING. Copyright © 2009 by Michael Fordham. All rights reserved. Manufactured in China. No part of this book may be used or reproduced in any manner whatsoever without written permission except in the case of brief quotations embodied in critical articles and reviews. For information address Transworld Publishers, 61-63 Uxbridge Road, London W5 5SA.

HarperCollins books may be purchased for educational, business, or sales promotional use. For information please write: Special Markets Department, HarperCollins Publishers, 195 Broadway, New York, NY 10007.

FIRST U.S. EDITION

Designed by A-Side Studio, www.a-sidestudio.co.uk

Library of Congress Cataloging-in-Publication Data has been applied for.

ISBN 978-0-06-182678-8

14   15   16   SCP   10 9 8 7 6 5 4 3 2